The Life and Works of
Charles Haddon Spurgeon

The Life and Works of

Charles Haddon Spurgeon

With John Ploughman's Talks and Pictures

by

Dr. Henry D. Northrop

Post Office Box 1099 • Murfreesboro, Tennessee 37133

Printed and Bound in the United States of America

CONTENTS

BOOK I

Charles H. Spurgeon: *His Life and Labors*

CONTENTS

BOOK II

Sermons and Lectures by C. H. Spurgeon

BOOK III

FOREWORD

When the name Spurgeon is spoken in Christian circles, it is rarely, if ever, necessary to inquire as to whom the name refers. It is almost always Charles Haddon Spurgeon, the English pastor, preacher and educator, whose ministry dominated his generation and whose written works still captivate readers more than a hundred years after his death.

Converted in 1850 at age fifteen in a small church during a snowstorm, Spurgeon was soon at the task of preaching. In 1854 he was called to the New Park Street pulpit, which would be moved to the corner of Elephant and Castle in South London and become famously known as the Metropolitan Tabernacle. There Spurgeon would preach to full-house crowds every week for thirty years. As his sermons were taken down by stenographers and published in newspapers, his influence grew far beyond his own church.

Were his notoriety only the result of his gifted pulpit oratory and his thriving congregation, Spurgeon's name would perhaps have faded quickly; but there was more to it than that. The thrust of what he did was always for the winning of souls and the care of those in his charge—all of which was indelibly etched in history by the stand he made to separate from the Baptist Union of Great Britain. The ministry was obviously no minor matter to him, and the stands he made demonstrated that he would not trivialize or compromise it.

Though loved by multitudes and honored by many of them, the fame into which he was vaulted never possessed him unduly or caused him to function arrogantly or pridefully. Amid the press and the pressure of his great work, he maintained a yielded heart and a humble spirit throughout his life. The public ministry so prominent and so powerful was truly a reflection of the person he was privately. Unmistakably, he was a man of God.

The Life and Works of Charles Haddon Spurgeon is a definitive work that will introduce you and acquaint you with one of God's choicest servants. The Sword of the Lord Publishers send it forth with the prayerful hope that it will be a wonderful blessing to all in whose hands it is held.

DR. SHELTON L. SMITH

President and Editor
Sword of the Lord Publishers

INTRODUCTION

I have always enjoyed reading biographies of great men, especially of great preachers. Seeing how God used these men builds one's faith and makes him believe that God can use him also. We recall a part of an old poem...

> **Lives of great men all remind us,**
> **We, too, can make our lives sublime;**
> **And in passing, leave behind us,**
> **Footprints on the sands of time!**

Several years ago we found this old biography of Charles Spurgeon written by Dr. Henry Davenport Northrop. It was the most complete biography that we have read of this prince of preachers. Since it was such a blessing to us, we thought it wise to reprint this old volume and make it available to our SWORD readers and others.

I particularly enjoyed reading about the young life of Spurgeon and about his conversion experience. We trust this biography will be an inspiration and challenge to all who read it, and we send it forth for that purpose.

DR. CURTIS HUTSON

Editor, 1980–1995
THE SWORD OF THE LORD

BOOK I

Charles H. Spurgeon:
His Life and Labors

CHAPTER I

Birth and Ancestry

Worldwide Fame—Unprecedented Success—The Great Preacher's Ancestors—Good Old Grandfather—Pen-picture of a Country Minister—Buckled Shoes and Silk Stockings—John, Father of Charles—A Good Mother—Reply of "Charley" to His Mother—Country Boys—Household Influence—Thirst for Knowledge—An Industrious Youth—A Remarkable Prophecy—"Old Bonner"

The fame of Mr. C. H. Spurgeon has filled the world. His name is known among all civilized peoples, and his sermons and writings have been translated into many languages. No other man of modern times preached to such multitudes of people; no other possessed a combination of gifts so rare. If success is the standard of merit, the great London preacher was the Saul among the prophets, standing head and shoulders above others.

Charles Haddon Spurgeon descended from the Essex branch of the same family. Early in his ministry in London he was introduced, at a bookstore in Paternoster Row, to Mr. John Spurgeon, a descendant of the Norwich branch of the family; and on comparing notes of their respective ancestors, piety, uprightness and loyalty were found alike in both.

The same spirit of religious intolerance which sent the immortal Bunyan to Bedford Jail for preaching the Gospel also in 1677 sent Job Spurgeon to Chelmsford Jail where, for conscience' sake, he lay on a pallet of straw for fifteen weeks in extremely severe winter weather, without any fire.

The great-grandfather of Pastor Spurgeon was contemporary with the opening period of the reign of King George III. The record preserved of his memory is that he was a pious man and ordered his household according to the will of God. From that day to this, the family has never wanted a man to stand before God in the service of the sanctuary.

A Good Old Grandfather

James, the grandfather of Pastor C. H. Spurgeon, was born at Halstead, in Essex, September 29, 1776. As a boy he was seriously inclined, and whilst yet a youth, became a member of the Independent church at Halstead.

JAMES SPURGEON
GRANDFATHER OF CHARLES HADDON

Whilst an apprentice at Coggeshall he was accepted as a member of the church there under the pastoral care of the Rev. S. Fielding. Following business pursuits till he was twenty-six years of age, his mind at that period was directed entirely to the work of the ministry; and in 1802 he entered Hoxton Academy. After two years' study, an application from Clare, in Suffolk, was made to him to try to raise a congregation which was very low; and in this he succeeded so far that in September, 1806, he was appointed pastor, and the church prospered under his pastorate.

The protracted ministry of Mr. Beddow in the Independent church at Stambourne, in Essex (a church which had only four ministers during the course of two hundred years), having terminated in 1810, Mr. Spurgeon received a unanimous call to the oversight of that church, which he accepted. In May, 1811, he was recognized as their pastor.

Himself the fourth of a succession of long-lived pastors in that village, he remained pastor over the church more than half a century, during which period he was peaceful, happy and successful in his labors. He frequently remarked, when more than fourscore years old, "I have not had one hour's unhappiness with my church since I have been over it."

Invitations from other churches were sent to him, but the love, harmony and prosperity which prevailed between pastor and people induced him to decline them all, and he remained true to the people of his choice.

Pen-picture of a Country Minister

It is a recorded fact and worthy of perpetuation that the venerable James Spurgeon never preached in any place away from his own church, but God fulfilled His promise and gave him to hear of some good being done to persons in the congregation.

He had a large head, and much that was good in it. He had a good voice and was very earnest and practical in preaching the glorious truths of the Gospel.

The great usefulness of his lifelong ministry will be known only in eternity. He was known widely in Essex as a man of the old school—staid, quiet and uniform in his dress and habits. He was the very picture of neatness, and in many particulars resembled John Wesley, especially in his manners and stature. He wore a dress cravat, a frilled shirt and had a vest with deep pockets, as if provided for large collections.

He was seldom without a packet of sweets, which he gave generously to the children wherever he went, so that they gathered round him and attached themselves to him with a firmness which riper years did not shake.

Last Days

He was always happy in the company of young people. He wore the breeches, buckled shoes and silk stockings which marked the reign of George III, and he really looked to be a venerable Nonconformist minister of a past age.

For more than half a century his life corresponded with his labors. His gentle manners, his sincere piety and his uniformity of conduct secured for him the good will of his neighbors, and he was as friendly with the parochial clergymen as with his attached Nonconformist friends. He often went to the parish church to hear the sermon when the prayers were over, especially when the cause of missions was to be advocated.

He was blessed with a wife whose piety and useful labors made her a valuable helpmeet to her husband in every good word and work. In his last illness he was sustained by divine grace, and the desire he had so often expressed, that he might speak of Christ on his dying bed, was granted to him.

He said the Gospel was his only hope; he was on the Eternal Rock, immutable as the throne of God. Those who were privileged to witness his departure from earth will never forget his joy and peace and the glorious prospect he had of Heaven.

The Senior Spurgeon

John Spurgeon, the father of Charles, was born at Stambourne in 1811. Second of ten children, he was a portly-looking man, a good specimen of a country gentleman, and was nearly six feet in height.

For many years he was engaged in business at Colchester; but with so excellent an example of a minister as was his father, it is not strange that his mind should have run in the same direction, though he did not fully enter on the ministry till he had reached the prime of life.

For sixteen years he preached on Sundays to a small Independent church at Tollesbury, being occupied with business during the week. He next accepted a call to the pastorate of the Independent church at Cranbrook, Kent, a village of three thousand persons, where he remained five years.

JOHN SPURGEON
FATHER OF CHARLES HADDON

The popularity of his son Charles in London was not without its influence on the father, whose personal worth and ministerial ability were not unknown in the metropolis, as he had spoken occasionally at meetings held by his son.

The pastorate of the Independent church in Fetter Lane, Holborn, became vacant and was offered to and accepted by Mr. Spurgeon, but his stay there was not long. A sphere more in accordance with his years and position was offered and accepted by him, and for some time he was pastor of the Independent church worshiping in the Upper Street, Islington. That position he resigned at the end of the year 1876.

He did good work in that locality and was much beloved by the people. His preaching was plain, earnest and pointed; and he manifested an affectionate solicitude for all under his pastoral care, especially the young people.

A Good Mother

There are many large places of worship in the locality, and preachers of distinction are numerous in that populous suburb; but even there Mr. Spurgeon gathered a large and important congregation twice on one Sunday, to whom his preaching was both acceptable and beneficial.

The various branches of church work were carried on with energy and fidelity; and those which required female agency were fostered and watched over with affectionate solicitude by Mrs. Spurgeon, whose motherly affection secured for her a welcome in the families of the church.

Mrs. John Spurgeon was the youngest sister of Charles Parker Jervis, Esq., of Colchester, in which town her husband carried on business for many years. Wherever she has resided she has been known and esteemed for her sincere piety, her great usefulness and humility.

She is short in stature, and in this respect her son Charles takes after her, but not in features, in which particular the other son, James Archer Spurgeon, assimilates more to his mother.

The prayerful solicitude with which she trained her children has been rewarded by each one of them making a public profession of his faith in Christ. Two of her sons occupy foremost places in the metropolis as preachers of the Gospel; one of her daughters, the wife of a minister, assists her husband in the preparation of his sermons.

Speaking one day to her son Charles of her solicitude for the best interests of all her children, Mrs. Spurgeon said, "Ah, Charley, I have often prayed that you might be saved, but never that you should become a Baptist." To this Charles replied, "God has answered your prayer, Mother, with His usual bounty and given you more than you asked."

Both Mr. and Mrs. Spurgeon made great sacrifices of personal comfort to give a good education to their children, and the children were taught habits of thrift and self-denial. The care thus bestowed on their training when young has been to the parents a source of much satisfaction; the good results of that care are manifested in the happy home lives of their children.

When at some future period the historian of the Metropolitan Tabernacle and of the Stockwell Orphanage is considering the primary causes of those great enterprises, the care which Mrs. Spurgeon bestowed on the early training of her family must be counted as a valuable auxiliary in preparing the way for such exemplary conduct.

The Country Boys

The villages of England, more than the towns, have the honor of producing our great men. In the village the faculties develop themselves as nature forms them, while in the large towns a thousand delusive influences are continually diverting the minds of the young into channels of danger and error.

The parents of Pastor Spurgeon were residing at the village of Kelvedon, in Essex, when on June 19, 1834, their son Charles was born. The population of the place is only two thousand souls, and the resident clergyman, at the time just stated, the Rev. Charles Dalton, lived long enough to celebrate his jubilee (50 years) as minister in that parish.

The Spurgeon family belonged to the Nonconformists, under whose teaching they were all brought up. Charles and James Spurgeon were much separated during their early years. Charles was of a larger and broader build than James, and the boys of the village are said to have given them names designative of character, which also indicated friendship or attachment.

Charles had as a boy a larger head than his brother, and he is represented as taking in learning more readily than James, whilst the latter excelled more in domestic duties. Besides the brothers there are six sisters living (the year 1890), two of whom are said to resemble Charles in mental energy.

Household Nurture

As the children were growing up, the father, like many professional and public men, feared his frequent absence from home would interfere with the religious education of the little ones. But happily for him he had a true helpmeet to cooperate with him in this important work, and happily for those children they had a noble mother who lived for

BIRTHPLACE OF C. H. SPURGEON

them and sought to build them up in true Christian character. Nor
has she lived unrewarded for her pains. Oh, that all mothers learned
the lesson well! Hear the good man speak thus of his wife:

> I had been from home a great deal, trying to build up weak congrega-
> tions, and felt that I was neglecting the religious training of my own
> children while I was toiling for the good of others. I returned home with
> these feelings.
>
> I opened the door and was surprised to find none of the children about
> the hall. Going quietly upstairs, I heard my wife's voice. She was engaged
> in prayer with the children; I heard her pray for them one by one by name.
> She came to Charles, and specially prayed for him, for he was of high
> spirit and daring temper. I listened till she had ended her prayer, and I
> felt and said, "Lord, I will go on with Thy work. The children will be
> cared for."

The Diligent Youth

When just old enough to leave home, Charles was removed to his
grandfather's house at Stambourne, where, under the affectionate
care of a maiden aunt and directed by the venerable pastor, he soon
developed into the thoughtful boy, fonder of his book than of his play.
He would sit for hours together gazing with childish horror at the grim
figures of *Old Bonner* and *Giant Despair*; or tracing the adventures of
Christian in the *Pilgrim's Progress*, or of Robinson Crusoe. The pious

THE OLD MANSE AND MEETING HOUSE, STAMBOURNE

precocity of the child soon attracted the attention of all around. He would astonish the grave deacons and matrons who met at his grandfather's house on Sunday evenings by proposing subjects for conversation and making pertinent remarks upon them.

At that early period in life he gave indications of that decision of character and boldness of address for which he has since become so remarkable.

In the spring of 1840 and before he was six years old, seeing a person in the village who made a profession of religion standing in the street with others known to be of doubtful character, he walked up to the big man and astonished him by asking, "What doest thou here, Elijah?"

In 1841 he returned to his father's house, then at Colchester, that he might secure what improved advantages in education a town could supply. His mental development was even then considerably in advance of his years, and his moral character, especially his love of truth, was very conspicuous.

Spending the summer vacation at his grandfather's in 1844, when he was just ten years old, an incident occurred which had a material influence on the boy at the time and even more so as divine Providence opened his way. Mr. Spurgeon's grandfather first related the incident to the writer, but it has since been written by Mr. Spurgeon himself with title of "The Rev. Richard Knill's Prophecy." The account is as follows:

A Puzzling Question

When I was a very small boy, I was staying at my grandfather's where I had aforetime spent my earliest days; and as the manner was, I read the Scriptures at family prayer.

Once upon a time when reading the passage in the book of Revelation which mentions the bottomless pit, I paused and said, "Grandpa, what can this mean?" The answer was kind but unsatisfactory: "Pooh, pooh, child, go on." The child intended, however, to have an explanation and therefore selected the same chapter morning after morning, Sunday included, and always halted at the same verse to repeat the inquiry.

At length the venerable patriarch capitulated at discretion, by saying, "Well, dear, what is it that puzzles you?" Now the child had often seen baskets with very frail bottoms, which in course of wear became bottomless and allowed the fruit placed therein to fall upon the ground.

Here, then, was the puzzle: If the pit aforesaid had no bottom, where would all the people fall who dropped out at its lower end?—a puzzle which rather startled the propriety of family worship and had to be laid aside for explanation at a more convenient season.

Questions of the like simple and natural character would frequently break up into paragraphs at the family Bible reading, and had there not been a world of love and license allowed to the inquisitive reader, he would soon have been deposed from his office. As it was, the Scriptures were not very badly rendered and were probably quite as interesting as if they had not been interspersed with original and curious inquiries.

A Walk Before Breakfast

On one of these occasions Mr. Knill, whose name is a household word and whose memory is precious to thousands at home and abroad, stayed at the minister's house on Friday, in readiness to preach at Stambourne for the London Missionary Society on the following Sunday.

He never looked into a young face without yearning to impart some spiritual gift. All love, kindness, earnestness and warmth, he coveted the souls of men as misers desire the gold their hearts pine for. He heard the boy read and commended: a little judicious praise is the sure way to a young heart.

An agreement was made with the lad that on the next morning, Saturday, he would show Mr. Knill over the garden and take him for a walk before breakfast: a task so flattering to juvenile self-importance was sure to be readily entered upon.

There was a tap at the door, and the child was soon out of bed and in the garden with his new friend, who won his heart in no time by pleasing stories and kind words and giving him a chance to communicate in return. The talk was all about Jesus and the pleasantness of loving Him. Nor was it mere talk; there was pleading too.

Into the great yew arbor, cut into the shape of a sugar-loaf, both went; and the soul winner knelt down and with his arms around the youthful neck, poured out vehement intercession for the salvation of the lad. The next morning witnessed the same instruction and supplication, and the next also, while all day long the pair were never far apart and never out of each other's thoughts.

The mission sermons were preached in the old Puritan meeting house, and the man of God was called to go to the next halting place in his tour as deputation for the Society.

Singular Prophecy

But he did not leave till he had uttered a most remarkable prophecy. After even more earnest prayer with his little *protégé*, he appeared to have a burden on his mind, and he could not go till he had eased himself of it. Writes Mr. Spurgeon:

> In after years he was heard to say he felt a singular interest in me and an earnest expectation for which he could not account.
>
> Calling the family together, he took me on his knee; and I distinctly remember his saying, "I do not know how it is, but I feel a solemn presentiment that this child will preach the Gospel to thousands and God will bless him to many souls. So sure am I of this, that when my little man preaches in Rowland Hill's chapel, as he will do one day, I should like him to promise me that he will give out the hymn commencing—
>
> > *"God moves in a mysterious way*
> > *His wonders to perform."*

This promise was of course made and was followed by another—namely, that at his express desire I would learn the hymn in question and think of what he had said.

The prophetic declaration was fulfilled. When I had the pleasure of preaching the Word of Life in Surrey Chapel and also when I preached in Mr. Hill's first pulpit at Wootton-under-Edge, the hymn was sung in both places.

Did the words of Mr. Knill help to bring about their own fulfillment? I think so. I believed them and looked forward to the time when I should preach the Word. I felt very powerfully that no unconverted person might dare to enter the ministry. This made me the more intent on seeking salvation and more hopeful of it; and when by grace I was enabled to cast myself on the Saviour's love, it was not long before my mouth began to speak of His redemption.

How came that sober-minded minister to speak thus to and of one into whose future God alone could see? How came it that he lived to rejoice with his younger brother in the truth of all that he had spoken? The answer is plain. But mark one particular lesson: would to God that we were all as wise as Richard Knill in habitually sowing beside all waters. Mr. Knill might very naturally have left the minister's little grandson on the plea that he had other duties of more importance than praying with children; and yet who shall say that he did not effect as much by that simple act of humble ministry as by dozens of sermons addressed to crowded audiences? To me his tenderness in considering the little one was fraught with everlasting consequences, and I must ever feel that his time was well laid out.

"Old Bonner"

During the fostering care of his Aunt Ann—his father's unmarried sister at Stambourne—an attachment grew up which was as sincere in affectionate regard as that which usually exists between parent and child. This aunt had charge of the infant Spurgeon during most of the first six years of his life. He was the first grandchild in the family. Care was taken by his aunt to instruct him gradually as the mind was capable of receiving impressions; but from his childhood his mind seems to have been framed after nature's model.

The book he admired at his grandfather's which had for one of its illustrations the portrait of Bonner, Bishop of London, was the cause of his mind receiving its first impressions against tyranny and persecution; and being told of the persecuting character of Bonner, the child manifested a great dislike to the name and called the picture which represented the bishop "Old Bonner."

Even at that early period of life before he was six years old, he exhibited a marked attachment to those who were known as the children of God.

Four years of the boy's life were spent at a school at Colchester, where he studied Latin, Greek and French. He was a diligent student, always carrying the first prize in all competitions.

ST. AUGUSTINE'S COLLEGE AT MAIDSTONE

In 1849 he was placed under the care of Mr. Swindell at Newmarket. There he learned to practice much self-denial. The privations he voluntarily submitted to at that time showed how decided were his purposes to acquire knowledge and, as far as he knew, to try to serve God.

But the struggle going on in his mind, preparatory to his giving his heart fully to God, can only be described in his own touching words, as recorded in one of his sermons. Speaking of a free-thinker, he remarks:

> I, too, have been like him. There was an evil hour in which I slipped the anchor of my faith: I cut the cable of my belief: I no longer moored myself hard by the coast of Revelation: I allowed my vessel to drift before the wind and thus started on the voyage of infidelity.
>
> I said to Reason, *Be thou my captain*; I said to my own brain, *Be thou my rudder*; and I started on my mad voyage.
>
> Thank God it is all over now; but I will tell you its brief history: it was one hurried sailing over the tempestuous ocean of free thought.

The result was: from doubting some things, he came to question everything, even his own existence.

But soon he conquered those extremes to which Satan often drives the sinner who is really repenting.

CHAPTER II

Conversion and Early Preaching

Mr. Spurgeon's Account of His Conversion and Early Preaching—A Desponding Penitent—Visit to a Primitive Methodist Chapel—"Look, Look!"—Preaching in the Old Place—Happy Days—Light in Darkness—Profession of Faith—Mission Work—Boy Preacher—The First Sermon—Cottage and Open-air Services—Escaping College—Poem

I will tell you how I myself was brought to the knowledge of the truth. It may happen that the telling of that will bring someone else to Christ.

It pleased God in my childhood to convince me of sin. I lived a miserable creature, finding no hope, no comfort, thinking that surely God would never save me.

At last the worst came to the worst—I was miserable; I could do scarcely anything. My heart was broken in pieces. Six months did I pray agonizingly with all my heart, but never had an answer. I resolved that, in the town where I lived, I would visit every place of worship in order to find out the way of salvation. I felt I was willing to do and be anything if God would only forgive me.

I set off, determined to go around to all the chapels and to all places of worship. Though I dearly venerate the men who occupy those pulpits now, and did so then, I am bound to say that I never heard them once fully preach the Gospel. I mean by that, they preached truth, great truths, many good truths that were fitting to many of their congregation—spiritually-minded people—but what I wanted to know was, How can I get my sins forgiven? And they never once told me that. I wanted to hear how a poor sinner, under a sense of sin, might find peace with God; but when I went I heard a sermon on "Be not deceived: God is not mocked," which cut me up worse but did not say how I might escape.

Earnestly Seeking

I went again another day. The text was something about the glories of the righteous, but nothing for poor me. I was something like a dog under the table—not allowed to eat of the children's food. I went time after time, and I can honestly say, I don't know that I ever went without prayer to God. And I am sure there was not a more attentive hearer in all the place than myself, for I panted and longed to understand how I might be saved.

At last one day it snowed so much that I could not go to the place I had determined to go to, so was obliged to stop on the way. It was a blessed stop to me! I found rather an obscure street and turned down a court. There was a little chapel—the Primitive Methodists' chapel. I had heard of these people from many and how they sang so loudly that they made people's heads ache; but that did not matter. I wanted to know how I might be saved; and if they made my head ache ever so much, I did not care.

ARTILLERY STREET PRIMITIVE METHODIST CHAPEL IN WHICH C. H. SPURGEON WAS CONVERTED

So, sitting down, the service went on, but no minister came. At last a very thin-looking man came into the pulpit, opened his Bible and read these words: "Look unto me, and be ye saved, all the ends of the earth." Just setting his eyes upon me, as if he knew me all by heart, he said, "Young man, you are in trouble." Well, I was, sure enough. Says he, "You will never get out of it unless you look to Christ."

"It Is Only Look"

Then, lifting up his hands, he cried out as only a Primitive Methodist could do, "Look, look, look! It is only look!"

I saw at once the way of salvation. Oh, how I did leap for joy at that moment! I know not what else he said: I did not take much notice of it—so possessed was I with that one thought. Like as when the brazen serpent was lifted up, they only looked and were healed, I had been waiting to do fifty things, but when I heard this word "Look!" what a charming word it seemed to me! I looked until I could almost have looked my eyes away! And in Heaven I will look on still in my joy unutterable.

I now think I am bound never to preach a sermon without preaching to sinners. I do think that a minister who can preach a sermon without addressing sinners does not know how to preach.

Preaching in the Old Place

On October 11, 1864, the pastor of the Metropolitan Tabernacle preached a sermon to five hundred hearers in the chapel at Colchester (in which he was converted) on the occasion of the anniversary in that place of worship. He took for his text the memorable words of Isaiah 45:22, "Look unto me, and be ye saved," then said, "That I heard preached from in this chapel when the Lord *converted* me." Then, pointing to a seat on the left hand under the gallery, he said, *"I was sitting in that pew when I was converted."*

This honest confession produced a thrilling effect upon the congregation and very much endeared the successful pastor to many hearts.

Best of All Days

Of his conversion, Mr. Spurgeon spoke on every fitting opportunity, hoping thereby to benefit others. As an example of the advantage which he takes, under the title of "A Bit for Boys," he says in *The Sword and the Trowel:*

> When I was just fifteen, I believed in the Lord Jesus, was baptized and joined the church. This is twenty-five years ago now, and I have never been sorry for what I then did; no, not even once.
>
> I have had plenty of time to think it over and many temptations to try some other course; and if I had found out that I had been deceived or had made a gross blunder, I would have made a change before now and would have done my best to prevent others from falling into the same delusion.
>
> I tell you, boys, the day I gave myself up to the Lord Jesus to be His servant was the very best day of my life.
>
> Then it was when I began to be safe and happy. Then I found out the secret of living and had a worthy object for my life's exertions and an unfailing comfort for life's troubles. Because I would wish every boy to have a bright eye, a light tread, a joyful heart and overflowing spirits, I plead with him to consider whether he will not follow my example, for I speak from experience.

Dawn of a New Life

Early in the month of January, 1856, Mr. Spurgeon preached a sermon to his own congregation on Sunday morning entitled "Sovereignty and Salvation." In that sermon he said:

Six years ago today, as near as possible at this very hour of the day, I was "in the gall of bitterness, and in the bond of iniquity," but had yet, by divine grace, been led to feel the bitterness of that bondage and to cry out by reason of the soreness of its slavery.

Seeking rest and finding none, I stepped within the house of God and sat there, afraid to look upward lest I should be utterly cut off and lest His fierce wrath should consume me.

The minister rose in his pulpit and, as I have done this morning, read this text: "Look unto me, and be ye saved, all the ends of the earth: for I am God, and there is none else."

I looked that moment; the grace of faith was vouchsafed to me in that instant, and

> 'Ere since by faith I saw the stream
> His flowing wounds supply,
> Redeeming love has been my theme
> And shall be till I die.

I shall never forget that day while memory holds its place; nor can I help repeating this text whenever I remember that hour when first I knew the Lord. How strangely gracious, how wonderfully and marvelously kind, that he who heard these words so little time ago for his own soul's profit, should now address you this morning as his hearers from the same text, in the full and confident hope that some poor sinner within these walls may hear the glad tidings of salvation for himself also and may today be 'turned from darkness to light, and from the power of Satan unto God'!

A Public Profession

All the letters he sent home at that period were full of the overflowings of a grateful heart; and although so young in years, he describes the operations of divine grace on the heart and life and the differences between the doctrines of the Gospel and the forms of the church in terms so precise and clear that no merely human teaching could have enabled him so to do.

Brought up, as he had been, among the Independents, his own views on one point of church ordinances now assumed a form differing materially from what his parents had adopted. Having experienced a change of heart, he felt it to be laid upon him as an imperative duty to make a full and public confession of the change by public baptism.

He had united himself formally with the Baptist people the year before; now he felt constrained to fully cast in his lot and become one of them entirely.

He wrote many letters home to his father, asking for advice and information, but striving to enforce his own conviction for making a public profession of his faith in Christ. At length the father was satisfied that his son had no faith in the dogma of baptismal regeneration; that his motives for seeking to be publicly recognized as a follower of the Lord Jesus were higher than those he had feared; therefore, no further opposition was made, and the necessary steps were taken for his immersion.

All the arrangements having been made, the young convert walked from Newmarket to Isleham, seven miles, on May 2; and, staying with the family of Mr. Cantlow, the Baptist minister there, he was by that gentleman publicly baptized in that village on Friday, May 3, 1851, being in his sixteenth year. He thus proceeds in his letter to his father:

> It is very pleasing to me that the day on which I shall openly profess the name of Jesus is my mother's birthday. May it be to both of us a fore-taste of many glorious and happy days yet to come.

School Duties and Mission Work

Having thus publicly devoted himself to the service of God, he was more earnest than ever in his efforts to do good. Besides having himself revived an old society for distributing tracts, he undertook to carry out this good work in Newmarket thoroughly. Whenever he walked out, he carried these messengers of mercy with him; he was instant in season and, indeed, was seldom out of season in his efforts to do good.

His duties in school occupied him three hours daily, the remainder of his time being spent in his closet or in some work of mercy. The Sunday school very soon gained his attention, and his addresses to the children were so full of love and instruction that they carried the good tidings home to their parents; and soon they came to hear the addresses in the vestry of the Independent chapel in that town. The place was soon filled.

The Boy Preacher

At one of the examinations of the school he had consented to deliver an oration on missions. It was a public occasion, and in the company was a clergyman.

During the examination, the clergyman heard of the death of his gardener and suddenly left for home. But on his way he thus reasoned with himself: *The gardener is dead; I cannot restore his life; I will return and hear what the young usher has to say on missions.* He returned, heard the oration, and was pleased to show his approval by presenting Mr. Spurgeon with a British gold coin.

Having at once identified himself as a member of the Baptist church in Cambridge, he soon found occupation suitable to his mind. His addresses to children, and afterwards to parents and children, had produced a love of the work; and he soon was called to exhort a village congregation. He was then sixteen years old.

Connected with the Baptist church meeting in St. Andrew's Street, Cambridge, formerly under the pastoral care of the late learned Robert Hall, there existed a society entitled "The Lay Preachers' Association." Although so young in years, Mr. Spurgeon was accepted as a member of this association. Here he at once found the occupation which his mind most desired, and he was soon appointed to address a congregation.

As this was one of the most important steps in Mr. Spurgeon's life, the reader will be glad to learn from his own pen the circumstances which led to his first attempted sermon. In introducing the text, "Unto you therefore which believe he is precious" (I Pet. 2:7), Mr. Spurgeon remarks, in 1873:

First Sermon

I remember well that, more than twenty-two years ago, the first attempted sermon I ever made was from this text.

I had been asked to walk out to the village of Taversham, about four miles from Cambridge, where I then lived, to accompany a young man whom I supposed to be the preacher for the evening. On the way I said to him that I trusted God would bless him in his labors. "Oh, dear," said he, "I never preached in my life; I never thought of doing such a thing. I was asked to walk with you, and I sincerely hope God will bless YOU in YOUR preaching." "Nay," said I, "but I never preached, and I don't know that I could do anything of the sort."

We walked together till we came to the place, my inmost soul being all in a trouble as to what would happen. When we found the congregation assembled and no one else there to speak of Jesus, though I was only sixteen years of age, as I found that I was expected to preach, I did preach, and the text was that just given.

Considering the results which have followed that sermon, it will be interesting to glance at some of the incidents belonging to that early period of his ministry.

COTTAGE AT TAVERSHAM WHERE SPURGEON FIRST PREACHED

Early Promise

In the summer of 1875, from inquiries made in the locality, a correspondent of the *Baptist* newspaper reports as follows:

> A gentleman informed me that he heard Mr. Spurgeon preach his first sermon when about sixteen years of age; and he then read, prayed and expounded the Word, being attired in a round jacket and broad turn-down collar, such as I remember to have been in fashion at that period.
>
> Mr. Spurgeon was then living near Cambridge, and his mode of preaching afforded promise that he would become a powerful and popular preacher.
>
> Mr. C., the schoolmaster of the village in 1850, was impressed with the precocious talent of the young preacher and his style of preaching.

Having once entered on this most solemn duty and finding acceptance with the people, he laid himself out for one service every evening, after attending to his duties in school during the day.

From an aged and experienced Christian who heard Mr. Spurgeon preach before his call to London, we learn that his addresses were very instructive and often included illustrations derived from history, geography, astronomy and from other branches of school occupation, evidently adapted from his daily duties, and thus made to serve as instruments in religion as well as in training and informing the mind.

His early ministry was not only gratuitous but often attended with demands on his small salary, which he willingly gave to God—not to be seen of men, did he help the needy.

In Cottages and the Open Air

In some of the thirteen village stations around Cambridge and Waterbeach to which Mr. Spurgeon devoted all his evenings, the preaching was held in a cottage; in others, a chapel; and occasionally the open common could furnish the accommodation required.

At the village of Waterbeach, Mr. Spurgeon was received in a marked manner of approval. In most of the places in which he had preached, the effect was very much alike in the large numbers attracted to hear the Word of God and in the success which God was pleased to bestow on his labors.

Even at that early period of his ministerial career, invitations to preach special sermons in towns and villages at a distance soon rapidly increased. At Waterbeach, however, the little church saw in the young man a suitability to their wants, so they gave him an invitation to become their pastor.

Pastorate at Waterbeach

He was well received by the people, and soon became quite popular. During the few months of his pastorate there, the church members were increased from forty to nearly one hundred.

Mr. Spurgeon has himself supplied an interesting reminiscence of his ministry at that village, which is worth preserving:

> When we had just commenced our youthful pastorate at Waterbeach in 1852, Cornelius Elven, as a man of mark in that region, was requested to preach the anniversary sermons in our little thatched meeting-house. Right well do we remember his hearty compliance with our desire.
>
> We met at the station as he alighted from a third-class carriage which he had chosen in order to put the friends to the least possible expense for his traveling. His bulk was stupendous, and one soon saw that his heart was as large in proportion as his body.

He gave us much sage and holy advice during the visit, which came to us with much the same weight as Paul's words came to Timothy. He bade us study hard and keep abreast of the foremost Christians in our little church, adding as a reason that if these men, either in their knowledge

WATERBEACH CHAPEL, 1851

of Scripture or their power to edify the people, once outstrip you, the temptation will arise among them to be dissatisfied with your ministry; and, however good they are, they will feel their superiority, and others will perceive it too, and then your place in the church will become very difficult to hold.

His sermons were very homely and preeminently practical. He told anecdotes of the usefulness of addressing individuals one by one about their souls.

Not Spoiled by Colleges

It has been remarked a hundred times by those not well informed on the matter that Mr. Spurgeon was an uneducated man and had no college instruction. The experience of a quarter of a century has demonstrated how erroneous were these remarks. Is there in England a man of education who has done more for the extension of the kingdom of Christ by the publication of numerous valuable theological and instructive books than Mr. Spurgeon? Let the list of his works determine.

On the question of not going to college, there is also some misconception. The exact facts are worthy of being placed on record. Mr. Spurgeon has himself so clearly stated the case in an article he wrote some time ago in his own magazine that the reader will be glad to see it here; it is curious and interesting:

Soon after I had begun in 1852 to preach the Word in Waterbeach, I was strongly advised by my father and others to enter Stepney, now Regent's Park College, to prepare more fully for the ministry. Knowing that learning is never an encumbrance but is often a great means of usefulness, I felt inclined to avail myself of the opportunity of attaining it. Although I believed I might be useful without a college training, I consented to the opinion of friends, that I should be more useful with it.

An Appointment Not Kept

Dr. Angus, the tutor of the college, visited Cambridge, where I then resided; and it was arranged that we should meet at the house of Mr. Macmillan, the publisher.

Thinking and praying over the matter, I entered the house at exactly the time appointed and was shown into a room, where I waited patiently for a couple of hours, feeling too much impressed with my own insignificance and the greatness of the tutor from London to venture to ring the bell and inquire the cause of the unreasonably long delay.

At last, patience having had her perfect work, the bell was set in motion, and on the arrival of the servant, the waiting young man of eighteen was informed that the doctor had tarried in another room and could stay no longer, so had gone off by train to London.

The stupid girl had given no information to the family that anyone called and had been shown into the drawing room; consequently, the meeting never came about, although designed by both parties. I was not a little disappointed at the moment, but have a thousand times since then thanked the Lord very heartily for the strange providence which forced my steps into another and far better path.

Strange Impressions

Still holding to the idea of entering the Collegiate Institution, I thought of writing and making an immediate application; but this was not to be.

That afternoon, having to preach at a village station, I walked slowly in a meditating frame of mind over Midsummer Common to the little wooden bridge which leads to Chesterton, and in the midst of the common I was startled by what seemed to me to be a loud voice, but which may have been a singular illusion. Whichever it was, the impression it made on my mind was most vivid. I seemed very distinctly to hear the words, "Seekest thou great things for thyself? Seek them not!"

This led me to look at my position from a different point of view and to challenge my motives and intentions. I remembered my poor but loving people to whom I ministered and the souls which had been given me in my humble charge; and although at that time I anticipated obscurity and poverty as the result of the resolve, yet I did there and then renounce the offer of collegiate instruction, determining to abide for a season, at least, with my people and to remain preaching the Word so long as I had strength to do it.

Had it not been for those words, I had not been where I am now. Although the ephod is no longer worn by a ministering priest, the Lord guides His people by His wisdom and orders all their paths in love. And in times of perplexity, by ways mysterious and remarkable, He says to them: "This is the way; walk ye in it."

The Turning Point

It is desirable to give one or two extracts from his letters, written at the same time, to show how anxiously the matter was considered. In his reply to his father, dated March 9, 1852, Mr. Spurgeon writes:

> I have all along had an aversion to college; and nothing but a feeling that I must not consult myself, but Jesus, could have made me think of it. It appears to my friends at Cambridge that it is my duty to remain with my dear people at Waterbeach; so say the church there unanimously, and so say three of our deacons at Cambridge.

During the summer his decision was taken, in the way previously related; and in a letter he sent to his mother in November following, he says:

> I am more and more glad that I never went to college. God sends such sunshine on my path, such smiles of grace, that I cannot regret if I have forfeited all my prospects for it. I am conscious I held back from love to God and His cause; and I had rather be poor in His service than rich in my own.
>
> I have all that heart can wish for; yea, God giveth more than my desire. My congregation is as great and loving as ever. During all the time I have been at Waterbeach, I have had a different house for my home every day. Fifty-two families have thus taken me in, and I have still six other invitations not yet accepted.
>
> Talk about the people not caring for me because they give me so little! I dare tell anybody under Heaven 'tis false! They do all they can.
>
> Our anniversary passed off grandly; six were baptized; crowds on crowds stood by the river; the chapel afterwards was crammed both to the tea and the sermon.

By these and other exercises of mind, God was preparing His young servant for greater plans of usefulness and a wider sphere of action.

The following stanzas were written by Mr. Spurgeon at the age of eighteen:

IMMANUEL

When once I mourned a load of sin;
When conscience felt a wound within;
When all my works were thrown away;
When on my knees I knelt to pray,
    Then, blissful hour, remembered well,
    I learned Thy love, Immanuel.

When storms of sorrow toss my soul;
When waves of care around me roll;
When comforts sink, when joys shall flee;
When hopeless griefs shall gape for me,
    One word the tempest's rage shall quell—
    That word, Thy name, Immanuel.

When for the truth I suffer shame;
When foes pour scandal on my name;
When cruel taunts and jeers abound;
When "Bulls of Bashan" gird me round,
    Secure within Thy tower I'll dwell—
    That tower, Thy grace, Immanuel.

When Hell enraged lifts up her roar;
When Satan stops my path before;
When fiends rejoice and wait my end;
When legioned hosts their arrows send,
    Fear not, my soul, but hurl at Hell
    Thy battle cry, Immanuel.

When down the hill of life I go;
When o'er my feet death's waters flow;
When in the deep'ning flood I sink;
When friends stand weeping on the brink,
    I'll mingle with my last farewell
    Thy lovely name, Immanuel.

When tears are banished from mine eye;
When fairer worlds than these are nigh;
When Heaven shall fill my ravished sight;
When I shall bathe in sweet delight,
    One joy all joys shall far excel,
    To see Thy face, Immanuel.

CHAPTER III

The Young Preacher in London

Speech at Cambridge—Invitation to London—Willing Hearers—Interesting Letters to New Park Street Church—Visitation of Cholera—Labors Among the Dying—Publication of Sermons—Eagerness of the Public to Obtain the Printed Discourses—Description of the Youthful Preacher—Thronging Crowds—Birthday Sermon—Preaching in Scotland—Good News From Printed Sermons—Reports of Many Conversions

The anniversary meeting of the Cambridge Union of Sunday Schools in 1853 was held at Cambridge, on which occasion Mr. Spurgeon was called upon to speak.

The part he took was of remarkable significance. Nothing in his manner or his remarks was specially attractive to his audience, but there was an unseen agency at work with the speaker as well as in the audience. There was present at that meeting a gentleman from Essex, on whose mind the address delivered by Mr. Spurgeon made a lasting impression.

Shortly afterwards he met in London with one of the deacons of the Baptist church of New Park Street, Southwark, a church which had once flourished like the ancient cedars of Lebanon, but which was then so far shorn of its former glory as to give cause of serious consideration. Anxiously did the thoughtful deacon tell his tale of a scattered church and a diminished congregation.

Fresh upon the mind of his hearer was the effect of the speech of the young minister at Cambridge, and he ventured to speak of the youthful evangelist of Waterbeach as a minister likely to be the means of reviving interest in the declining church at New Park Street.

The two friends separated, the deacon not much impressed with what he had heard; and things grew worse.

Invited to London

But finally a correspondence was commenced between Deacon James Low and Mr. Spurgeon, which soon resulted in the latter receiving an invitation to come to London and preach before them in their large chapel. The work was altogether of God; man only made the arrangements. The motto of Julius Caesar may be modified to express the results of the visit: Mr. Spurgeon came; he preached; he conquered.

C. H. SPURGEON WHEN HE FIRST
CAME TO LONDON

For some months the pulpit had been vacant, the pews forsaken, the aisles desolate and the exchequer empty. Decay had set in so seriously that the deacons lost heart; and until Mr. Spurgeon arrived, the cause seemed hopeless.

In the autumn of 1853 he first occupied New Park Street pulpit. The chapel, capable of holding twelve hundred people, had about two hundred occupants at the first service. The preacher was a young man who had just passed his nineteenth year. In his sermon he spoke with the freedom and boldness which evinced that he believed what he preached and believed that his message was from God.

Some were disappointed; others resolved to oppose, and did oppose; but by far the greater proportion were disposed to hear him again.

Instant Success

The result of the first sermon was proved, in a few hours, to have been a success. The evening congregation was greatly increased, partly from curiosity, partly from the youth of the preacher and his unusual style of address.

Mr. Spurgeon was again invited to take the pulpit on another

Sunday as early as possible; for a feeling of excitement was created, and it required to be satisfied. After consulting with his church at Waterbeach, he arranged to supply the New Park Street pulpit during three alternate Lord's days.

Because the desire to hear the young preacher had greatly extended, it was determined to invite Mr. Spurgeon from his rustic retreat to undertake the heavy responsibility of pastor of one of the most ancient Baptist churches in London and formerly the most influential; and he entered on that duty in the month of April, 1854.

We are permitted to give two of Mr. Spurgeon's letters to the church at the time of his appointment, which will most clearly state the facts relating to his coming to London.

The first of the following letters was written to Deacon Low shortly before Mr. Spurgeon left Cambridge, and the second is dated from his first lodgings immediately after his permanent arrival in London. It will be seen that these letters exhibit a wisdom and maturity scarcely to be expected from a youth of twenty.

No. 60 Park Street, Cambridge, Jan. 27, 1854.
To James Low, Esq.

MY DEAR SIR:

I cannot help feeling intense gratification at the unanimity of the church at New Park Street in relation to their invitation to me. Had I been uncomfortable in my present situation, I should have felt unmixed pleasure at the prospect Providence seems to open up before me; but having a devoted and loving people, I feel I know not how.

One thing I know, namely, that I must soon be severed from them by necessity, for they do not raise sufficient to maintain me in comfort. Had they done so, I should have turned a deaf ear to any request to leave them, at least for the present. But now my Heavenly Father drives me forth from this little Garden of Eden; and while I see that I must go out, I leave it with reluctance and tremble to tread the unknown land before me.

When I first ventured to preach at Waterbeach, I only accepted an invitation for three months on the condition that, if in that time I should see good reasons for leaving or they on their part should wish for it, I should be at liberty to cease supplying or they should have the same power to request me to do so before the expiration of the time.

With regard to a six months' invitation from you, I have no objection to the length of time, but rather approve of the prudence of the church in wishing to have one so young as myself on an extended period of approbation.

But I write after well weighing the matter, when I say positively that I cannot—I *dare* not—accept an unqualified invitation for so long a time. My objection is not to the length of time of probation, but it ill becomes a youth to promise to preach to a London congregation so long until he knows them and they know him. I would engage to supply for three months of that time and then, should the congregation fail or the church disagree, I would reserve to myself liberty, without breach of engagement, to retire; and you would on your part have the right to dismiss me without seeming to treat me ill.

Should I see no reason for so doing and the church still retain their wish for me, I can remain the other three months, either with or without the formality of a further invitation; but even during the second three months I should not like to regard myself as a fixture, in case of ill success, but would only be a supply, liable to a fortnight's dismissal or resignation.

Perhaps this is not businesslike—I do not know; but this is the course I should prefer, if it would be agreeable to the church. Enthusiasm and popularity are often the crackling of thorns, and soon expire. I do not wish to be a hindrance if I cannot be a help.

With regard to coming at once, I think I must not. My own deacons just hint that I ought to finish the quarter here; though, by ought, they mean simply—pray do so if you can. This would be too long a delay. I wish to help them until they can get supplies, which is only to be done with great difficulty; and, as I have given you four Sundays, I hope you will allow me to give them four in return. I would give them the first and second Sundays in February and two more in a month or six weeks' time. I owe them much for their kindness, although they insist that the debt lies on their side. Some of them hope, and almost pray, that you may be tired in three months so that I may be again sent back to them!

Thus, my dear sir, I have honestly poured out my heart to you. You are too kind. You will excuse me if I err, for I wish to do right to you, to my people and to all, as being not mine own but bought with a price.

I respect the honesty and boldness of the small minority and only wonder that the number was not greater. I pray God that, if He does not see fit that I should remain with you, the majority may be quite as much the other way at the end of six months, so that I may never divide you into parties.

Pecuniary matters I am well satisfied with. And now one thing is due to every minister, and I pray you to remind the church of it, namely, that in private, as well as public, they must all wrestle in prayer to God that I may be sustained in the great work.

I am, with the best wishes for your health and the greatest respect,

Yours truly,

C. H. SPURGEON

Call to New Park Street Chapel

Viewed in the light of subsequent results, it will not surprise the reader to learn that it did not take the church six months to determine their part of the contract. Before three months had passed away, "the small minority" had been absorbed into the majority, and the entire church united in giving their young minister, not yet twenty years old, an invitation to accept the pastorate, both cordial and unanimous.

Mr. Spurgeon's second letter at this period will best explain the real facts:

75 DOVER ROAD, BOROUGH, April 28, 1854.
To the Baptist Church of Christ worshiping in
New Park Street Chapel, Southwark:

DEARLY BELOVED IN CHRIST JESUS:

I have received your unanimous invitation, as contained in a resolution passed by you on the 19th instant, desiring me to accept the pastorate among you. No lengthened reply is required; there is but one answer to so loving and cordial an invitation. I ACCEPT IT. I have not been perplexed as to what my reply shall be, for many things constrain me thus to answer.

NEW PARK STREET CHAPEL, SOUTHWARK

I sought not to come to you, for I was the minister of an obscure but affectionate people. I never solicited advancement. The first note of invitation from your deacons came to me quite unlooked for, and I trembled at the idea of preaching in London. I could not understand how it came about, and even now I am filled with astonishment at the wondrous Providence.

I would wish to give myself into the hands of our covenant God, whose wisdom directs all things. He shall choose for me; and so far as I can judge, this is His choice.

I feel it to be a high honor to be a pastor of a people who can mention glorious names as my predecessors, and I entreat of you to remember me in prayer, that I may realize the solemn responsibility of my trust.

Remember my youth and inexperience; pray that these may not hinder my usefulness. I trust also that the remembrance of these may lead you to forgive the mistakes I may make or unguarded words I may utter.

Blessed be the name of the Most High! If He has called me to this office, He will support me in it; otherwise, how should a child, a youth, have the presumption thus to attempt a work which filled the heart and hands of Jesus?

Your kindness to me has been very great, and my heart is knit unto you. I fear not your steadfastness; I fear my own. The Gospel, I believe, enables me to venture great things, and by faith I venture this.

I ask your cooperation in every good work—in visiting the sick, in bringing in inquirers and in mutual edification.

Oh, that I may be no injury to you, but a lasting benefit! I have no more to say, only this: if I have expressed myself in these few words in a manner unbecoming my youth and inexperience, you will not impute it to arrogance, but forgive my mistake.

And now, commending you to our covenant-keeping God, the triune Jehovah, I am yours to serve in the Gospel,

C. H. SPURGEON

Before three months of the new pastorate had expired, the fame of the young minister had spread over the metropolis, crowds of people flocked to his chapel at every service, and the newspapers, week by week for some time, were asking, "Who is this Spurgeon?"

For a long time that question was a puzzle to many minds, but one thing was certain: he had secured the ear and attention of the public, who waited upon his ministry by thousands.

The Black Flag

The summer of 1854 will long be remembered for the frightful scourge of Asiatic cholera with which the great city was visited. The black flag could be seen stretched across streets to warn strangers of the close proximity of plague-stricken dwellings.

On all sides there was anxious foreboding, sorrow or bereavement. The young pastor's services were eagerly sought for, his time and strength taxed to their utmost; but he discharged the duties of the emergency with a true and manly courage. A paragraph from his *Treasury of David* on Psalm 91 most graphically describes this trying period:

In the year 1854, when I had scarcely been in London twelve months, the neighborhood in which I labored was visited by Asiatic cholera, and my congregation suffered from its inroads. Family after family summoned me to the bedsides of the smitten, and almost every day I was called to visit the grave.

I gave myself up with youthful ardor to the visitation of the sick and was sent for from all corners of the district by persons of all ranks and religions. I became weary in body and sick at heart. My friends seemed falling one by one, and I felt or fancied that I was sickening like those around me. A little more work and weeping would have laid me low among the rest. I felt that my burden was heavier than I could bear, and I was ready to sink under it.

As God would have it, I was returning mournfully home from a funeral when my curiosity led me to read a paper which was wafered up in a shoemaker's window in the Dover Road. It did not look like a trade announcement, nor was it; for it bore in a good bold handwriting these words: "Because thou hast made the Lord, which is my refuge, even the most High, thy habitation; There shall no evil befall thee, neither shall any plague come nigh thy dwelling."

The effect upon my heart was immediate. Faith appropriated the passage as her own. I felt secure, refreshed, girt with immortality.

I went on with my visitation of the dying in a calm and peaceful spirit. I felt no fear of evil, and I suffered no harm. The Providence which moved the tradesman to place those verses in his window I gratefully acknowledge, and in the remembrance of its marvelous power I adore the Lord my God.

Publishing Sermons

In the autumn of the first year's pastorate he preached a sermon from the words, "Is it not wheat harvest today?" The sermon attracted attention, was much talked about by his hearers; and during the following week it appeared under the title of "Harvest Time," and had a large sale. This led the publisher shortly afterwards to print another of his sermons under the title of "God's Providence."

The public at once took to these sermons, and by the end of the year about a dozen had thus been issued. This greatly increased his popularity, for many who had not heard him read those sermons, were interested in them and soon found opportunity to go and hear him.

Since the demand for his sermons was considerably greater than for the sermons of other ministers then being published, Mr. Spurgeon made arrangements with the first friend he met in London, who was a printer and a member of his church, to commence the publication of one sermon of his every week, beginning with the new year, 1855.

Through the good providence of God, the sermons have appeared continuously week by week, without interruption, for more than twenty-seven years, with a steady, improving and large circulation, which is in itself a marked indication of divine favor. No other minister the world has ever known has been able to produce one printed sermon weekly for so many years. The work still goes on with unabated favor and unceasing interest.

The Preacher Described

The following description of the preacher's style at this period is one of the earliest we have met with:

NEW PARK STREET PULPIT

His voice is clear and musical; his language plain; his style flowing, but terse; his method lucid and orderly; his matter sound and suitable; his tone and spirit cordial; his remarks always pithy and pungent, sometimes familiar and colloquial, yet never light or coarse, much less profane.

Judging from a single sermon, we supposed he would become a plain, faithful, forcible and affectionate preacher of the Gospel in the form called Calvinistic; and our judgment was the more favorable, because, while there was a solidity beyond his years, we detected little of the wild luxuriance naturally characteristic of very young preachers.

Want of order and arrangement was a fault the preacher soon found out himself, and he refers to it when he says:

> Once I put all my knowledge together in glorious confusion, but now I have a shelf in my head for everything; and whatever I read or hear, I know where to stow it away for use at the proper time.

Intense Interest Excited

Amongst the multitudes who assembled to hear the popular preacher was a member of the Society of Friends who, being deeply impressed by what he saw and heard, wrote a lengthened article on the subject. The writer observes:

> The crowds which have been drawn to hear him, the interest excited by his ministry, and the conflicting opinions expressed in reference to his qualifications and usefulness have been altogether without parallel in modern times.
>
> It was a remarkable sight to see this round-faced country youth thus placed in a position of such solemn and arduous responsibility, yet addressing himself to the fulfillment of its onerous duties with a gravity, self-possession and vigor that proved him well fitted for the task he had assumed.

Within one year, New Park Street Chapel had to be enlarged. During the enlargement, Exeter Hall was taken, and it was filled to overflowing every Sunday morning to hear the young preacher. The chapel, which had been enlarged to the fullest extent of the ground, was soon found to be far too limited for the thousands who flocked to hear him; and by the end of the summer it became necessary to seek for a much larger place to satisfy the demand of the public.

Twenty-first Birthday

On June 19, 1855, Mr. Spurgeon came of age, and he improved the occasion by preaching a sermon relating thereto. A large congregation heard it, and it was printed with an excellent likeness of the young preacher, pale and thin as he then was. The sermon was published with the title, "Pictures of Life and Birthday Reflections." It had a large sale. That was the first portrait of him which had been issued.

At that period the first attempt to issue a penny weekly newspaper was made by Mr. C. W. Banks, and the *Christian Cabinet* was a very spirited publication.

The value of a pure and cheap press was fully appreciated by Mr. Spurgeon, who generously furnished articles for the columns of that serial during nearly the whole of its first year's existence. They show a clear and sound judgment on many public events passing more than twenty years ago, and they are the first buddings of that genius which has since ripened so fully and yielded such an abundant harvest of rich mental food. The books which have since come from Mr. Spurgeon's pen are equally marvelous for their number, variety and usefulness; and some of them have had most unprecedentedly large sales.

Visit to Scotland

In July of this year, 1855, he paid his first visit to Scotland. A lively description of his congregation and preaching was printed in the *Cabinet*.

On the bright evening of September 4, Mr. Spurgeon preached to about twelve thousand people in a field in King Edward's Road, Hackney. The sermon was printed under the title of "Heaven and Hell" and had a very large sale, doing at the same time a large amount of good.

The sermon was closed by the preacher giving the following account of his own conversion, which had a good effect on his audience, proving that experience is the best teacher. Thousands of young people present were astonished at what they heard, and many turned that night from their sins. The preacher said:

> I can remember the time when my sins first stared me in the face. I thought myself the most accursed of all men. I had not committed any very great open transgression against God; but I recollected that I had been well trained and tutored, and I thought my sins were thus greater than other people's.
>
> I cried to God to have mercy, but I feared that He would not pardon me. Month after month I cried to God; but He did not hear me, and I knew not what it was to be saved.
>
> Sometimes I was so weary of the world that I desired to die, but I then recollected that there was a worse world after this and that it would be an ill matter to rush before my Maker unprepared.
>
> At times I wickedly thought God a most heartless tyrant because He

did not answer my prayer; then at others I thought, *I deserve His displeasure; if He sends me to Hell, He will be just.*

But I remember the hour when I stepped into a place of worship and saw a tall, thin man step into the pulpit. I have never seen him from that day and probably never shall till we meet in Heaven.

He opened the Bible and read with a feeble voice: "Look unto me, and be ye saved, all the ends of the earth: for I am God, and there is none else." *Ah!* thought I, *I am one of the ends of the earth*; and then, turning round and fixing his gaze on me, as if he knew me, the minister said, "Look, look, look!"

I thought I had a great deal to *do*, but I found it was only to *look*. I thought I had a garment to spin out for myself; but I found that, if I looked, Christ could give me a garment. Look, sinner, that is the way to be saved. Look unto Him, all ye ends of the earth, and be saved.

Preaching is the ordained means for the salvation of sinners: the power of appeal by the human voice is greater than any other; but there is another influence which is potent.

Before Mr. Spurgeon had issued more than half a year's sermons from the press, letters reached him from far-off places reporting the good which had been effected by reading them.

On one of Mr. Spurgeon's visits to Scotland, he was taken to visit Anne Sims, an aged saint living at the Brae of Killiecrankie, far away up the mountains. She had expressed intense delight in reading his sermons and prayed for his success in the work, little thinking that, in her mountain solitude and in her ninetieth year, she should ever see the preacher himself, whose visit was to her like that of an angel.

It would be difficult to chronicle the results which have followed the reading of the sermons.

Tidings of Good Done

In the first article in *The Sword and the Trowel* for 1872, the editor himself says, "Our ministry has never been without large results in conversion."

Twenty conversions have been reported to him by letter in one week. The last Sunday sermon he preached in 1855, with which the first volume of his printed discourses is closed, had special reference to the war in the Crimea, and it commanded a large sale. Its title was "Healing for the Wounded." It contributed materially to allay public anxiety about the war.

Mr. Spurgeon closed the year by holding a watchnight service in his chapel. It was a happy and memorable service, and it was afterward repeated at the close of every year, the last hours of the closing year and the first moments of the opening new year being devoted to the worship of God, in acts of personal consecration.

It is a gratifying fact, not generally known, that from the first year of Mr. Spurgeon's ministry in London several clergymen have used his sermons weekly, with a little adaptation, in their own churches. This testimony has been given by the clergymen themselves, in person and by letter, to the writer. Some are using the sermons in that way at the present time; and though delivered secondhand in this manner, yet they are not without fruit.

CHAPTER IV

A Wife and a New Tabernacle

Mr. Spurgeon's Marriage—Twelve Sermons Weekly—Not an Ascetic—Surrey Gardens Music Hall—The Great Metropolitan Tabernacle—Praying Among Bricks and Mortar—Preaching to the Aristocracy—Note From Mr. Gladstone—Offer From an American Lecture Bureau—How the Preacher Appeared in His Pulpit—Pastors' College—Poem Addressed to Mrs. Spurgeon—Revivals and Colportage—Talk of Founding a New Sect—Visit to Paris—Preaching to Costermongers

The year 1856 was a remarkable one in the life of Mr. Spurgeon. It was the year of his marriage, the year in which he preached his grandfather's jubilee sermon and one of the centenary sermons in Whitefield's Tabernacle in Tottenham Court Road.

During the first week of the year, Mr. Spurgeon was delighting large audiences at Bath. The second week was made memorable by a service held in his own chapel, in which the young people, more particularly, took a very lively interest. Early in the forenoon of January 8, Mr. Spurgeon was married to Miss Susanna Thompson, daughter of Mr. Robert Thompson of Falcon Square, London. Twin boys, Charles and Thomas Spurgeon, are the only additions to their family. Both are now settled pastors.

At this period Mr. Spurgeon was daily in the pulpit, often traveling many miles between the services held; and for months together he preached twelve sermons weekly, with undiminished force and unflagging zeal. In the achievement of such herculean tasks, he has doubtless been indebted to an excellent constitution and to his simple habits of living. He is the very embodiment of nature, without the usual makeup of art. He throws himself on the tide of social interchange

SPURGEON AND HIS WIFE IN THEIR
GARDEN SOON AFTER THEIR MARRIAGE

with the freedom of one who has no tricks to exhibit and no failings to conceal.

He is one of the most pleasant of companions: pious without any of the shams of piety; temperate without a touch of asceticism; and devout without the solemnity of the devotee.

Preaching for his poorer brethren in the country, he declined to receive any contribution towards his personal outlay, excepting only in cases where the church could well afford to pay his traveling expenses.

Preaching in Surrey Music Hall

New Park Street Chapel, when enlarged, soon became utterly inadequate to receive the crowds which flocked to hear Mr. Spurgeon, so the deacons found it necessary to take the largest available building in London—the Royal Surrey Gardens Music Hall—and in October, 1856, Mr. Spurgeon commenced to preach every Sunday in that vast audience-room, continuing the morning service there till the great Metropolitan Tabernacle was opened.

What is known as the Surrey Gardens catastrophe, we need not do more than allude to. On October 19 a sad and fatal accident had well nigh put an end to the large Sunday gatherings drawn to hear Mr. Spurgeon; but that fatality was overruled for good. Previous to this Mr. Spurgeon knew not what illness was; but this calamity, joined with the wicked calumnies of a portion of the press, laid prostrate even the strong man.

In October, 1856, the first meeting was held for considering the steps necessary to be taken for erecting a great Tabernacle. The proposal was very heartily taken up by Mr. Spurgeon's friends, and in every part of the country sympathy was largely shown with the movement.

Many laughed at the idea of erecting as a place of worship an edifice to hold five thousand persons. Regardless of these objections, the work went on, Mr. Spurgeon traveling all over the land, preaching daily, with the promise of half the proceeds of the collection being devoted to the new Tabernacle.

The foundation stone of the great building was laid by Sir Samuel Morton Peto, August 16, 1859.

Strange Place for a Prayer Meeting

During the progress of the work, Mr. Spurgeon met on the ground, one evening after the workmen had left, one of his deacons. After some consultation and meditation, surrounded by planks, piles of timber and bricks, in the dim twilight, they both knelt down where no eye could see them but that of God. With only the canopy of Heaven for their covering, the pastor and his friend each poured out most earnest supplications for the prosperity of the work, the safety of the men engaged on the building, and a blessing on the church. Their prayers were not offered in vain, but were abundantly answered. Out of so large a number of men engaged on the work, not one of them suffered harm.

ROYAL SURREY GARDENS MUSIC HALL

In 1860 a large and enthusiastic meeting was held in the building before it was finished, at which much money was given and more promised. Great preparations were made during the winter for the holding of a large bazaar in the spring, which was probably one of the largest and most productive of the kind ever held in London. The opening services were commenced on March 25, 1861, and were continued without interruption for five weeks.

As the result of all these efforts, the great Tabernacle, to hold five thousand, was free from debt at the end of the special services, and

METROPOLITAN TABERNACLE—C. H. SPURGEON, PASTOR.

INTERIOR VIEW OF THE METROPOLITAN TABERNACLE.

$155,000 of free-will offerings had been poured into the hands of the treasurer.

Since then various improvements have been made in the audience-room; and, using every facility modern invention could suggest, seats have been provided for 5,500 and standing room for 1,000 more—total, 6,500.

Immense Congregations

Large as is the accommodation provided, the Tabernacle has always been filled. All the prophets of evil have been found false, and the spirit of faith with which the work was begun has had its full reward in results even greater than ever had been anticipated.

When the church removed from New Park Street in 1861, it numbered 1,178 members. In ten years from the commencement of his ministry, Mr. Spurgeon has received into fellowship by baptism 3,569 persons.

During the period in which he was preaching in the Surrey Music Hall, large numbers of the aristocracy attended his ministry, amongst whom were Lord Chief Justice Campbell, the Lord Mayor and Sheriffs of London, Earl Russell, Lord Alfred Paget, Lord Panmure, Earl Grey, Earl Shaftesbury, the Marquis of Westminster, the Duchess of Sutherland, Lord Carlisle, Earl of Elgin, Baron Bramwell, Miss Florence Nightingale, Lady Rothschild, Dr. Livingstone and many others of learning and distinction, some of whom sought and obtained interviews with the preacher.

It was during that interim that Mr. Spurgeon paid one of his visits to Holland, was privileged to preach before the Dutch Court, and had a lengthened interview with the queen of that country. It was reported that some members of the English Royal Family also occasionally attended on his preaching, and not a few distinguished clergymen and professors.

Gladstone and Spurgeon

On one occasion Mr. Gladstone and his son formed part of the congregation, and a mutual interview was held at the close of the service between the great premier and the humble pastor. Mr. Gladstone has often spoken very highly of Mr. Spurgeon, calling him "the last of the Puritans."

During Mr. Spurgeon's illness in 1891, in a letter to Mrs. Spurgeon, Mr. Gladstone said:

> In my own home, darkened at the present time, I read with sad interest the accounts of Mr. Spurgeon's illness. I cannot help conveying to you an earnest assurance of my sympathy and of my cordial admiration, not only for his splendid powers, but still more for his devoted and unfailing character. I humbly commend you and him in all contingencies to the infinite stores of divine love and mercy.

Mrs. Spurgeon replied with a note of thanks, a postscript to which was traced by Mr. Spurgeon, as follows:

> Yours is a word of love such as those only write who have been into the King's country and seen much of His face. My heart's love to you.

Dr. David Livingstone, the great African explorer, said on one occasion, after hearing Mr. Spurgeon, that no religious service he ever remembered had so deeply impressed his own mind as that he had witnessed and participated in that morning, adding that, when he had retired again into the solitudes of Africa, no scene he had ever witnessed would afford him more consolation than to recall the recollection that there was one man God had raised up who could so effectively and impressively preach to congregated thousands, whilst he should have to content himself by preaching to units, or at most tens, under a tropical sky in Africa. He was implying that Mr. Spurgeon's sphere of religious influence was a hundred times greater than that of the great and good traveler.

No Time to Lecture in America

Mr. Spurgeon has often been invited to lecture in this country, but has always declined. The managers of the Redpath Lyceum Bureau, having noticed a paragraph in the Boston papers stating that Mr. Spurgeon was about to visit the United States, enclosed it to him and wrote as follows:

BOSTON, MASS., JUNE 22, 1876

DEAR SIR:

> Is the above paragraph true? We have tried so long and so hard for many years to secure you that we thought it impossible and long since gave up

all hope. We are the exclusive agents of all the leading lecturers in America. We will give you *a thousand dollars in gold* for every lecture you deliver in America and pay all your expenses to and from your home and place you under the most popular auspices in the country. Will you come?

To this invitation Mr. Spurgeon returned the following reply:

CLAPHAM, LONDON, ENGLAND, JULY 6
GENTLEMEN:

I cannot imagine how such a paragraph should appear in your papers, except by deliberate invention of a hard-up editor; for I never had any idea of leaving home for America for some time to come. As I said to you before, if I could come, I am not a lecturer, *nor would I receive money for preaching.*

In the year 1857 Mr. Spurgeon preached two sermons—one in the ordinary course of his ministrations, the other on a special occasion— both of which commanded a sale of more than a hundred thousand copies. The first, preached in the autumn, was entitled "India's Ills and England's Sorrows" and had reference to the mutiny in India. The second was preached in the Crystal Palace at Sydenham on the fast day relating to the war in India, when probably not fewer than twenty thousand formed the preacher's audience.

Marvelous Gifts

It will doubtless interest many to learn something of the personal appearance of the preacher as he stood before that vast audience. One who had some skill in depicting natural life wrote of him:

He is of medium height, at present quite stout, has a round and beard- less face, not a high forehead, dark hair parted in the center of the head. His appearance in the pulpit may be said to be interesting rather than commanding. He betrays his youth and still wears a boyish countenance. His figure is awkward—his manners plain—his face (except when illumined by a smile) admitted to be heavy.

His voice seems to be the only personal instrument he possesses, by which he is enabled to acquire such a marvelous power over the minds and hearts of his hearers. It is powerful, rich, melodious and under per- fect control. Twelve thousand have distinctly heard every sentence he uttered in the open air, and this powerful instrument carried his burning words to an audience of twenty thousand gathered in the Crystal Palace.

"Soon as he commences to speak," says an English critic, "tones of richest melody are heard. A voice, full, sweet and musical, falls on every ear and awakens agreeable emotions in every soul in which there is a sympathy for sounds. That most excellent of voices is under perfect control and can whisper or thunder at the wish of its possessor.

SPURGEON IN TABERNACLE PULPIT

"Then there is poetry in every feature and every movement, as well as music in the voice. The countenance speaks, the entire form sympathizes. The action is in complete unison with the sentiments. And the eye listens scarcely less than the ear to the sweetly flowing oratory."

To the influence of this powerful voice he adds that of a manner characterized by great freedom and fearlessness, intensely earnest and strikingly natural. When to these we add the influence of thrilling description, touching anecdote, sparkling wit, startling episodes, striking similes, all used to illustrate and enforce the deep, earnest home truths of the Bible, we surely have a combination of elements which must make up a preacher of wonderful attraction and of marvelous power.

Pastors' College

Amidst his incessant duties and almost daily journeys and sermons, the devoted pastor still found time to give instruction to the young men he kept under his careful ministry. With Mr. Spurgeon it was work almost night and day and all day long, with but little intermission, for several years in succession.

The germs of what is now known as Pastors' College were never absent from his mind and frequently occupied his attention when in London. In 1857 the first student was sent out in charge of a church; in 1858 Mr. Silverton went forth; in 1859 Mr. Davies and Mr. Genders followed, both of whom have left their mark on society.

On January 1, 1865, appeared the first number of *The Sword and the Trowel*: a record of combat with sin and labor for the Lord. It had an ornamental cover representing a Jewish doorway of stone; beyond and within were seen the zealous Jews at work rebuilding the walls of Jerusalem, the sword in one hand, the trowel in the other.

The work was so wisely planned and it has been so ably conducted that it now occupies a prominent, if not a foremost, place amongst the periodical literature of the land and has a circulation of several thousand copies monthly, with a steady advancement.

Literary Labors

Besides the other works daily undertaken by Mr. Spurgeon himself and all his journeys in the country to preach special sermons, he found time to write no less than nineteen articles for the first year's volume of his magazine.

At the end of the year the editor was ill at home, but he informed his friends through the magazine that he had finished writing his new book, *Morning by Morning*, by which means he hoped to hold hallowed communion with thousands of families all over the world every morning at the family altar. He has since added to it a companion volume, *Evening by Evening*, both of which works have had a large sale.

Amongst his articles in 1865 were two poems, one titled "The Fall of Jericho"; the other will find a fitting place in these pages. It was written while on a visit to Hull in Yorkshire during the summer and tenderly expresses the young pastor's love to his wife.

MARRIED LOVE—TO MY WIFE

Over the space that parts us, my wife,
I'll cast me a bridge of song,
Our hearts shall meet, O joy of my life,
On its arch unseen, but strong.

The wooer his new love's name may wear
Engraved on a precious stone;
But in my heart thine image I wear,
That heart has long been thine own.

The glowing colors on surface laid,
Wash out in a shower of rain;
Thou need'st not be of rivers afraid,
For my love is dyed ingrain.

And as every drop of Garda's lake
  Is tinged with sapphire's blue,
So all the powers of my mind partake
  Of joy at the thought of you.

The glittering dewdrops of dawning love
  Exhale as the day grows old,
And fondness, taking the wings of a dove,
  Is gone like a tale of old.

But mine for thee, from the chambers of joy,
  With strength came forth as the sun,
Nor life nor death shall its force destroy,
  Forever its course shall run.

All earth-born love must sleep in the grave,
  To its native dust return;
What God hath kindled shall death out-brave,
  And in Heaven itself shall burn.

Beyond and above the wedlock tie
  Our union to Christ we feel;
Uniting bonds which were made on High,
  Shall hold us when earth shall reel.

Though He who chose us all worlds before,
  Must reign in our hearts alone,
We fondly believe that we shall adore
  Together before His throne.

During the year 1865 Mr. Spurgeon held in the Tabernacle united meetings for prayer through one entire week, attended by over six thousand persons, which were a source of so much blessing to those attending them that a second series followed a month later.

Revival Services

Conscious of the power of prayer, the pastor commenced the year 1866 with a month's continuous revival services, at which 120 ministers and students were present. Knowing that he should have the sympathy and cooperation of his church in conducting them, in September the whole church had a day of fasting and prayer.

An important work which had for a long time occupied Mr. Spurgeon's attention was brought out this year under the title *Our Own*

Hymn Book. The preparation of a new collection of psalms and hymns for congregational use was felt to be an urgent necessity, but there was a nervous fear about the success of such a work. It was prepared with great care, and no pains were spared to make it complete in every respect, giving correct text, author's name to each hymn, with date of first publication and other interesting particulars in the large edition of the book.

The public at once saw the value of the collection; and since that time it has had a very large sale, having been adopted by and is now in use in scores, if not hundreds, of congregations.

Colportage Association

As a student of the times in which Puritanism began to take hold of the mind of the English people, Mr. Spurgeon knew how great a work was accomplished by the Nonconformists by book hawking. Having learned by several visits to Scotland how useful and valuable that agency was in the north of England, he therefore in January, 1866, issued a circular stating his intention to establish a system of colportage, by which his sermons and other works of a moral and religious character might be more widely distributed.

At first it was intended to be confined to London and the neglected villages and small country towns around, where access to religious literature was difficult. The result of the appeal made in January led to the formation in October of THE COLPORTAGE ASSOCIATION which has ever since been one of the important agencies of the Tabernacle and which is every year increasing its operations and usefulness. It employs colporteurs, whose whole time is directed to the work and who are paid a moderate salary; also book agents, who are constantly delivering books to purchasers, for which service they receive a liberal discount on sales and by which they are enabled to make a satisfactory living.

The wisdom of the course taken by Mr. Spurgeon in this matter has since been abundantly demonstrated. That association has been a blessing to thousands and has done a noble work in very needy localities.

Not a Sectarian

At this time there was a feeling abroad which manifested itself in several articles in public papers, notably in a New York religious weekly, that, by means of his College and large number of new chapels being erected all over the land for his students, Mr. Spurgeon was aiming at founding a sect after the example of Wesley. So soon as this notion reached Mr. Spurgeon, he took the earliest opportunity of repudiating the idea. In a short article entitled "Spurgeonism," he thus records his views:

> There is no word in the world so hateful to our heart as that word *Spurgeonism* and no thought further from our soul than that of forming a new sect. Our course has been, and we hope ever will be, an independent one; but to charge us with separating from the general organization of the religious world, and even of the Baptist denomination, is to perpetrate an unfounded libel.

> We preach no new gospel, we desire no new objects and follow them in no novel spirit. We love Christ better than a sect and truth better than a party, and so far are not denominational; but we are in open union with the Baptists for the very reason that we cannot endure isolation. He who searches all hearts knows that our aim and object is not to gather a band around self, but to unite a company around the Saviour. "Let my name perish, but let Christ's name last forever," said George Whitefield; and so has Charles Spurgeon said a hundred times.

> We aid and assist the Baptist churches to the full extent of our power, although we do not restrict our energies to them alone; and in this, those churches are far enough from blaming us. Our joy and rejoicing is great in the fellowship of all believers; and the forming of a fresh sect is work which we leave to the Devil, whom it befits far more than ourselves.

> It is true that it has long been in our power to commence a new denomination, but it is not true that it has ever been contemplated by us or our friends. We desire as much as possible to work with the existing agencies; and when we commence new ones, our friends must believe that it is with no idea of organizing a fresh community.

Work in Paris

The closing days of the year 1866 Mr. Spurgeon spent in Paris in a successful effort to get the Baptist church in that city brought out of an obscure corner, in which property could not be respected, into a place of prominence, where there was hope of its becoming known and being useful. This effort had long exercised the mind of Pastor Spurgeon, and he had the joy of seeing the work he aimed at fully accomplished.

He spent his Christmas in Paris, getting rest for himself and doing a good work for the Parisians.

Reinvigorated by his short trip to the Continent, he returned to his duties at the Tabernacle with renewed energy and a stronger faith, having gained fresh courage from his success in France.

The month of February, 1867, witnessed the usual week of prayer, which that year, on the 18th, was marked by a whole day of fasting and prayer, commencing at seven in the morning and continuing, without a pause or breaking up for meals, until nine at night—a day of prayer in which the Holy Spirit was manifestly present all day. The account of the services held during that week reads like a new chapter of the Acts of the Apostles.

Reaching the Common People

The readiness with which Mr. Spurgeon can adapt himself to his audience, whether consisting of the educated or affluent, the poor or the ignorant, was never more distinctly seen than when, in the Evangelists' Tabernacle, Golden Lane, City, he preached to a congregation of costermongers (those who hawk fruit or vegetables). Mr. Orsman, the missionary there, had distributed tickets among the street dealers in Whitecross Street so as to secure the class for whom the service was intended.

An amusing article might be written to describe the singular variety of countenances and callings of those present. The hymns were heartily sung, and the prayer won the hearts of the audience when Mr. Spurgeon offered supplication for those who had bodily aches and pains and whose poverty deprived them of many desired comforts. Many deep sighs followed those prayers.

The sermon was preached from St. John 4:15, illustrated by allusions to the habits and manner of life of his congregation, whose acuteness relished the anecdotes and homely hits which the preacher so freely used.

A costermonger's living depends much upon his voice. After the service the costers were free in their comments on the preacher's voice, which was described as "Wot a woice!" "Wonderful!" "Stunnin'!" "I never!" "Would make a fine coster!" etc.

After the sermon about two hundred remained to be prayed with, and much spiritual good was done that night.

Great Assemblies in Agricultural Hall

Six years had elapsed since the Tabernacle was opened. Since the building had suffered much from the massive congregations which had assembled there, it became necessary to close it for several weeks for repairs. During that period Mr. Spurgeon preached to immense congregations in the Agricultural Hall, Islington. The first of the five special services was held on Sunday, March 24, 1867, when about twelve thousand were present.

The preacher's delivery was slow, measured and emphatic; nothing labored; and his voice lost none of its accustomed music. Many thousands heard the Gospel at that time who were not accustomed to attending any place of worship. More than twenty thousand were in attendance on the final day.

The heavy responsibilities which rested on the pastor of the Tabernacle in the early part of the year made it necessary for him to seek a little recreation. With that he blended a friendly service for his esteemed friend Pastor Oncken by preaching for him at the opening of his new Baptist church at Hamburg.

He included in his travels a visit to Heligoland, which furnished for his ready and fertile pen most interesting matter for an article containing information both curious and valuable and not to be found elsewhere.

CHAPTER V

Successful Labors

Orphan Houses—Impressive Spectacle—"On My Back"—Liberal Gifts—Illness of Mrs. Spurgeon—Silly Tales—"A Black Business"—Laid Aside by Illness—New Year's Letter—The Pastor Prostrate—Discussion Concerning Future Punishment—The Bible and Public Schools—A Victim to Gout—Visit to the Continent—Pastors' College— Ingatherings at the Tabernacle—Fisk Jubilee Singers—Pointed Preaching—Great Missionary Meeting—A New Cornerstone

Returning home, the industrious pastor found an abundance of important work awaiting him. During the April previous the land had been secured at Stockwell for the ORPHAN HOUSES. The work of preparation for their erection had been so far advanced that a great festival was arranged. On Monday, September 9, 1867, a party of some four thousand persons assembled at Stockwell, a large proportion of the company being collectors; and it was part of the program for the foundation stones of three of the houses to be laid and for the numerous collectors to lay on the stones their respective contributions.

It was an auspicious day for Mr. Spurgeon, for his deacons and church members. A widely extended interest had been felt in the work, and the occasion became a grand holiday in that southern suburb of London. Three of the houses were thus far advanced in their progress, namely, the Silver Wedding House, the Merchants' House and the Workmen's House. The united sum the collectors laid upon the stones amounted to eleven thousand dollars.

A Home for Orphans

The entire spectacle was both novel and touching. Prayers were offered on the occasion, the influence of which it is believed will be felt throughout all time. Appropriate hymns were sung, each ceremony being conducted with verses specially prepared, the first of which was as follows:

> *Accept, O Lord, the grateful love*
> *Which yields this house to Thee;*
> *And on the Silver Wedding House*
> *Let blessings ever be.*

It was announced at the close of the ceremony that in addition to the $100,000 given by Mrs. Hillyard, the money in hand was then $27,500.

JAMES A. SPURGEON, CO-PASTOR

The assembly returned home high-ly delighted with the service and the glad tidings they had heard, whilst the pastor, worn out with fatigue and anxiety, retired home to rest.

The mental and physical strain of such heavy responsibilities was too much for Mr. Spurgeon. Soon after he was laid aside quite ill. Although physically prostrate, his mind was in active exercise. After suffering for two months, he wrote an article for his magazine entitled "On My Back," in which he submissively said that, after two months of ill health and severe pain, yet he believed there was a limit to sickness and that Jesus knew all about it, feeling assured that the design of sickness was divinely good.

This long absence from the pulpit led to the appointment of his brother, James Archer Spurgeon, as co-pastor to the church at the Tabernacle, who officially entered on those duties in January, 1868.

Busy With Pen and Voice

Although the year 1868 did not furnish occasion for such important events as the preceding one, yet was there much earnest work done by Mr. Spurgeon at his Tabernacle. Not able to do so much physical work, he used his pen very freely, writing two articles for his magazine to advocate the claims of the Colportage Association.

In March he delivered at the Tabernacle a lecture on "Our History and Work," with Mr. W. McArthur, M.P., in the chair. He also wrote an interesting article relating incidents in the life of his grandfather.

In the month of May he preached the "Sermon to Young Men" at Mr. Martin's Chapel, Westminster, on behalf of the London Missionary Society—a service rendered the more cheerfully, remembering, as he did, the prophetic words of good Richard Knill, that he would preach in the largest chapel in London.

That was probably the largest chapel he had preached in, excepting his own. During the same month he spoke at the Breakfast Meeting of the Congregational Union.

Generous Donations

In the month of March a generous friend sent to the pastor five thousand dollars for the College and five thousand dollars for the Orphanage—such instances of liberality amply testifying the high estimation in which the noble enterprises of Mr. Spurgeon were held by the public. On his birthday, June 19, a great meeting was held and liberal contributions made for the Orphanage.

Bright as are these spots in the life of the pastor and in his work at the Tabernacle and its belongings, yet there hung over his home all the time a dark shadow which divine Providence saw fit to place there.

Mrs. Spurgeon had long been a great sufferer; and to alleviate her sorrows, if possible, a very painful operation had to be undertaken. The most skillful surgeons of the land were engaged, under the direction of Sir James Simpson of Edinburgh.

Prayer was made for her by the whole church; and by the blessing of God, the operation was so far successful that her sufferings were alleviated and her life prolonged; but it has been a life of pain and weakness, though with less of anguish.

A Jubilant Note

A gratifying fact is recorded by Mr. Spurgeon this year, who publicly acknowledges the kindness of Dr. Palfrey of Finsbury Square for his gratuitous and generous professional attendance on the poor members of the Tabernacle.

At Christmastide and at the opening of the year, the claims of

Mr. Spurgeon's benevolent agencies were remembered by his many friends, who sent him of their worldly substance with generous hands so that he commences the first number of *The Sword and the Trowel* for 1869 with a most jubilant note: "Bless the Lord, O my soul!"

He also made the announcement that a gentleman in Australia had written to say he intended to reprint his sermons weekly in that far-off land, to give them a yet wider circulation.

From the very commencement of his ministry, strange tales had been put into circulation by his detractors, most of which Mr. Spurgeon passed by in silence. Several very ludicrous speeches were attributed to him soon after he became popular in London. In the midst of his work, at the opening of the year 1869, the voice of the slanderer was again heard, and many were troubling the busy pastor to know how true were the statements in circulation respecting him.

Absurd Stories

In reply to all these, under the head of "Silly Tales," he wrote in his magazine:

> Friends who write us about silly tales may save themselves the trouble. We have been enabled in our ministry and in our walk before God so to act, through grace, that we have given no occasion for the slanderers, save only that we have kept the Faith and been very jealous for the Lord God of Israel.
>
> Many of the absurd stories still retailed everywhere are the very same libels which were repeated concerning Rowland Hill and others long gone to their rest.

Having seen much of the folly too frequently exhibited at funerals, he published his views, with the apt title, "Funerals, or a Black Business." After exposing the folly of using feathers and goldheaded sticks in carrying a dead body to the grave, he observes:

> I would sooner be eaten by crows than have pride and pomp feeding on my little savings, which are meant for my bereaved wife and children and not for unsuitable, untimely and unholy show.
>
> I have heard that more than four millions of money are squandered every year in funeral fopperies. The money buys or hires silk scarfs, brass nails, feathers for horses, kid gloves and gin for the mutes, white satin and black cloth for the worms. It seems to me to be mighty fine nonsense, more

for the pride of the living than the honor of the dead; more for the profit of the undertaker than anyone else.

Attack of Smallpox

In June of that year the first report of the Orphanage was issued, plainly setting forth how earnestly the work had been carried on for it in having the houses erected and in getting them furnished and occupied. Twenty-nine boys were then in residence, one of whom was the son of one of the workmen who had assisted in building the Workmen's House. The father had died after the house was erected.

Taking a short holiday in July, accompanied by a friend, Mr. Spurgeon climbed the summit of Hindhead in the South of England, then paid a brief visit to the Continent.

Soon after his return home in October, he was entirely laid aside from pastoral work by a slight attack of smallpox. His friends became seriously anxious about him, and special prayer was made again and again for his recovery. It came slowly, but in anticipation thereof the first article in the magazine for November was "A Sermon From a Sick Preacher." Possessed of such mighty faith in God and with such indomitable courage, Pastor Spurgeon found opportunities for doing good, whilst others considered what had best be done. He even wrote directions on "How to Bear Affliction."

New Year's Letter

During the progress of his recovery, he wrote a New Year's Letter to his ministering brethren. This commences his magazine for 1870. With much affectionate earnestness, he urges them, even by special means, if ordinary ones fail, to aim at the salvation of the souls of their congregations, enforcing this duty upon them by the example of the Ritualists, who are zealous, working to spread their delusions, especially amongst the poor with whom they know how to succeed by bribes of bread and clothing. He says he writes as a sick man but feels the urgency and importance of soul winning.

The prostrate condition of the pastor's health for nearly three months made it necessary for him to appeal with his pen for the aid of his friends in sustaining the benevolent works of the Tabernacle. In March, 1870, his appeal took the following form:

The pastorate of a church of four thousand members, the direction of all its agencies, the care of many churches arising from the College work, the selection, education and guidance in their settlements of the students, the oversight of the Orphanage, the editing of a magazine, the production of numerous volumes, the publication of a weekly sermon, an immense correspondence, a fair share in public and denominational action, and many other labors, besides the incessant preaching of the Word, give us a right to ask of our friends that we be not allowed to have an anxious thought about the funds needed for our enterprises.

Future Punishment

This remarkable picture of energy and activity will scarcely be surpassed by any man living, if indeed it can be equaled by more than one in a million even in this industrious age. But there were other duties pressing on Mr. Spurgeon's mind at the time which he could not throw off.

For some months previously a controversy had been warmly carried on in the columns of the *Christian World* newspaper, advocating a curious system of future punishment ending in annihilation. The editor of the paper prohibited in his columns the publication of any letters on the opposite side, excepting only what Mr. Spurgeon might write.

Mr. Spurgeon wrote to the editor, pointing out that his conduct was not quite frank and declining on his part to help the agitation, telling him that the words of our Lord—"These shall go away into everlasting punishment"—finally settled the point. He held that the publication of views which are opposed to that declaration and the views themselves, were equally dangerous.

A Controversy

Greatly were the funds of the College aided by the lectures which its president gave from time to time on its behalf. After one of his visits to Italy, Mr. Spurgeon delivered a very interesting and lively lecture on "Rome—What I Saw and Heard There."

Some of the reporters for the daily press—not a few of whom are Jesuits—misrepresented some very material portions of the lecture in their abridged account. Mr. Spurgeon was obliged to defend himself. What he said against such insidious foes in the pages of his own magazine led to another kindred topic being brought before the public about the same time, when these same reporters misled the public mind by applying to King Victor Immanuel of Italy a prayer which belonged only to Immanuel, Victor over sin, the Man Christ Jesus.

In May, 1870, Mr. Spurgeon sent forth a new work entitled *Feathers for Arrows*, intended to supply preachers and teachers with useful material for filling up their sermons, lectures and addresses. Ten thousand copies of the book were sold in three months.

The Bible in the Public Schools

The public mind was considerably agitated at that time by the action of the School Board in reference to religious teaching in their schools. Some wanted to exclude the reading of the Bible from them and so deprive the upgrowing population of the use of the best Book in the language.

A large meeting was held in Exeter Hall in July, in defense of the Bible being daily read in elementary schools. Mr. Spurgeon took the chair on the occasion. The result of the meeting was, the Bible retains its place as a daily school Book.

The wisdom of the decision then made has been abundantly manifested since, especially so by the great gathering of Board-School children in the Crystal Palace in July, 1877, when some thousands of prizes were publicly given to the pupils for proficiency in knowledge of the Bible and when it was most convincingly shown that parents in London (excepting only a few Jews) do not object to their children being taught daily from the Word of God.

The special religious services held in February at the Tabernacle were seasons of much blessing. More than one hundred members were added to the church in one month. The people went to the services expecting to receive good, and they were not disappointed.

Severe Attack of Gout

Soon after the annual College supper, held in March, 1871, at which the sum of $7,500 was given, Mr. Spurgeon was laid aside by a more than usually severe attack of gout. This confined him indoors for three long, weary months. Yet in the midst of all his pain and suffering he wrote in July of the great mercies he had received from the hand of God and by the bounty of his friends to the Orphanage and College.

It was at the close of this protracted attack of bodily pain that he published discourses. Its second title is "Bread Enough and to Spare," and it is based on Luke 15:17.

In honor of the event just named, it was the delight of the pastor to receive from a friend five thousand dollars on behalf of the College. Who would not pray that God's blessing may rest forever on that friend?

Taking the advice of his friends, Mr. Spurgeon proceeded to the Continent for a short tour and rest. His observant eye was constantly discovering some passing beauty which his ever-ready pencil recorded in his notebook, a book containing a store of incidents which serve to enrich his conversation and fill up his magazine. Accordingly, taking Jersey and Guernsey on his way, we find before the end of the year an interesting article from his pen on St. Brelade's Bay.

Pilgrimage to Sunny Italy

As the cold raw winter weather set in, the beloved pastor was urged by friends to seek a warmer climate. When illness in a severe form again overtook him, on the second day he received a telegram from Boston, America, offering most liberal terms if he would go to that country and deliver a series of lectures. So large a sum would have been a strong temptation to most men, but not so to this minister of Jesus Christ, whose prompt reply was that he "had neither time nor strength to go to America."

Instead of journeying westward for personal gain, he started on a pilgrimage to sunny Italy and the south of France, taking what he designated a scriptural holiday, a forty days' rest. Accordingly, leaving gloomy December in England, he spent that month in visiting Pompeii, Venice, Florence, Rome, Naples and France—a fitting holiday after having completed nineteen years' labor in London.

In taking a survey of the work of the year for the preface to his magazine, Mr. Spurgeon sums up the record by saying it had been a year of spiritual drought in the churches generally, but at the Tabernacle they had witnessed much prosperity, and the trained pastors who had gone out from them had been also blessed in like manner.

Eleven students were appointed to pastoral duty during 1872. Also during this year Archibald G. Brown opened his large Tabernacle in the east of London, a building for extent and variety of Christian work second only to Mr. Spurgeon's. Mr. Brown is one of the most successful students trained in the Pastors' College.

Results of Overwork

In the hope that the genial sunshine of Southern Europe, in which he has passed out of the old into the new year, would have established his health for renewed efforts, the pastor appeared once more at the Tabernacle.

At the church meeting in January, 1873, he had the gratification of finding 135 new members to be received into fellowship, thus demonstrating that there was life in the church, though its chief pastor had been away.

The cold, raw, damp weather continuing with the new year, he was again prevented from leaving his own home and for many weeks was unable to preach. How great a trial that silence was to the preacher, none so well knew as himself. Sorrowing greatly at the privation both to himself and his church, he yet submitted without murmur to the will of God.

C. H. SPURGEON IN HIS STUDY

Shut in from the outer world, he had an opportunity of surveying the progress of the work which was being done at the Tabernacle. The College reports exhibited the outposts which had already been reached by the students, one of whom was laboring to set forth Jesus as the only Saviour of sinners in China, one in Sydney, one in Tasmania, one in Adelaide, two in Madrid, one in Ontario, one in Ohio, one in Philadelphia, one in South Africa, and one in Toronto. What a vast prospect of work to be done in the intermediate spaces between each one of those missionary agents and the Tabernacle!

Thousands of Church Members

At the Annual Church Meeting held in February, 1873, the total membership was reported at 4,417. The losses during the previous year had been 263, the additions were 571, leaving a net increase for the year of 308 living members. Well might both pastor and deacons rejoice at the presence of the Lord God in their midst.

At this date came a renewed application from the United States to come over and lecture. Note the preacher's reply:

> An American firm offers Mr. Spurgeon $25,000 to deliver twenty-five lectures in that country, $1,000 each, and further arrangements can be made for one hundred lectures. Although the remuneration offered is very far beyond anything our beloved people are likely to give us, we prefer to have the Gospel according to our Lord's words preached freely, rather than to use the Lord's time for earning money for our own purse.

Fisk Jubilee Singers

Always sympathizing with the oppressed, it did not surprise anyone to learn that the Fisk Jubilee Singers received an early invitation from the pastor and deacons to give one of their concerts in the Metropolitan Tabernacle. It would be difficult to determine which party experienced the most delight, the singers to go and see and hear Mr. Spurgeon speak in his own church, or his congregation to welcome, with all the heartiness they could manifest, those liberated slaves, whose vocal powers had by anticipation preceded their visit, to insure them a hearty greeting.

It was indeed a pleasant hour when the singers were introduced to the vast mass of people which crowded every inch of space in the building to hear them. Indeed, hundreds had to go away, unable to crowd in anywhere within sight or hearing.

And the collection which followed it was right royal in amount. They cleared about $1,100 for their University by singing at the Tabernacle alone.

The effect on the mind of the pastor was thus described in his own magazine:

> The melodies were rendered by our emancipated friends in a manner altogether unique: we have never heard anything like it; pure nature untrammeled by rule, pouring forth its notes as freely as the wild birds in the spring. The people were charmed: our communication with the choir was very pleasant.

As soon as the singers arrived in London on their second tour, they received an earnest invitation to repeat their visit to the Metropolitan Tabernacle.

Pointed Preaching

As the practical pastor was again charged with being too personal in preaching, in one of his articles on "Personal Preaching" Mr. Spurgeon remarks:

> We aim at speaking personally and pointedly to all our hearers, and they are the best judges whether we accomplish it and also as to whether we use language at which any man ought to be offended.
>
> Very seldom does a week occur without our receiving letters from persons unknown to us, thanking us for advising or comforting them in our sermons, the parties evidently being under the impression that some friend had communicated their cases to us, though, indeed, we knew nothing whatever of them.
>
> Frequently we have had apologetic notes acknowledging the justice of the rebuke and correcting us in some minor details of a description supposed to refer to a special sinner; whereas we were unaware of the writer's existence. We have ceased to regard these incidents as curious, for we remember that the Word of God is "a discerner of the thoughts and intents of the heart."

A Rally for Missions

Strange and interesting facts often reached him.

At the commencement of Mr. Spurgeon's ministry he related having received a letter from a poor shoemaker who said that he was the man who had kept his shop open on Sunday and had sold only one pair of old boots for one-and-eight-pence. Having desecrated the Lord's day for so small a sum and been so publicly exposed, none but God could have told the facts to the preacher; so he had resolved to keep open his shop no longer. He became converted and joined the church. But the preacher had no knowledge of the man till he wrote about himself.

During the spring weather of '73 Mr. Spurgeon did not recover his accustomed health, neither did he give up his accustomed work, excepting when really unable to leave home.

At the end of April he preached one of the annual sermons before the Wesleyan Missionary Society in Great Queen Street Chapel to the largest congregation ever assembled on a similar occasion. At the close the collection reached an amount greater than had ever before been made for that object.

In June he took part in the services connected with laying memorial stones for a new Baptist chapel near his own residence at Clapham. He stated that it had long been in his heart to build a chapel in that locality, and he had laid aside one thousand dollars to commence the work, but all his efforts had failed. He was glad that others were doing what he had not been able to do. He had himself been delighted that year to preach for the Wesleyans and to speak for the Independents; but he urged all Baptists residing in that district to give to the church which intended to assemble in that new erection.

In the early part of the year Mr. Spurgeon had made a collection at the Tabernacle on behalf of the new Surrey Chapel for Mr. Newman Hall, which reached five hundred dollars.

Laying a Cornerstone

In taking a survey of the literary work of *The Sword and the Trowel* for the year, in his preface for 1873 the editor remarks:

> I have been hunting up topics of interest with no small degree of anxiety, sending forth the magazine with earnest desires to win a hearing and to produce good results of all kinds. I edit the periodical most conscientiously, giving it my personal attention, and I spare no pains to make it as good as I can.

The applications made to the College for pastors during 1873 were more numerous than had before been made. Thirty of these were supplied. Out of that number, two were sent to Spain, one to India, one to China, one to Prince Edward Island, one to Ireland and one to Scotland.

On October 14 the foundation stone of the new College buildings was laid by the president. It was a day long to be remembered with delight. The people on the occasion gave five thousand dollars, and the students fifteen hundred more; but the chief joy of the day was the whole-day prayer meeting which the students held, that the divine blessing might rest on the work and upon all connected with the College.

The month of January, 1879, will long be remembered. Having completed the twenty-fifth year of his pastorate, it was decided to celebrate the occasion, which was termed THE PASTORAL SILVER WEDDING, by presenting Mr. Spurgeon with a liberal testimonial. The amount proposed to be raised was $25,000.

A large bazaar was opened, which was well supported. With the subscription lists, the proceeds exceeded the amount originally proposed.

With his usual largeheartedness he declined accepting the amount for his private benefit. There was one important institution connected with the Tabernacle that needed to be placed on a surer footing, and this was a fitting opportunity for securing that end. The Almshouses, affording homes for nineteen poor widows, required a more permanent support, so all the proceeds of the "Pastoral Silver Wedding Fund" were devoted to this laudable object, thereby insuring its future maintenance.

CHAPTER VI

The Pastors' College

The First Student—Call for Preachers to the Masses—A Faithful Instructor—Growth of the College—Efforts to Secure Funds—Generous Gifts—Unknown Benefactor— Provision for Students—Opinion of Earl Shaftesbury—New Churches Founded— Mr. Spurgeon's Annual Report—Milk and Water Theology—Rough Diamonds— Course of Study—Earnest Workers—A Mission Band—Interesting Letters—Help for Neglected Fields

In the early part of his career Mr. Spurgeon founded a school for the education of young men for the ministry. It has been a very successful institution, the training place of a large number who have gone forth, some even to the ends of the earth, bearing the "glad tidings." The object, methods and results of the school are stated by Mr. Spurgeon.

The College was the first important institution commenced by the pastor, and it still remains his firstborn and best-beloved. To train ministers of the Gospel is a most excellent work; and when the Holy Spirit blesses the effort, the result is of the utmost importance both to the church and to the world.

The Pastors' College commenced in 1856. During this long period it has unceasingly been remembered of the God of Heaven, to whom all engaged in it offer reverent thanksgiving. When it was commenced, I had not even a remote idea of whereunto it would grow. There were springing up around me, as my own spiritual children, many earnest young men who felt an irresistible impulse to preach the Gospel, yet with half an eye it could be seen that their want of education would be a sad hindrance to them. It was not in my heart to bid them cease preaching. Had I done so, they would in all probability have ignored my recommendation. As it seemed that preach they would, though their attainments were very slender, no other course was open but to give them an opportunity to educate themselves for the work.

A Young Apollos

The Holy Spirit evidently had set His seal upon the work of one of them by conversions wrought under his open-air addresses; it seemed therefore to be a plain matter of duty to instruct this youthful Apollos still further, that he might be fitted for wider usefulness.

No college at that time appeared to me to be suitable for the class of men that the providence and grace of God drew around me. They were mostly poor, and most of the colleges involved necessarily a considerable outlay to the student; for even where the education was free, books, clothes and other incidental expenses required a considerable sum per annum.

THE PASTORS' COLLEGE

Moreover, it must be frankly admitted that my views of the Gospel and of the mode of training preachers were and are somewhat peculiar.

I may have been uncharitable in my judgment, but I thought the

Calvinism of the theology usually taught to be very doubtful, and the fervor of the generality of the students to be far behind their literary attainments.

Preachers for the Masses

It seemed that preachers of the grand old truths of the Gospel, ministers suitable for the masses, were more likely to be found in an institution where preaching and divinity would be the main objects, not degrees and other insignia of human learning. I felt that, without interfering with the laudable objects of other colleges, I could do good in my own way.

These and other considerations led me to take a few tried young men and put them under some able minister that he might train them in the Scriptures and in other knowledge helpful to the understanding and proclamation of the truth. This step appeared plain; but how the work was to be conducted and supported was the question—a question, be it added, solved almost before it occurred.

Two friends, both deacons of the church, promised aid which, with what I could give, enabled me to take one student.

An Able Tutor

I set about to find a tutor. In Mr. George Rogers, God sent us the very best man. He had been preparing for such work and was anxiously waiting for it.

MR. GEORGE ROGERS

This gentleman, who has remained during all this period our principal tutor, is of Puritanic stamp, deeply learned, orthodox in doctrine, judicious, witty, devout, earnest, liberal in spirit, and withal juvenile in heart to an extent most remarkable in one of his years.

My connection with him has been one of uninterrupted comfort and delight. The most sincere affection exists between us. We are of one mind and of one heart. What is equally important, he has in every case secured not merely the respect but the filial love of every student.

Into this beloved minister's house the first students were introduced, and for a considerable period they were domiciled as members of his family.

Encouraged by the readiness with which the young men found spheres of labor and by their singular success in soul winning, I enlarged the number; but the whole means of sustaining them came from my own purse. The large sale of my sermons in America, together with my dear wife's economy, enabled me to spend from three thousand dollars to four thousand dollars in a year in my own favorite work; but on a sudden, owing to my denunciations of the then existing slavery in the States, my entire resources from that "brook Cherith" were dried up.

Shunning Debt

I paid as large sums as I could from my own income and resolved to spend all I had, then take the cessation of my means as a voice from the Lord to stay the effort, as I am firmly persuaded that we ought under no pretense go into debt.

On one occasion I proposed the sale of my horse and carriage, although these were almost absolute necessities to me on account of my continual journeys in preaching the Word. This my friend Mr. Rogers would not hear of, actually offering to be the loser rather than this should be done.

Then it was that I told my difficulties to my people. The weekly offering commenced, but the incomings from that source were so meagre as to be hardly worth calculating upon.

I was brought to the last pound, when a letter came from a banker in the city informing me that a lady, whose name I have never been able to discover, had deposited a sum of one thousand dollars to be used for the education of young men for the ministry.

How my heart leaped for joy! I threw myself then and henceforth upon the bounteous care of the Lord, whom I desired with my whole heart to glorify by this effort.

Some weeks after, another five hundred dollars came in from the same bank from another hand.

The College Grows

Soon after Mr. Phillips, a beloved deacon of the church at the

Tabernacle, began to provide an annual supper for the friends of the College, at which considerable sums have from year to year been given. A dinner was also given by my liberal publishers, Messrs. Passmore and Alabaster, to celebrate the publishing of my five-hundredth weekly sermon, at which $2,500 was raised and presented to the funds.

The College grew every month, and the number of students rapidly advanced from one to forty. Friends known and unknown, from far and near, were moved to give little or much to my work. The funds increased as the need enlarged.

Then another earnest deacon of the church espoused as his special work the weekly offering. And by the unanimous voice of the church under my care the College was adopted as its own child. Since that hour the weekly offering has been a steady source of income, till in the year 1869 the amount reached exactly $9,345.

The Trial of Faith

There have been during this period times of great trial of my faith; but after a season of straitness, never amounting to absolute want, the Lord has always interposed and sent me large sums (on one occasion five thousand dollars) from unknown donors.

When the Orphanage was thrust upon me, it did appear likely that this second work would drain the resources of the first; and it is very apparent that it does attract to itself some of the visible sources of supply; but my faith is firm that the Lord can as readily keep both works in action as one.

My own present inability to do so much, by way of preaching abroad, occasions naturally the failure of another great source of income; and as my increasing labors at home will in all probability diminish that stream in perpetuity, there is another trial of faith.

Yet if the Lord wills the work to be continued, He will send His servant a due portion of the gold and silver which are all His own; therefore, as I wait upon Him in prayer, the All-sufficient Provider will supply all my needs. About $25,000 is annually required for the College, and the same sum is needed for the Orphanage; but God will move His people to liberality, and we shall see greater things than these.

An Unknown Benefactor

While speaking of pecuniary matters, it may be well to add that, as many of the young men trained in the College have raised new congregations and gathered fresh churches, another need has arisen—namely, money for building chapels.

It is ever so in Christ's work; one link draws on another, one effort makes another needed. For chapel building, the College funds could do but little, though they have freely been used to support men while they are collecting congregations; but the Lord found for me one of His stewards who, on the condition that his name remains unknown, has hitherto, as the Lord has prospered him, supplied very princely amounts for the erection of places of worship, of which more than forty have been built or so greatly renovated and enlarged as to be virtually new structures.

Truly may it be said, "What hath God wrought!"

Pecuniary needs, however, have made up but a small part of our cares. Many have been my personal exercises in selecting the men. Candidates have always been plentiful, and the choice has been wide; but it is a serious responsibility to reject any, and yet more to accept them for training.

When mistakes have been made, a second burden has been laid upon me in the dismissal of those who appeared to be unfit. Even with the most careful management and all the assistance of tutors and friends, no human foresight can secure that in every case a man shall be what we believed and hoped.

Weak Brethren

A brother may be exceedingly useful as an occasional preacher; he may distinguish himself as a diligent student; he may succeed at first in the ministry; yet, when trials of temper and character occur in the pastorate, he may be found wanting. We have had comparatively few causes for regret of this sort, but there have been some such, and these pierce us with many sorrows.

I devoutly bless God that He has sent to the College some of the holiest, soundest and most self-denying preachers I know, and I pray that He may continue to do so; but it would be more than a miracle if all should excel.

While thus speaking of trials connected with the men themselves, it is due to our gracious God to bear testimony that these have been comparatively light and are not worthy to be compared with the great joy which we experience in seeing so many brethren still serving the Lord according to their measure of gift, and all, it is believed, earnestly contending for the Faith once delivered unto the saints. Nor is the joy less in remembering that eleven have sweetly fallen asleep after having fought a good fight.

At this hour some of our most flourishing Baptist churches are presided over by pastors trained in our College. As years shall add ripeness of experience and stability of character, others will be found to stand in the front rank of the Lord's host.

Separate Lodgings

The young brethren are boarded generally in twos and threes in the houses of our friends around the Tabernacle, for which the College pays a moderate weekly amount. The plan of separate lodging we believe to be far preferable to having all under one roof. By the latter mode, men are isolated from general family habits and are too apt to fall into superabundant levity.

The circumstances of the families who entertain our young friends are generally such that they are not elevated above the social position which in all probability they will have to occupy in future years, but are kept in connection with the struggles and conditions of everyday life.

Devotional habits are cultivated to the utmost, and the students are urged to do as much evangelistic work as they can. The severe pressure put upon them to make the short term as useful as possible leaves small leisure for such efforts, but this is in most instances faithfully economized.

Although our usual period is two years, whenever it is thought right the term of study is lengthened to three or four years. Indeed, there is no fixed rule, all arrangements being ordered by the circumstances and attainments of each individual.

Fields White for the Harvest

As before hinted, our numbers have greatly grown and now range from eighty to one hundred. Very promising men who are suddenly thrown in our way are received at any time, and others who are selected from the main body of applicants come in at the commencement of terms.

The church at the Tabernacle continues to furnish a large quota of men. As these have usually been educated for two or more years in our evening classes, they are more advanced and better able to profit by our two years of study.

We have no difficulty in finding spheres for men who are ready and fitted for them. There is no reason to believe that the supply of trained ministers is in advance of the demand.

Able Educators

Even on the lowest ground of consideration, there is yet very much land to be possessed. When men break up fresh soil, as ours are encouraged to do, the field is the world, and the prayer for more laborers is daily more urgent.

If the Lord would but send us funds commensurate, there are hundreds of neighborhoods needing the pure Gospel, which we could by His grace change from deserts into gardens. How far this is a call upon the reader, let him judge as in the sight of God. Shall there be the gifts and graces of the Spirit given to the church, and shall there not also be sufficient bestowed of the earthly treasure? How much owest thou unto my Lord?

The College was for some little time aided by the zealous services of Mr. W. Cubitt of Thrapstone, who died among us, enjoying our highest esteem. A most able brother, Mr. Gracey, the classical tutor, is one of ourselves and was in former years a student, though from possessing a solid education he needed little instruction from us except in theology. In him we have one of the most efficient tutors living, a man fitted for any post requiring thorough scholarship and aptness in communicating knowledge.

In the English elementary classes, Mr. Fergusson does the first work upon the rough stones of the quarry. From the men whom he has taught in the evening classes, we have heard speeches and addresses which would have adorned any assembly, proving to demonstration his ability to cope with the difficulties of uncultured and ignorant minds.

Mr. Johnson, who zealously aids in the evening, is also a brother precisely suited to the post which he occupies.

These evening classes afford an opportunity to Christian men engaged during the day to obtain an education for nothing during their leisure time, and very many avail themselves of the privilege. Nor must I forget to mention Mr. Selway, who takes the department of physical science and by his interesting experiments and lucid descriptions gives to his listeners an introduction to those departments of knowledge which most abound with illustrations.

Last, but far from least, I adore the goodness of God which sent me so dear and efficient a fellow-helper as my brother in the flesh and in the Lord, J. A. Spurgeon. His work has greatly relieved me of anxiety, and his superior educational qualifications have tended to raise the tone of the instruction given.

Earl of Shaftesbury's Testimony

As to the quality of the preachers whom we have been enabled to send forth, we need no more impartial witness than the good Earl of Shaftesbury, who was kind enough to express himself publicly in the following generous terms:

> It was an utter fallacy to suppose that the people of England would ever be brought to a sense of order and discipline by the repetition of miserable services, by bits of wax candle, by rags of popery and by gymnastics in the chancel; nothing was adapted to meet the wants of the people but the gospel message brought home to their hearts, and he knew of none who had done better service in this evangelic work than the pupils trained in Mr. Spurgeon's College. They had a singular faculty for addressing the population and going to the very heart of the people.

Each year the brethren educated at the Pastors' College are invited to meet in conference at the Tabernacle, and they are generously entertained by our friends. The week is spent in holy fellowship, prayer and communication. By this means men in remote villages, laboring under discouraging circumstances and ready to sink from loneliness of spirit, are encouraged and strengthened: indeed, all the men confess that a stimulus is thus given which no other means could confer.

Breaking Up New Soil

All things considered, gratitude and hope are supreme in connection with the Pastors' College. And with praise to God and thanks to a thousand friends, the president and his helpers gird up the loins of their minds for yet more abundant labors in the future. To every land we hope yet to send forth the Gospel in its fullness and purity. We pray the Lord to raise up missionaries among our students and make every one a winner of souls. Brethren, remember this work in your prayers and in your allotment of the Lord's portion of your substance.

When the necessity for new College buildings was plainly indicated, a friend in May, 1873, sent $5,000 towards that object. On October 14, 1873, the foundation stone of those buildings was laid, when the people contributed $5,000 and the students gave $1,500 and undertook to raise the amount to $5,000. In 1874 Messrs. Cory and Sons of Cardiff sent for the benefit of the fund $5,000 worth of paid-up shares in their colliery company. In July, 1875, the president received $25,000 for the same object as a legacy from the late Mr. Matthews. These are named as examples of the various ways in which God has answered prayer and rewarded the faith of His servant in that important work.

Founding Churches

Shortly before the new College buildings were commenced, by an article in *The Sword and the Trowel*, Mr. Spurgeon directed public attention to the institution. The following extract will suffice:

> The supply of men as students has been always large, and at this time more are applying than ever. Our one aim has been to train preachers and pastors. The College is made into a home missionary society for the spread of the Gospel. One of our students, Mr. F. E. Suddard, was first, in 1872, among seven competitors for one of Dr. Williams' scholarships at the Glasgow University. In the metropolis alone, forty-five churches have been founded.
>
> One of the students has commenced a cause in Turk's Island; he is now carrying on evangelistic work in St. Domingo where, if he is spared, he is likely to become the apostle of that island and also of Haiti. One brother has gone to serve the Lord in China, two are laboring in Spain, several are doing a good work in Canada, more than twenty brethren have become pastors in America, and seven others have gone as far south as Australia. One is a missionary in India, another in Prince Edward Island.

How the Money Came

The suitable and commodious new buildings which have been erected and furnished cost about $75,000, all of which is paid. Here we have a fine hall, excellent classroom, a handsome library and, in fact, all that a college can require.

The way in which the money was raised was another instance of divine goodness: $15,000 was given as a memorial to a dear and lamented husband; $10,000 was a legacy to the College from a reader of the sermons. The ministers who had been formerly students came to our help in a princely fashion. Large amounts were made up by the unanimous offerings of Tabernacle friends on days when the pastor invited the members and adherents to be his guests at the College. In answer to prayer, the gold and the silver have been ready when needed. How our heart exults and blesses the name of the Lord!

The evening classes are in a high condition of prosperity, there being about two hundred men in regular attendance and a considerable number among them of hopeful ability. Out of this class city missionaries, lay preachers, writers for the press and colporteurs are continually coming. It is an eminently useful part of the College work.

There are now hundreds of men proclaiming the Gospel who have been trained in the College. We are daily expecting more missionaries to be raised up among us.

One of Mr. Spurgeon's Annual Reports of the College

Our statistics, which are far from being complete, show that these brethren baptized 20,676 in ten years (1865-74), that the gross increase to their churches was 30,677, and the net increase 19,498. *LAUS DEO.*

On inquiring the other day for the secretary of one of our largest societies, I was informed that he had gone to the seaside for a month in order that he might have quiet to prepare the report. I do not wonder at this if he has aforetime written many descriptions of the same work, for every year increases the difficulty unless a man is prepared to say the same thing over and over again.

Very few can, like Paganini, perform so admirably on one string that everybody is charmed with the melody. The task grows still harder when the year has been peaceful and successful. It has been truly said, "Happy is the nation which has no history," because it has been free from changes, wars, convulsions and revolutions; but I may remark, on the other hand, unhappy is the historian who has to produce a record of a certain length concerning a period which has been innocent of striking events—making bricks without straw is nothing to it.

No Milk and Water Theology

The Pastors' College has of late maintained the even tenor of its way, knowing little of external attack and nothing of internal strife. Regular in its work and fixed in its purpose, its movement has been calm and strong. Hence there are no thrilling incidents, painful circumstances or striking occurrences with which to fill my page and thrill my reader's soul. *Gratitude writ large* is about the only material at hand out of which to fashion my report.

"Bless the Lord, O my soul!" is my one song, and I feel as if I could repeat it a thousand times.

The College started with a definite doctrinal basis. I never affected to leave great questions as moot points to be discussed in the hall and believed or not believed, as might be the fashion of the hour. The creed of the College is well known, and we invite none to enter who do not accept it. The doctrines of grace, coupled with a firm belief in human responsibility, are held with intense conviction; and those who do not receive them would not find themselves at home within our walls.

The Lord has sent us tutors who are lovers of sound doctrine and zealous for the truth. No uncertain sound has been given forth at any time, and we would sooner close the house than have it so.

An Army of Prophets

Heresy in colleges means false doctrine throughout the churches; to defile the fountain is to pollute the streams. Hesitancy, which might be tolerated in an ordinary minister, would utterly disqualify a teacher of teachers. The experiment of Doddridge ought to satisfy all godly men that colleges without dogmatic evangelical teaching are more likely to be seminaries of Socinianism than schools of the prophets.

Old Puritanic theology has been heartily accepted by those received into our College, and on leaving it they have almost with one consent remained faithful to that which they have received. The men are before the public in every part of the country, and their testimony well known.

This institution has now reached its twenty-fifth year, and its object, spirit and manner of work remain the same. It was intended from the first to receive young men who had been preaching for a sufficient time to test their abilities and call to the work of the ministry; and such young men have been forthcoming every year in growing numbers.

Some bodies of Christians have to lament that their ministry is not adequately supplied: I know of one portion of the church which is sending up to Heaven bitter lamentations because as the fathers depart to their rest there is scanty hope that their places will be filled. But among the Baptists, the candidates for the ministry are, if possible, too plentiful.

Object of the College

This is a new state of things and is to be interpreted as indicating growth and zeal. Certainly the applicants are not tempted by rich livings or even by the prospect of competent support. If they are, I take abundant pains to set before them the assured truth that they will find our ministry to be a warfare abounding in long marches and stern battles, but equally notable for meager rations. Still they come, and it needs a very hard heart to repel them and to refuse to eager brethren the drill and equipment which they covet so earnestly. If it were wise to increase the number of students, another hundred of suitable men could at once be added to those who are already under tuition.

From the start our main object was to help men who, from lack of funds, could not obtain an education for themselves. These have been supplied not only with tuition and books, gratis, but with board and lodging and in some cases, with clothes and pocket money. Some very successful brethren needed everything; and if they had been required to pay, they may have remained illiterate preachers to this day. Still, year by year the number of men who are ready to support themselves in whole or in part has increased, and I believe that it is increasing and will increase.

As a College we have had to struggle with a repute based upon falsehood and created by jealousy; but this has not injured us to any great extent, for men come to us from America, Australia and the Cape. Also applications have frequently been made from other foreign countries. German students have attended our classes during their own vacations, and members of other colleges are usually to be seen at our lectures.

The institution never deserved to be charged with giving a mere apology for an education; and if ever that reproach could have been justly cast upon us, it is utterly undeserved now that the time of study has become more extended and a fuller course of training has thus become possible.

Diamonds in the Rough

Scholarship for its own sake was never sought and never will be within the Pastors' College; but to help men to become efficient preachers has been and ever will be the sole aim of all those concerned in its management. In order to increase our prestige, I shall not refuse poor or zealous young Christians whose early education has been neglected. Pride would suggest that we take "a better class of men"; but experience shows that they are not better, that eminently useful men spring from all ranks, that diamonds may be found in the rough, and that some who need most pains in the polishing reward our labor a thousandfold.

My friends will still stand by me in my desire to aid the needy but pious brother, and we shall rejoice together as we continually see the ploughman, the fisherman and the mechanic taught the way of God more perfectly and enabled through divine grace to proclaim in the language of the people the salvation of our God.

Period of Preparation

During the past year about 120 men have been with us; but as some have come and others have gone, the average number in actual residence has averaged one hundred. Of these, a few have been with us three years, and more have entered upon the third year. The rule is that a man's usual period terminates at the end of two years, and his remaining longer depends upon the judgment formed of him.

Certain men will never get beyond an English education, and to detain them from their work is to repress their ardor without bestowing a compensatory advantage. In other cases, the longer the period of study, the better. Probably the third year is to many a student more useful than the other two, and he goes forth to his life work more thoroughly prepared.

I could not lengthen the course in former days when churches tempted the brethren away before the proper time, as they too often did. They told these raw youths that it was a pity to delay, that if they left their studies, souls might be saved, and I know not what else besides. Some were induced to run away, as Rowland Hill would have said, before they had pulled their boots on. If I constrained them to remain, the good deacons of the eager churches thought me a sort of a harsh jailer who locked up his prisoners and would not give them up at the entreaty of their friends.

One wrote and bade me loose the brother, for the Lord had need of him; and I would have let the young man go if I had thought that he was one of the donkeys to whom the passage referred.

That a number of brethren may have entered upon their ministry prematurely was no fault of mine but of those who tempted them to quit their classes too soon. However, there have been periods in which there is a lull in the demand of the churches for ministers; then we have been able to retain the men for a longer season. Such a time is passing over us just now, and I do not regret it, for I am persuaded it is good to give the brethren a longer space for preparatory study.

I have been very ill through the greater part of the past year, therefore have been unable to give so much personal service to the College as I have usually done. This has been a sore trial to me, but it has been much alleviated by my beloved brother, J. A. Spurgeon, the vice-president, who has looked after everything with great care. I have also been greatly comforted by the knowledge that the tutors are as deeply concerned about the holy service as ever I can be.

Digging Up the Weeds

It has been my joy to learn that the College was never in a better state in all respects than now and that the men under training give promise of becoming useful preachers. I have had very little weeding work to do on my coming back to my place, and those whom I have removed were not chargeable with any fault, but their capacity was questioned by the tutors. All through the year this painful operation has to be carried on, and it always causes me much grief; but it is a necessary part of my official duty as president.

Young men who come to us loaded with testimonials are occasionally found after awhile to be lacking in application or in spiritual power; and after due admonition and trial, they have to be sent back to the place from whence they came. Others are as good as gold, but their heads ache and their health fails under hard study, or from lack of mental capacity they cannot master the subjects placed before them. These must be kindly but firmly set aside; but I always dread the task.

This thinning-out process is done with conscientiousness, under the guidance of the tutors; but this year there has been little need of it, and I have rejoiced in the fact, since frequent depression of spirit has made it undesirable to have much trying work to do.

I am glad to say that very rarely have I had to deal with a case of *moral* failure. Bad young men have crept in among us, and no men are perfect; but I have great comfort in seeing the earnest and prayerful spirit which has prevailed among the brotherhood.

Foremost among our aims is the promotion of *a vigorous spiritual life* among those who are preparing to be undershepherds of Christ's flock. By frequent meetings for prayer and by other means, we labor to maintain a high tone of spirituality.

I have endeavored in my lectures and addresses to stir up the holy fire; *for well I know that if the heavenly flame burns low, nothing else will avail.*

The earnest action of the College Missionary Society has been a source of great joy to me; for above all things I desire to see many students devoting themselves to foreign work. The Temperance Society also does a good work and tends to keep alive among the men a burning hatred of England's direst curse.

The Divine Anointing

We need the daily prayer of God's people that much grace may be with all concerned in this important business; for what can we do without the Holy Spirit? How few ever pray for students! If ministers do not come up to the desired standard, may not the members of the churches rebuke themselves for having restrained prayer on their account?

When does a Christian worker more need prayer than in his early days, when his character is forming and his heart is tenderly susceptible both of good and evil influences? I would beseech all who have power with God to remember our colleges in their intercessions.

The solemn interests involved in the condition of these schools of the prophets compel me to entreat, even unto tears, that the hopeful youth of our ministry may not be forgotten in the supplications of the saints. For us also who have the responsible duty of guiding the minds of these young men, much prayer is requested, that we may have wisdom, love, gentleness, firmness and abounding spiritual power. It is not every man who can usefully influence students, nor can the same men have equal power at all times. The Divine Spirit is needed, and He is given to them that ask for His sacred teaching.

A Missionary Society

In Great Britain hundreds of our former students are preaching the Word, some in the more prominent pulpits of the denomination and others in positions where their patience and self-denial are severely tested by the present depression in trade and the consequent inability of rural congregations to furnish them with adequate support.

The College has reason to rejoice not only in the success of her most honored sons, but in the faithfulness and perseverance of the rank and file, whose services, although they are little noticed on earth, will receive the "well done" of the Lord.

This institution is not alone a College, but a Home and Foreign Missionary Society. Our three evangelists have traversed the land with great diligence, and the Lord has set His seal to their work.

It is my greatest pleasure to aid in commencing new churches. The oftener brethren can create their own spheres, the more glad shall I be.

It is not needful to repeat the details of former reports; but many churches have been founded through the College, with more to follow. I announced at the beginning of this enterprise that it was not alone for the education of ministers, but for the general spread of the Gospel; and this has been adhered to, a part of the income being always expended in that direction.

An Interesting Letter

A very considerable number of Pastors' College men are to be found at the Antipodes. I cannot forget that there I have a beloved son; but next to that in nearness to my heart is the fact that so many of my spiritual sons are there, prospering and bringing glory to God.

It was with no little delight that I received the following letter from some of them. Readers must kindly excuse expressions of affection which are so natural from friends; I could not cut them out without destroying the spirit of the letter:

MELBOURNE, VICTORIA
NOVEMBER 2, 1880
REV. C. H. SPURGEON:

HONORED AND BELOVED PRESIDENT:

A number of former students at the College being met together at this metropolis of the Antipodes, it was most heartily agreed that we should send you an expression of our warm love. For truly we can say that instead of distance or even time causing any abatement of love towards you personally or towards the institution which we may with truth style our *Alma Mater*, we find it intensified and hallowed.

The meetings of the Victorian Baptist Association are now being held in this city, which has brought most of us together; but the Melbourne Exhibition has brought to us Brother Harry Woods from South Australia, and Brother Harrison from Deloraine, Tasmania.

Our Brother A. J. Clarke's house is the rendezvous for all the brethren, and the cheery hospitality of himself and wife prove them to be called to the episcopate. Though all the brethren, so far as we know, have had blessing this year, some of them wonderfully so, yet our Brother A. J. Clarke, here at West Melbourne, has experienced a year of toil and harvesting in which we all rejoice and which exercises a stimulating effect upon all who hail from "the College."

When a number of us were bowing in prayer together, we felt how thoroughly you would have been with us in spirit, as we prayed that we might oppose, in the might of God, the awful world-spirit of this region, and that our souls might be kept wholly loyal to King Jesus, having no "fellowship with the unfruitful works of darkness."

Finally, beloved servant of God, we hail you in the name of our Triune Jehovah! No words of ours can express our personal obligation to you. But by fidelity to Christ and to truth, by manifesting that we have caught the spirit of burning love to souls which burns in your own breast, and by serving to our utmost ability and to the last day of life, in the kingdom and patience of Jesus, we hope to show that all your care and that of the tutors and friends of the Tabernacle has not been ill-bestowed. We remain,

Yours, in the bonds of eternal love,

WM. CHRISTR. BUNNING, Geelong.
WILLIAM CLARK, Ballarat.
ALFRED J. CLARKE, West Melbourne.
H. H. GARRETT, Brighton.
HENRY MARSDEN, Kew.
J. S. HARRISON, Deloraine, Tasmania.
HARRY WOODS, Saddleworth, S. Australia.
F. G. BUCKINGHAM, Melbourne.

Similarly in Canada the Lord has been with those who have gone from the College. During his visit to Canada, my brother, J. A. Spurgeon, formed a branch of our Conference there, and from it the annexed loving epistle has lately come:

567 YORK STREET, LONDON,
EAST ONTARIO, CANADA
APRIL 6, 1881

BELOVED PRESIDENT:

We, the members of the Canadian branch of the Pastors' College Brotherhood, herewith greet you lovingly (and our brethren through you) on the occasion of your Annual Conference, which we hope may surpass even the best of by-gone gatherings, in all holy joy and such spiritual refreshing as may fit all for more abundant service.

Need we say how deeply we feel for all the sufferings by which our president is made to serve, the while we gratefully recognize "the peaceable fruit" of those sufferings in such enriched utterances as we have lately read?

We love our dear president as of yore, remembering days of prayerful tryst in which we heard him sigh and groan his longings for our course.

During another year we have been "kept by the power of God" and used in service; and although we are in some cases separated even here by many dreary miles of continent, we still hold and are held to and by the old-time kindness and, better still, "the form of sound words."

We "shake hands across the vast," loved president and brethren, and wish you every joy in Conference.

For the Canadian Brethren.
Yours affectionately,

JOSEPH FORTH,
President of the Canadian Branch of the Pastors' College Brotherhood

Help for the Heathen

A point of great interest to which I hope the Lord may turn the attention of many of His servants is that of English evangelists for India. Mr. Gregson, the well-known missionary, has urged upon me the great utility of sending out young men who should preach the Gospel to those in India who understand the English language, whether British, Eurasian or educated Hindoo.

He advises that the men should be sent out for five years, and therefore be subjected to no remark should they return at the end of that period. He thinks it probable that they would acquire a language and remain abroad as missionaries; but if not, they would be missionary-advocates on their return home and arouse among our churches fresh enthusiasm.

It is believed that in many cities churches could be gathered which would support these men as their ministers, or that at least a portion of their expenses would be found on the spot.

I have determined to enter upon this field as God shall help me; and Mr. H. R. Brown, who has been for years the pastor of the church at Shooter's Hill, has reached Calcutta on his way to Darjeeling in the hill country. If the Lord shall prosper him there, I hope he will live long in that salubrious region, build up a church and become the pioneer of a little band of evangelists.

Our native tongue is sure to spread among the educated Hindoos, hence many a heathen may be brought to Jesus by evangelists who do not understand any of the languages of the East, that meanwhile our countrymen, too often irreligious, may be met with by divine grace and find Christ where the most forget Him. I hope many friends will take an interest in this effort and assist me to carry it out.

Funds have come in as they have been needed; but apart from a legacy, now nearly consumed, the ordinary income has not been equal to the expenditure of the year. The balance at the banker's is gradually disappearing; but I do not mention this with any regret, for He who has sent us supplies hitherto will continue His bounty, and He will move His stewards to see that this work is not allowed to flag from want of the silver and the gold. With a single eye to His glory I have borne this burden hitherto and found it light; and I am persuaded from past experience that He will continue to keep this work going so long as it is a blessing to His church and to the world.

A Legacy Lost

I am greatly indebted to the generous donors at the annual supper and quite as much to the smaller weekly gifts of my own beloved congregation, which, in the aggregate, have made up the noble sum of $9,100. I am sorry to say that a considerable legacy left to the College will in all probability be lost through the law of mortmain. This is a great disappointment; but if one door is shut, another will be opened.

Into the hands of Him who worketh all our works in us we commit the Pastors' College for another year.

CHAPTER VII

Stockwell Orphanage

A Large Gift—New Home for Children—Process of Building—Laying the Corner-stone—The Little Ones Happy—Generous Givers—Daily Life in the Orphanage—What Becomes of the Boys—Rules of Admission—Not a Sectarian Institution—Successful Anniversary

It is the Lord's own work to care for the fatherless. Those who have faith in God never need be without success in undertaking the care of the orphan. God helps the helpless; but He uses man as His agent in arranging details.

Soon after *The Sword and the Trowel* was commenced, Mr. Spurgeon indicated in one of his articles published in its pages several forms of Christian usefulness, amongst them being the care of the orphan.

Shortly afterwards, in September, 1866, Mr. Spurgeon received a letter from a lady offering to place at his command the sum of $100,000 with which to commence an orphanage for fatherless boys. At first he felt disposed to avoid the onerous responsibilities of such a work and, calling at the address given by the lady, tried to prevail upon her to give the money to Mr. Mueller of Bristol. The claims of London for such an institution were urged; and, unable to refuse the request of the generous donor, the money was accepted on trust for the purpose named.

Mrs. Hillyard, the widow of a clergyman of the Church of England, was the lady whose benevolence thus originated the Orphanage. The money was in railway debentures, which were not at that time available for use other than as an investment.

Birth of the Orphanage

After consulting with the leading friends at the Tabernacle, a body of twelve trustees was chosen, in whose names the money was invested and a resolution agreed upon to purchase a suitable plot of land at Stockwell, on which to erect an orphanage.

In March, 1867, the deed of incorporation was signed by the trustees, and in May the claims of the projected buildings were urged with so much force and urgency that the people belonging to the Tabernacle took up the case with loving zeal and energy.

By the month of August $5,350 was in hand, and the whole church at the Tabernacle was engaged in collecting on this behalf. Prayer, faith and prompt, energetic action were all combined in the efforts made, and pastors, trustees and congregation were of one mind in their purpose to make the work a success.

Within the space of a year the plan of the Orphanage was matured, the foundations laid, the work was making rapid progress, and a large amount of money was in hand for the purpose. Donations from $5 to $1,250 had been generously forwarded to help on the work, and a great meeting was held in September, 1867, when the public generally had an opportunity of showing their sympathy with the proceedings. Previously to that large meeting, the foundation stones of three of the houses were laid under circumstances of more than usual interest.

Mrs. Tyson, a lady who had often aided Mr. Spurgeon in the work of the College and in other enterprises, had been spared to see the twenty-fifth anniversary of her marriage day, on which occasion her beloved husband, a wealthy merchant, presented her with $2,500. The lady at once took this money to Mr. Spurgeon to be dedicated to God for the erection of one of the orphan houses, to be called Silver-Wedding House.

About the same time a merchant in the city called upon the pastor at the Tabernacle and, after transacting some business with him, left with Mr. Spurgeon's secretary a sealed envelope in which was $3,000, to be used in building another house which, it was afterwards determined, should be called Merchant's House, as the donor refused to have his name given.

The way in which God was answering the prayers of His people was further shown by an offer made by the workmen who had built the Tabernacle to give the labor necessary for erecting a third house, whilst their employer volunteered to give the necessary material: this to be called the Workmen's House.

Such manifest tokens of the divine favor attending the work greatly encouraged the pastor and the trustees; so on Monday afternoon, August 9, 1867, the foundation stones of the three houses named were laid—one by Mrs. Hillyard, one by Mr. Spurgeon, one by Mr. Higgs.

The scene presented at Stockwell on that day was exceedingly picturesque and intensely interesting. At the monster tea meeting which followed, the tables extended 330 feet in length, and the bright sunshine made the scene one of joy and delight which will long be remembered, though the rain, which came down so bountifully just as tea was over, caused much discomfort.

The subscriptions brought in that day reached $12,000. In *The Sword and the Trowel* for October the names of 1,120 collectors are printed, with the amounts on their cards, stated to be $14,010. Amongst the collectors were members of the Church of England, Congregationalists, Methodists, Baptists and others, so general had been the sympathy which was felt in the work.

The Work Grows

The faith of the pastor and trustees of the Orphanage was greatly strengthened by the wonderful manner in which God had answered their prayers and rewarded their efforts. It was announced that eight houses were contemplated, to provide for not less than 150 orphans, requiring an outlay of $15,000 per annum. Messrs. Olney & Sons gave $2,500 to erect a fourth house, to be called Unity House, after the sainted and venerable Mrs. Olney.

By the end of the year 1867 the trustees had no less than two hundred names of orphans from whom to select fifty in the following April. The pressing need of providing for these children made the way easier for extending the work. Accordingly, at the meeting of the Baptist Union early in 1868, it was resolved than an effort should be made to raise the funds necessary for erecting two houses, at a cost of $3,000 each.

Whilst these efforts were being made amongst the Baptists, Mr. Thomas Olney, Superintendent of the Tabernacle Sunday school, aided by the teachers and scholars, was collecting the funds necessary for erecting a house to represent the young children. Simultaneously with that effort was another amongst the students at the college, who had resolved to show their affection for their pastor by raising money sufficient to erect a house on their behalf and to perpetuate their institution by having it named the College House.

Laying a Cornerstone

Two meetings were held at the Orphanage in June, 1868—one on the first of June, when the venerable Thomas Olney, Sr., laid the foundation stone of the building which was to form the lecture and dining hall, the master's house and the entrance gateway. It was a gladsome sight to witness the joy of the venerable man, who had for nearly three-score years been connected with the church, worshiping at the Tabernacle, as he performed the pleasing duty assigned to him.

On the same day the Rev. John Aldis of Reading and Alexander B. Goodall, Esq., each laid one of the foundation stones of the two Testimonial Houses, subscribed for by the Baptist churches as a token of regard to Mr. Spurgeon.

A monster tea-meeting followed the proceedings, after which addresses were delivered by the Revs. Thomas Binney, Dr. Raleigh, J. T. Wigner, W. Brock, D. D., W. Howieson, A. Mursell, Henry Varley, W. Scott, S. H. Booth, G. Gould, J. Raven, J. H. Millard, John Spurgeon, Sr., C. H. Spurgeon and James A. Spurgeon.

Mr. Wigner presented to the pastor an address of affectionate sympathy from the Baptist churches, which was signed by Mr. Goodall and himself on behalf of the subscribers to the fund, and with the address was the sum of $6,000. That sum was afterwards increased to $8,720 so as to include the furniture and fittings for the two houses, that the offering might be in every respect complete in all its parts.

Happy Children

The meeting held on June 19, the thirty-fourth birthday of Mr. Spurgeon, was, if possible, a more joyous and enthusiastic one than any of the preceding. On that day Mr. Thomas Olney, Jr., surrounded by a huge mass of children forming the Tabernacle Sunday schools, laid the foundation stone of the Sunday School House amidst the enthusiastic applause of the delighted children.

It was a time of joy they will all long remember. Dear Mrs. Spurgeon, so long a suffering invalid, was there to witness the happiness of the assembly; and by request from the students at the college and the ministers who had gone from it, she was induced to lay the foundation stone of the College House. She was graciously upheld on the occasion, although the surpassing kindness displayed was enough to overcome one of a stronger frame.

After the stone laying was over, twenty-six sweet little girls in white advanced one by one and presented Mrs. Spurgeon with money which their parents had subscribed as a token of their affectionate rejoicing at her temporary restoration. It was a touching, beautiful and unexpected sight, which deserves to be recorded.

A large sum of money was presented to Mr. Spurgeon as a birthday offering, *which he put into the Orphanage treasury.*

Funds Flow In

Another incident occurred at that period which deserves to be placed on record. The Baptist church at Liverpool, over which the Rev. Hugh Stowell Brown presides, was about to be reopened, and Mr. Spurgeon consented to preach the sermon. He did so; but the church and congregation resolved to defray the cost of the repairs and gave to Mr. Spurgeon for the Orphanage the whole of the collection, which amounted to $1,250.

The manner in which the funds have been contributed, first to erect the Orphanage buildings, and since then to maintain the children and officers and keep the whole establishment in continuous operation, most clearly indicates that, from the commencement of the work up to the present time, the hand of God has been directing the whole.

Each house was occupied as soon as it was finished; but unable to wait until the first was ready, so soon as the plan of the Orphanage was matured and trustees appointed, four orphans were selected and placed under the charge of a sister in her own house. As money came in, others were added to them.

To manifest still further the interest which Mrs. Hillyard took in the work, when she found several orphans already in charge of a matron, she sold some household plate to give the money for their support.

Thus encouraged, by the month of July, 1867, before the foundation stones were actually laid, seven boys were chosen by the trustees as a commencement. It was wonderful how the money was sent in.

One day, just as Mr. Spurgeon finished his sermon in the open air, a lady put into his hand an envelope containing $100 for the Orphanage and $100 for the College. In January, 1868, Mr. Spurgeon announced

BOYS' HOME—STOCKWELL ORPHANAGE.

in his magazine that an unknown gentleman had given him $5,000 towards two of the houses. In March another sum of $5,000 was announced, and in June the Baptist churches sent in $6,000. In September, a year after the work began, a great bazaar was held, which brought in a net profit of $7,000.

How many loving hearts and willing hands were employed to bring about such a result, it would be impossible to tell, though there were but few of the eleven hundred collectors who so nobly came forward at the first meeting a year before, who did not lend a helping hand to the bazaar.

By the end of the year the president announced in his magazine that only $5,000 more was required to complete the eight houses. "And this," says he, "will surely be sent in; for the Lord will provide." And so it came to pass.

The Right Man in the Right Place

In January, 1869, fifty children had been chosen to occupy the houses as soon as they should be ready, but up to the month of June only twenty-nine orphans were in residence. The chief difficulty, which for some time had given anxiety to the trustees, was to find a suitable superintendent. Several persons had presented themselves, but not one had satisfied the claims of the institution.

When the difficulty seemed to be the greatest, Divine Providence sent the right man.

Vernon J. Charlesworth, who had been for seven years co-pastor at Surrey Chapel with Newman Hall, offered his services, and they were accepted. Mr. Charlesworth was at once appointed: and the ability which he has manifested in managing the affairs of the institution is very satisfactory evidence that he is the right man in the right place. By his influence within the Orphanage and by his pen outside, he has shown himself to be the orphan's friend.

Up to the spring of the year 1870, some 154 orphans had been admitted, six of whom had been removed, leaving 148 in residence. In 1877 the resident orphans numbered 230.

How the Children Live

Each of the eight houses forms a separate family, that plan having after mature consideration been resolved upon as the best. Each family is complete in its own arrangements; each dwelling having a large sitting and four lofty bedrooms for the boys, with lockers which, when closed, form handy seats in the middle of the room; and a sitting room, bedroom and kitchen for the matron in charge. A large covered playroom adjoins the houses on the east, and separate from that is the infirmary, forming the east end of the quadrangle. At the west end is the schoolroom and dining hall, the master's house and entrance gateway; and in the rear of the dining hall is the suite of offices for cooking and other domestic purposes.

In selecting the most needy boys for the benefits of the institution, the trustees are in no way influenced by the religious opinions of their parents. Those showing the most pressing want have the preference.

A Big Family

A judicious writer has said of the Stockwell Orphanage:

How superior any real approach to the family ideal is to the barrack system was apparent to us on a mere glance at these fatherless lads. The families are large, about thirty boys in each house; but they are under the care of affectionate and diligent matrons, and everything is done to compensate for the loss of parental rule and training.

There is more of the "home" than of the "institution" in the atmosphere. To encourage home ideas and for the sake of industrial training, the boys in turn assist in the domestic work during the morning of the day; each boy's period of service being restricted to one week in six, servants being entirely dispensed with. A working cook superintends the kitchen, aided by the boys.

No regimental uniform is allowed. The boys differ in the clothes they wear, in the cut of the hair, and show all the variety of a large family. The boys do not look like loosely connected members of a huge and miscellaneous crowd, but sons and brothers.

No traces of ill-disguised dissatisfaction, as though in perpetual restraint, always under orders, were apparent; but a free, healthy and vigorous homeliness, as if under the genial and robust influence of love, made itself everywhere manifest.

With all the care of a Christian father, situations are chosen for the lads where their spiritual interests will not be in danger; and when they have been passed into them, the master corresponds with them and gives them counsel and assistance as they need. Like a true home, its benediction follows every inmate throughout his life.

We were specially pleased with our visit to the school. The boys are well drilled in elementary knowledge, reading, writing, arithmetic, grammar, history, geography, vocal music, Latin, shorthand, science of common things and Scripture.

A French class is held for the elder boys. Military drill is given daily. Drawing is successfully taught, and many boys excel in it. The singing class did very great credit to its instructor—singing at sight, with great accuracy and sweetness, music of some difficulty.

Two of Her Majesty's Inspectors were deputed from the Local Government Board to visit the institution, and they gave the following report, which reflects the highest credit upon Mr. Spurgeon for his wisdom and prudence: "An admirable institution, good in design, and, if possible, better in execution."

Nonsectarian and Financially Efficient

The children are admitted between the ages of six and ten years, and they remain until they are fourteen. From an abstract drawn up by the master in 1873 it was found that the creeds of the parents of the children admitted to that date were in the following proportions: 69 were members of the Church of England; 26 Independent; 19 Wesleyan; 51 Baptist; four Presbyterian; one Catholic; and 35 made no profession of religion.

In the management of the Orphanage will be found one of its chief attractions, and one which ought to commend its plans to other similar institutions. The author of a book called *Contrasts* cites the Stockwell School as a specimen of admirable administration, proving that large expenditure in some public institutions does not guarantee thorough satisfaction.

In some orphan schools and pauper schools the rate of expense per head is from $115.00 to $145.00, whilst in the Stockwell Orphanage, with complete organization and highly satisfactory results in each department, the cost is only $72.00 per head, inclusive of everything. This is the highest testimonial which could be given of its efficiency.

Rules of Admission

Looking over the list of applications which are entered in the books at Stockwell, it was ascertained that two only out of every dozen cases could be received. What becomes of the other ten? Think of widows, some of them sickly and unable to work, with four or five children;

BOYS' SCHOOL—STOCKWELL ORPHANAGE.

families of orphans deprived of both parents; and yet the Stockwell trustees had to decline them because there were more necessitous cases. But there was one comfort: they had not to pay any election expenses.

On that subject Mr. Spurgeon has written the following judicious remarks:

> No widow ever goes away lamenting over time, labor and money spent in vain. The worst that can happen is to be refused because there is no room or her case is not so bad as that of others. Not a shilling will have been spent in purchasing votes, no time lost in canvassing, no cringing to obtain patronage. Her case is judged on its merits, and the most necessitous wins the day.
>
> We have now so many applicants and so few vacancies that women with two or three children are advised not to apply, for while there are others with five, six or seven children depending upon them, they cannot hope to succeed.

A dozen orphanages as large as the one at Stockwell could be filled at once with children needing such help.

A Good Investment

The economy with which the Orphanage has been managed has excited the admiration of many who are familiar with the details of kindred institutions. Those who honor Mr. Spurgeon with their contributions make a good investment and will share in the blessedness of the return.

The office expenses are reduced to a minimum, and no paid canvassers are employed. Offerings find their way into the exchequer from all parts of the globe; and though at times there has been a little tightness felt, the children have never lacked a meal.

Mr. Spurgeon is a man of unwavering faith in the living God; and though his faith has been put to the severest test, it has never failed him. Friends who have not been able to give money have sent gifts in kind. Flour and potatoes, meat and preserves are always gladly received. One manufacturer has given all the coverlets for the beds, and the proprietors and pupils of a young ladies' school have endeavored to keep the boys supplied with shirts.

The Orphanage has now existed long enough to form a correct opinion of its merits in every department. Hundreds of boys have left the school and entered on the duties of life. The reports which have been received annually from those businessmen who have taken them have been most gratifying. With few exceptions, those who have left keep up communication with the home. Summing up these results, a recent report says:

> Almost every boy who has gone into a situation has given satisfaction. Where failure has occurred, it has arisen from a craving for the sea or from the interference of an unwise mother. Some of the lads are in good positions and command the esteem of their employers.

Nearly all the boys have sent a portion of their first earnings as a donation to the orphanage, in sums varying from one dollar to five dollars, thus manifesting a spirit of gratitude. Some of the letters received from them are read to the boys and produce on their minds beneficial results. Many of the boys have, before they have left, become decided Christians; and some have made public confession of their faith by baptism. The headmaster himself was publicly baptized in 1874, and five of the boys joined him in the same act of dedication.

Others have become members of Christian churches in the towns and villages where they have gone to reside. One of the first boys converted is now devoting his evenings and Sundays to missionary work in South London, and showed so much talent for preaching that he was received into the College in January, 1876.

It is gratifying to be able to record that the health of the orphans has been graciously maintained, with but little interruption, through the several years of its existence.

The 1875 anniversary of the schools was held at the Orphanage on the pastor's birthday, June 19, which was preceded by a bazaar. The attendance was so large that it was necessary to hold two public meetings to accommodate those persons present. The Earl of Shaftesbury was present and spoke at both the services. The contributions added $2,500 to the funds.

CHAPTER VIII

Annual Report of Stockwell Orphanage

A Devoted Woman—Faith Insures Success—Story of an Old Puritan—Need of a Double Income—Health of the Orphanage—An Appeal Hard to Resist—Young Choristers— Spontaneous Charity—A Notable Year—Enlarging the Bounds—Girls' Orphanage— Liberal Response to Appeals for Help—The Miracle of Faith and Labor

In issuing the twelfth annual report of the Stockwell Orphanage, the Committee writes:

With profound gratitude to our Heavenly Father we issue the Twelfth Report of the Stockwell Orphanage. Our gratitude will be shared, we doubt not, by all who have given of their substance towards the maintenance and development of the institution. We therefore invite all our readers to "rejoice with us" in the tokens of the divine favor which has crowned our labors during another year. "The Lord hath been mindful of us: He will bless us."

When we remember how this gracious work began by the consecrated thought of a holy woman, then grew into an actual gift from her hand, and further developed, by the large help of others, into houses and schools, infirmary and dining hall, and all manner of provision for destitute children, we feel bound to cry, "What hath God wrought!"

Our God has supplied all our need according to His riches in Glory by Christ Jesus. The story of the Stockwell Orphanage will be worth telling in Heaven when the angels shall learn from the church the manifold wisdom and goodness of the Lord.

Incidents which could not be published on earth will be made known in the heavenly city, where every secret thing shall be revealed. How every need has been supplied before it has become a want; how guidance has been given before questions have become anxieties; how friends have been raised up in unbroken succession, and how the One Great Friend has been ever present, no single pen can ever record.

To care for the fatherless has been a work of joyful faith all along; and in waiting upon God for supplies, we have experienced great delight. The way of faith in God is the best possible. We could not have carried on the work by a method more pleasant, more certain, more enduring. If we had depended upon annual subscribers, we should have had to hunt them up and pay a heavy poundage or perhaps fail to keep up the roll. If we had advertised continually for funds, our outlay might have brought in a scanty return. But dependence upon God has been attended with no such hazards.

We have done our best as men of business to keep the Orphanage before the public, but we have desired in all things to exercise faith as servants of God. Whatever weakness we have personally to confess and deplore, there is no weakness in the plan of faith in God. Our experience compels us to declare that He is the living God; the God who heareth prayer; the God who will never permit those who trust in Him to be confounded.

The business world has passed through trying times during the last few years, but the Orphanage has not been tried. Men of great enterprise have failed, but the home for the fatherless has not failed, for this enterprise is in the divine hand; an eye watches over it which neither slumbers nor sleeps.

Let the people of God be encouraged by the fact of the existence and prosperity of the Stockwell Orphanage. Miracles have come to an end, but God goes on to work great wonders. The rod of Moses is laid aside, but the rod and staff of the Great Shepherd still compass us.

An Old Puritan

The son of an old Puritan rode some twenty miles to meet his father, who came a similar distance to the halfway house. "Father," said the son, "I have met with a special providence, for my horse stumbled at least a dozen times, yet it did not fall."

"Ah," replied the father, "I have had a providence quite as remarkable, for my horse did not stumble once all the way."

This last is the happy picture of the Orphanage for some time past and, indeed, throughout its whole career; we have never had to issue mournful appeals because of exhausted resources, and in this we must see and admire the good hand of the Lord.

STOCKWELL ORPHANAGE PLAY AREA

We now enter more fully upon a fresh stage of our existence; we shall need to double the amount of our present income, and we shall have it from the ever-opened hand of the Lord our God. Friends will be moved to think of our great family, for our Great Remembrancer will stir them up. The duty of each Christian to the mass of destitute orphanhood is clear enough; and if pure minds are stirred up by way of remembrance, there will be no lack in the larder, no want in the wardrobe, no failing in the funds of our Orphan House.

We labor under one great difficulty. Many people say, "Mr. Spurgeon will be sure to get the money, and there is no need for us to send." It is clear that if everybody talked so, our president's name would be a hindrance instead of a help. He will be the means of finding money for our institution, for the Lord will honor his faith and hear his prayers and be glorified in him; but there will be no thanks due to those who fabricate an excuse for themselves out of the faithfulness of God.

THE INFIRMARY OF STOCKWELL ORPHANAGE

This difficulty, however, does not distress us. We go forward believing that, when we have twice our present number of children, the Lord will send us double supplies. We cannot entertain the suspicion that the girls will be left without their portion; for we, being evil, care as much for our daughters as for our sons, and our Heavenly Father will do the same. It is well, however, to remind our friends of this, that each helper of the Orphanage may try to interest another generous heart, and so enlarge the circle of our friends. It may be that by such means the Great Provider will supply us; for we know that when our Lord fed the multitude He first said to His disciples, "Give ye them to eat."

The sanitary condition of the Orphanage has been all that we could desire. Considering that so large a proportion of the children come to us in a delicate condition, and some with the taint of hereditary disease, it is a matter for devout thankfulness that their general health is so good and that so few deaths have occurred. Out of the entire number who have left, only one boy was unable to enter upon a situation in consequence of an enfeebled constitution. We owe it to an ever-watchful Providence that, during the prevailing epidemic, not a single case of fever or smallpox has occurred in the institution.

Religious Culture

Family worship is conducted twice daily, before the morning and evening meals, by the headmaster or his assistants, the service being taken occasionally by the president or a member of the committee or a visitor to the institution who may happen to be present. The Word of God is read and expounded, hymns sung, prayer offered; and the whole of the boys repeat a text selected for the day. A service is conducted for the elder boys every Wednesday evening by Mr. W. J. Evans, when addresses are given by ministers and other friends.

During their term of residence in the institution all the boys are total abstainers, no alcoholic liquors being allowed except by order of the doctor; but most of them are pledged abstainers, with the approval of their friends.

Band of Hope meetings are held every month, when the children receive instruction from competent speakers; and lectures are given at intervals during the winter months.

The Cry of the Orphan

The operations of the institution reveal to the managers the widespread necessity which exists. The cry of the orphan comes from every part of our beloved land, and the plea of the widow for Christian sympathy and help is restricted to no one class of the community. Faces once radiant with smiles are saddened with grief, for the dark shadow which death casts falls everywhere. How true are the lines of the poet:

> There is no fireside, howsoe'er defended,
> But has one vacant chair.

It is a constant joy to the president and the committee that they are able to mitigate to such a large extent the misery and need which

are brought under their notice; and it must be an equal joy to the subscribers to know that their loving contributions furnish the sinews for
this holy war.

As our Sunday school is affiliated to the Sunday School Union, we
allow the boys who desire to do so to sit for examination. Of the candidates who were successful at the last examination, three gained prizes,
twelve first-class certificates and thirty-eight second-class certificates.

Young Choristers

During the year the boys took part in the Crystal Palace Musical
Festivals, arranged by the Band of Hope Union and the Tonic Sol-fa
Association.

A SCHOOLROOM OF STOCKWELL ORPHANAGE

In order to make the character and claims of the institution more widely known, the headmaster and the secretary have held meetings in London and the provinces. The success which has crowned their efforts is of a very gratifying character. The boys who accompany them to sing and to recite furnish a powerful appeal by their appearance and conduct and commend the institution to which they owe so much. The local papers speak in terms of the highest praise of their services, and thus a most effective advertisement is secured without any cost to the institution.

So far as the boys are concerned, these trips have an educational value, for they get to know a great deal of the products and industries of different parts of the country, besides securing the advantage of being brought into contact with Christian families where they reside during their visit.

After defraying all expenses, the amount realized during the year is $3,320. Our thanks are hereby tendered to all who assisted in any way to secure such a splendid result.

Spontaneous Benevolence

The committee records with thankfulness that there has been no lack in the funds contributed for the efficient maintenance of the institution. Friends prefer to give donations rather than pledge themselves to send annual subscriptions, and the benevolence thus manifested is purely spontaneous.

The admirable custom of making shirts for the boys is still continued by the young ladies of an educational establishment, who send in a supply of two hundred shirts every year. Their efforts are supplemented by several working associations, but the supply is not yet equal to the demand, and we cordially invite the cooperation of others, to whom we shall be glad to send samples and patterns.

The work of caring for the widow and the fatherless is specially mentioned by the Holy Spirit as one of the most acceptable modes of giving outward expression to pure religion and undefiled before God and the Father. Therefore, the Lord's people will not question that they should help in carrying it out.

Will it need much pleading? If so, we cannot use it, as we shrink from marring the willinghood which is the charm of such a service. The work is carried on in dependence upon God, and as His blessing evidently rests upon it, we are confident the means will be forthcoming as the need arises.

While commending the work to our Heavenly Father in prayer, we deem it right to lay before the stewards of His bounty the necessities and claims of the institution.

A Memorable Year

The year 1880 will be a memorable one in the history of the institution, and we record with gratitude the fact that the foundation stones of the first four houses for the Girls' Orphanage were laid on the 22nd of June, when the president's birthday was celebrated.

It was a joy to all present that Mrs. Spurgeon was able to lay the memorial stone of "The Sermon House, the gift of C. H. Spurgeon and his esteemed publishers, Messrs. Passmore and Alabaster."

The memorial stone of another house, the gift of Mr. W. R. Rickett and called "The Limes, in tender memory of five beloved children," was laid by C. H. Spurgeon, who made a touching allusion to the sad event thus commemorated.

Mrs. Samuel Barrow laid the memorial stone of the house called "The Olives," the amount for its erection having been given and collected by her beloved husband.

The trustees of the institution, having subscribed the funds for the erection of a house, the treasurer, Mr. William Higgs, laid, in their name, the memorial stone which bears the inscription, "Erected by the Trustees of the Orphanage to express their joy in this service of love."

Plans for Enlarged Usefulness

At the present moment the buildings of the Orphanage form a great square, enclosing a fine space for air and exercise. Visitors generally express great surprise at the beauty and openness of the whole establishment. Much remains to be done before the institution is completely accommodated. There is needed an infirmary for the girls; and till that is built, one of the houses will have to be used for that purpose, thus occupying the space which would otherwise be filled by thirty or forty children. This should be attended to at an early date.

Baths and washhouses will be urgently required for the girls. We propose to make them sufficiently commodious for the girls to do the

THE GIRLS' HOME—STOCKWELL ORPHANAGE

washing for the entire community of five hundred children, thus instructing them in household duties and saving considerable expense.

We would not spend a sixpence needlessly. No money has been wasted in lavish ornament or in hideous ugliness. The buildings are not a workhouse or a county jail, but a pleasant residence for those children of whom God declares Himself to be the Father.

The additional buildings which we contemplate are not for luxury but for necessary uses; and as we endeavor to lay out money with judicious economy, we feel sure that we shall be trusted in the future as in the past.

Are there not friends waiting to take a share in the Stockwell Orphanage Building? They cannot better commemorate personal blessings, nor can they find a more suitable memorial for departed friends. No storied urn or animated bust can half so well record the memory of beloved ones as a stone in an Orphan House. Most of the buildings are already appropriated as memorials in some form or other, and only a few more will be needed. Very soon all building operations will be complete, and those who have lost the opportunity of becoming shareholders in the Home of Mercy may regret their delay.

At any rate, none who place a stone in the walls of the Stockwell Orphanage will ever lament that they did this deed of love to the little ones for whom Jesus cares. Honored names are with us already engraven upon the stones of this great Hostelry of the All-merciful; and many others are our co-workers whose record is on high, though unknown among men.

Who will be the next to join us in this happy labor?

When the whole of the buildings are complete, the institution will afford accommodation for five hundred children and prove a memorial of Christian generosity and of the lovingkindness of the Lord.

The following description of the Girls' Orphanage is from Mr. Spurgeon's own pen:

> In our address at the presentation of the late testimonial, we disclaimed all personal credit for the existence of any one of the enterprises over which we preside, because each one has been forced upon us. "I could not help undertaking them," was our honest and just confession. This is literally true, and another illustration of this fact is now to come before the Christian public.

Several of us have long cherished the idea that the time would come in which we should have an Orphanage for girls as well as for boys. It would be hard to conceive why this should *not* be. It seems ungallant, not to say unrighteous, to provide for children of one sex only; for are not all needy little ones dear to Christ, with whom there is neither male nor female? We do not like to do such things by halves, and it is but half doing the thing to leave the girls out in the cold.

We have all along wished to launch out in the new direction, but we had not quite enough on hand for the time being and were obliged to wait. The matter has been thought of, talked about and more than half promised; but nothing has come of it till this present. Now, as we believe at the exact moment, the hour has struck, and the voice of God in providence says, "Go forward."

The Work Begun

The fund for the Girls' Orphanage has commenced, and there are about a dozen names upon the roll at the moment of our writing. The work will be carried on with vigor as the Lord shall be pleased to send the means, but it will not be unduly pushed upon anyone so as to be regarded as a new burden, for we want none but cheerful helpers who will count it a privilege to have a share in the good work. We shall employ no collector to make a percentage by dunning the unwilling and shall make no private appeals to individuals.

There is the case: if it be a good one and you are able to help it, please do so; but if you have no wish in that direction, our Lord's work does not require us to go a-begging like a pauper, and we do not intend to do so.

We have never been in debt yet, nor have we had a mortgage upon any of our buildings, nor have we even borrowed money for a time; but we have always been able to pay as we have gone on. Our prayer is that we may never have to come down to a lower platform and commence borrowing.

Abundance of Girls

It has often happened that we have been unable to assist widows in necessitous circumstances with large families because there did not happen to be a *boy* of the special age required by the rules of our Boys' Orphanage. There were several girls, but then we could not take girls; and however deserving the case, we have been unable to render any assistance to very deserving widows simply because their children were not boys. This is one reason why we need a Girls' Orphanage.

Everywhere also there is an outcry about the scarcity of good servants, honest servants, industrious servants, well-trained servants. We know where to find the sisters who will try to produce such workers out of the little ones who will come under their care.

We have succeeded by God's grace and the diligent care of our masters and matrons in training the lads so that they have become valuable to businessmen: why should not the same divine help direct us with the lassies, so that domestics and governesses should go forth from us as well as clerks and artisans?

We believe that there are many friends who will take a special interest in the girls, and that there are some whose trades would more readily enable them to give articles suitable for girls than those which are useful to boys.

Here is a grand opportunity for Christian people with means to take your places among the first founders of this new institution; and if you judge that such a work will be good and useful, we hope that you will without fail *and without delay* come to our assistance in this fresh branch of service. We cannot afford to lose a single penny from the funds for the boys, but this work for the girls must be something extra and above. You helped Willie and Tommy: will you not help Mary and Maggie?

(It is very needful to add that foolish persons often say, "Mr. Spurgeon can get plenty of money and needs no help." If all were to talk in this fashion, where would our many works drift to? Mr. Spurgeon does get large sums, but not a penny more than the various works require, and he gets it because God moves His people to give it. He hopes, good reader, He may move you also.)

We have no personal end to serve; we do not, directly or indirectly, gain a single penny by the Orphanage, College or any other societies over which we preside; neither have we any wealthy persons around us who are at loss to know how to dispose of their property; but our hard-working church keeps continually consecrating its offerings, and our friends far and near think upon us.

Our treasury is the bounty of God; our motto is: THE LORD WILL PROVIDE. Past mercy forbids a doubt as to the future, and so in the name of God we set up our banners.

Work, Not Miracles

The girls' part is not yet fully complete, but it soon will be so; then we must take in the girls. Now it occurs to me to let my friends know the increased need which has arisen and will arise from the doubling of the number of children. The income must by some means be doubled.

My trust is in the Lord alone, for whose sake I bear this burden. I believe that He has led me all along in the erection and carrying on of this enterprise, and I am also well assured that His own hand pointed to the present extension and supplied the means for making it. I, therefore, rest in the providence of God alone.

But the food of the children will not drop as manna from Heaven; it will be sent in a way which is more beneficial, for the graces of His children will be displayed in the liberality which will supply the needs of the orphans.

God will neither feed the children by angels nor by ravens, but by the loving gifts of His people. It is needful, therefore, that I tell my friends of our need, and I do hereby tell them. The institution will need, in rough figures, about one thousand dollars a week. This is a large sum; and when I think of it, I am appalled if Satan suggests the question: "What if the money does not come in?"

But it is nothing to the Lord of the whole earth to feed five hundred little ones. He has kept 250 boys for these years, and He can do the like for the same number of girls. Only let not His stewards say that there is no need at Stockwell, for there is great and crying need that all my friends should inquire whether they may not wisely render me much more aid than they have done.

The buildings are not all finished yet, nor the roads made; but this will soon be accomplished. Then the institution will be in full operation, and its requirements will be great.

I have written these lines with a measure of reluctance; and I hope that it is not in unbelief, but as a reasonable service, that I have thus stated the case.

CHAPTER IX

The Great Preacher's Last Illness and Death

Alarming Reports—Messages of Sympathy—Cheering Words From the Christian Endeavor Convention of the United States—Message From International Congregational Council—Letters From the Prince of Wales and Mr. Gladstone—Rays of Hope—Anxiety and Fervent Prayers—Glowing Eulogies—Removal to Mentone—Unfavorable Reports—The Closing Scene—Immense Literary Labors

Early in July, 1891, alarming reports became current concerning Mr. Spurgeon's health. It was known that for a long time he had been a sufferer from gout and kidney complaint, and the gravest fears were felt lest these complaints should undermine his otherwise strong constitution and end his great work.

Daily reports were issued from the sick chamber; all the newspapers throughout Christendom contained references to the illustrious sufferer, and among all classes of persons profound sympathy was awakened. Thousands besides Mr. Spurgeon's own congregation prayed earnestly for his recovery. On the 16th of July the *Christian World*, the leading religious newspaper of London, reported as follows: "The condition of Mr. Spurgeon is now regarded as quite beyond human aid. Last evening he had further relapsed, and there was much difficulty in getting him to take nourishment."

On Thursday Mr. Spurgeon was in a very critical condition. The bulletin issued on Friday stated that, although the kidneys were acting more freely, the delirium continued, and he was still very prostrate.

On Saturday Mrs. Spurgeon considered him "no worse." The report of Sunday afternoon showed a slight change for the better.

On Monday night the doctors considered his condition less favorable. Tuesday's bulletin was as follows: "Rev. C. H. Spurgeon has had a very restless night, with delirium. The waste of albumen from the kidneys suddenly increased, and the prostration of strength is very great."

The next day's official bulletin was still more alarming: "After a restless night, Mr. Spurgeon is very weak this morning. The heart's action is becoming more feeble, and the amount of nourishment taken is less."

Messages of Sympathy

The intense interest felt in Mr. Spurgeon's condition is shown by the messages of sympathy that literally pour in on Mrs. Spurgeon. On Friday the telegraph office at Beulah Hill was completely blocked for a considerable part of the day. Telegrams were sent from: the committee of the Baptist Missionary Society, the Nonconformist ministers of Wrexham, the South London Presbytery, the Primitive Methodist General Committee, the British and Foreign Sailors' Society, an assembly of ministers at Grimsby, a meeting of the Loyal Orange Institution at Netley Abbey, the London Wesleyan Council, the Chesham Sunday School Alliance, the Lambeth Auxiliary of the Sunday School Union and the Council of the Evangelical Alliance.

Letters and telegrams were also received from Chicago, Ontario, Massachusetts and many other places. General Booth sent a message: "Four thousand officers of the Salvation Army, assembled in council at Congress Hall, Clapton, assure you of their hearty sympathy and united prayers for Mr. Spurgeon's recovery."

The rector of Newington, the parish in which the Tabernacle is situated, between whom and Mr. Spurgeon the most kindly feeling has existed, wrote to Mrs. Spurgeon expressing his sympathy and hope that her husband's life, so precious to her and his flock, might be spared.

The Bishop of Rochester telegraphed: "As I am myself ill and unable to call and inquire for Mr. Spurgeon, I am anxious to express to you my warm sympathy in your anxiety."

The Young People's Society of Christian Endeavor, in convention, more than 12,000 strong, sent "love and prayers" from Minneapolis, U.S.A.

M. le Pasteur Saillens of Paris telegraphed: "We offer constant prayers for your dear husband and yourself."

Dr. Maclagan, Archbishop-Designate of York, sent "prayerful sympathy."

The International Congregational Council sent an expression of profound affection for, and tender sympathy with, Mr. and Mrs. Spurgeon, before commencing business at the Memorial Hall.

During the opening services of the Council, earnest prayer was offered for the recovery of Mr. Spurgeon; and after the elections had been disposed of, a resolution expressive of sympathy with Mrs. Spurgeon was given, telling her of the earnest prayers of the Assembly that the valuable life of her husband might be spared to the churches. The hearty manner in which the resolution (which was forwarded by telegram) was carried showed how brotherly feeling could dominate denominational distinctions and theological differences.

From Mr. Spurgeon

Later, the following letter was heard with sympathetic interest:

> Mrs. Spurgeon is very grateful for the sympathy and Christian love expressed in the resolution passed by the International Council of Congregationalists. The way is very dark just now, but the light of God's love is beyond the darkness. The prayers of all are still needed, for the dear patient's condition is still very critical. Nothing is impossible with God, and we still hope, saying with all our hearts, "God's will be done." Please to accept the warmest thanks of Mrs. Spurgeon and of yours sincerely,
>
> C. SPURGEON

Prayer meetings, held through the week at the Tabernacle, were largely attended. On Monday Dr. Clifford, Rev. Newman Hall, Rev. Arthur Mursell and Mr. Cuff were among those present. On Tuesday numbers of people were waiting as early as half-past six for the seven o'clock prayer meeting, many of these being old pensioners from the neighboring almshouses. The loving sympathy of friends from all parts of the world is greatly appreciated, not only by Mrs. Spurgeon and Rev. J. A. Spurgeon, but by the church deacons, who expressed their gratitude in a statement issued on Sunday.

Inquiries From the Prince of Wales

By command of the Prince of Wales, Colonel Knollys wrote to Dr. Kidd, making inquiries concerning Mr. Spurgeon's condition, asking the doctor, in the event of his having an opportunity, to convey the expression of His Royal Highness' sympathy to Mr. Spurgeon in his illness. Dr. Kidd read that letter at his patient's bedside, when Mr. Spurgeon remembered having on a former occasion received a communication from the Heir-Apparent.

Mrs. Spurgeon seems to have been specially strengthened for the ordeal she has been passing through. Those only to whom he has been accustomed have been allowed to be in attendance on Mr. Spurgeon. One of these is the faithful man-servant known to all visitors as George, while the other men-servants have taken turns by night.

Mr. Spurgeon has never been unconscious, nor has he all along ever been delirious in the sense of not knowing those about him. He has often asked for his private secretary; he has sometimes been attended by his other secretary, Mr. Keys. And when visited by Dr. Russell Reynolds, he remembered having seen the doctor on a certain occasion at Mentone.

One Catholic priest in charge of a garden party prayed for Mr. Spurgeon's permanent recovery. Ritualists have likewise remembered him in their devotions.

Letter From Mr. Gladstone

Mrs. Spurgeon has received the following letter from Mr. Gladstone:

Corton, Lowestoft
July 16

My dear Madam:

In my own home, darkened at the present time, I have read with studied interest daily accounts of Mr. Spurgeon's illness. I cannot help conveying to you the earnest assurance of my sympathy with you and with him and of my cordial admiration not only of his splendid powers, but still more of his devoted and unfailing character.

May I humbly commend you and him, in all contingencies, to the infinite stores of Divine love and mercy, and subscribe myself, my dear Madame, faithfully yours,

W. E. GLADSTONE

Mrs. Spurgeon sent the following reply, the postscript being in her husband's handwriting:

Westwood, Upper Norwood
July 18, 1891

Dear Mr. Gladstone:

Your words of sympathy have a special significance and tenderness coming from one who has just passed through the deep waters which seem now to threaten me. I thank you warmly for your expression of regard for my beloved husband, and with all my heart I pray that the consolations of God may abound toward you even as they do to me.

Although we cannot consider the dear patient out of danger, the doctors have today issued a somewhat more hopeful bulletin. I feel it an honor to be allowed to say that I shall ever be your grateful friend.

S. SPURGEON

P.S. Yours is a word of love such as those only write who have been in the King's country and have seen much of His face. My heart's love to you.

C. H. SPURGEON

A Gleam of Hope

On giving the news of Mr. Spurgeon's condition to the congregation on Sunday morning, Mr. Stott said that hope of the pastor's recovery was being strengthened, but they must keep on praying rather than yield to too pleasurable excitement, for Mr. Spurgeon was not yet "out of the wood." Under the most happy circumstances, it would still be some time before the patient could become convalescent.

Rev. W. Stott presided at the Monday evening prayer meeting in the Tabernacle. Rev. J. A. Spurgeon, with a sore throat and a voice weak from cold, told of seeing his brother in the course of the day; and although he was seriously ill, he did not look like a dying man; that, weak as he was, he might yet be restored; that he was very seriously ill, and their hope was only in God, who could restore him; that when at prayer concerning his brother, he had had a struggle, but he had at last left it in God's hands.

They left all to God; but when they had done that, they felt that they could not let Him go until they had their pastor back.

Mr. James Spurgeon went on to say that his brother was happy in his mind and was contented. Notwithstanding all that they had heard about his wanderings, his heart had not wandered from Christ. He was not in trouble and not in much pain, and God was to be thanked that in that respect he was as he was. They wanted him back, but would still say, "Thy will be done."

He said that the Lord has never made a mistake and never would do so. How many were thinking of the sick pastor and how many were reading his sermons who had not done so for years! Thus good would come out of the affliction.

If in the end prayers did not avail and the physicians found that they could do nothing more, then they would have to believe that it was as the pastor had himself hinted some time ago, namely, that his time was come and his work was done.

The number of letters and telegrams received at Westwood was marvelous. God was speaking to the nation, and it might be to the church. People now saw what a servant England had in C. H. Spurgeon. If he was raised up again to preach the Gospel, perhaps the nation would learn more to appreciate his testimony.

As regarded the prayer meetings they were holding, they could not fail to be a mighty lesson to those who took part in them, apart from Mr. Spurgeon. How little earth seemed in comparison with eternal things! God might have a purpose in dealing with them as He was doing.

Then what a wonderful spirit of prayer was manifest! There had been one hundred and fifty prayers offered on the preceding Monday, and one hundred had been offered in their meetings of that day. It was decided that their meetings should be continued until there was a decided change in their pastor's condition one way or the other—till their Father in Heaven should say, "It is enough."

Cheering News

Shortly before nine o'clock a telegram arrived from Westwood giving the cheering news of a slight improvement in Mr. Spurgeon's general state. The internal congestion was somewhat diminished, the gout was less painful, while the delirium was milder, intervals of accurate memory occurring. The condition was one of grave danger, but there was said to be some hope.

Words of Appreciation

One of the foremost journals of the metropolis gave expression to the public sympathy and voiced the estimate of Mr. Spurgeon's life and work, as follows:

"While there is life there is hope"; and we rest in confidence that, unless the will of God our Saviour see that the kingdom of His dear Son will be better served by His true and faithful servant's being removed to the Sanctuary above, our beloved and honored brother, C. H. Spurgeon, will be raised up to continue his labors in the Gospel on earth.

But if he should be taken up, a crowning testimony will have been given to the profound impression made upon his fellow-Christians and upon his fellowmen throughout the world, of all denominations and of all shades of thought, by his long and faithful witness to the truth.

Men and women of all sects and creeds, of every rank and position, have, from all parts of the world, written, telegraphed or called to express their deep sympathy; and tens of thousands expect with eager interest the morning paper, and the first thing they look for is the bulletin describing Mr. Spurgeon's condition.

Why People Are Moved

This phenomenal interest is not due alone to personal affection for a beloved brother or father in Christ; to admiration of his fearless character, his marked individuality, his English tenacity; to Christian reverence for one who has scattered the Gospel broadcast throughout the world, largely by his voice, and far more largely by the press; to regard for the orphans' friend; to respect for the gifted evangelist, pastor and teacher who has exercised his God-given gifts of perfecting other men for the work of ministering, though all these elements are included in it.

But lying beneath them all is a conviction of the truth of the Gospel which he has ministered—the Gospel of the atonement; the good tidings of the kingdom of God; the unwavering witness of a man true to the core to 'the precious blood of Christ, as of a lamb without blemish and without spot, by whom we believe in God who raised him up from the dead, and gave him glory that our faith and hope may be in God.'

No higher honor could be accorded to a man than that, lying helpless, suffering, delirious, upon his bed of death, the world was moved with sympathy and tender love because, like Daniel, he was found faithful to his God; because he chose to have the Gospel pure and plain, as pulse and water, rather than spiced with delicacies for the great and wise.

Yet though we speak of the possibility of his being taken, we fervently unite in the universal, loving prayer that God may restore His servant to years of better health and greater usefulness than before he was laid so low.

Removal to France

Mr. Spurgeon continued to improve and was finally able to make the journey to Mentone, where the climate and surroundings had proved on several occasions to be highly beneficial to his health. Here he spent the last months of 1891, apparently gaining strength, yet very slowly, and hopes were entertained that he would ultimately recover. He became well enough to correct the proofs of his sermons, the publication of which was continued; but his progress towards recovery was so slow as to be scarcely perceptible.

Suddenly in the latter part of January, 1892, news came that he had met with a serious relapse. At once the fears of his multitude of friends and admirers were revived. For several days reports were received which were far from reassuring. The following dispatch relates the story of his death:

> MENTONE, FRANCE, Jan. 31.—The celebrated divine, Charles Haddon Spurgeon, died here fifteen minutes before midnight tonight. Mrs. Spurgeon, his private secretary, and two or three friends were present at the last moment. He was unconscious when the end came and had not spoken for some hours.
>
> Mr. Spurgeon did not recognize his wife throughout the day; he refused all food, and although milk was given him, it was not retained. A large number of telegrams of inquiry and sympathy were received by the pastor's family.

Thus ended the life of the celebrated divine, whose voice had held listening thousands spellbound and whose influence had been felt in all the earth.

Enormous Literary Work

Glancing at Mr. Spurgeon's work, it will be seen that it was enormous. Besides editing and furnishing most of the matter for his monthly magazine, *The Sword and the Trowel*, since January 1, 1865, he wrote *The Saint and His Saviour*, *The Treasury of David*, an Exposition of the Psalms in seven octavo volumes; *The New Park Street Pulpit*, and the

Metropolitan Tabernacle Pulpit, which contains about two thousand of his weekly sermons from 1855 to 1889, making thirty large volumes. Also *Lectures to My Students*, *Commenting and Commentaries*, *John Ploughman*, the *Cheque Book of the Bank of Faith* and various other publications. Many of these have been translated into various tongues.

In October, 1887, Mr. Spurgeon withdrew from the Baptist Union. In announcing his decision to withdraw and replying to his critics, he said:

> To pursue union at the expense of the truth is treason to Jesus. To tamper with His doctrines is to become traitors to Him. We have before us the wretched spectacle of professedly orthodox Christians publicly avowing union with those who deny the faith and deny the personality of the Holy Ghost.

Mr. Spurgeon had long been contemplating the act of secession. He announced his determination of withdrawing if certain other clergymen, who were for some reason distasteful to him, were not excommunicated. This, of course, the Union refused to do.

The resignation which he tendered was accepted, and the great church which he had built up went with him without question.

Mr. Spurgeon's Obsequies

Upon the death of the celebrated divine, the newspapers throughout the world, both secular and religious, contained lengthy obituary notices which were highly eulogistic of the man and his work. He had died at the very height of his power and usefulness, yet his life had been so busy that the labor of half a dozen ordinary men had been condensed into it.

It was difficult for his congregation to believe that they never would again hear the rich, magnetic voice of their beloved pastor. There were demonstrations of sorrow on every hand; the great heart of the public was moved and throbbed with sympathy and grief.

The announcement was made at once that the body would be removed from Mentone to London and that a public funeral would be held. The obsequies were attended by thousands of all religious denominations and all classes of people. Such a demonstration has seldom been witnessed even in the great metropolis. Every evidence of the respect in which Mr. Spurgeon was held was manifested, while all expressed sincere sorrow that his wonderful life's work was finished.

It was gratifying to know that his last days were cheered by the tender ministries of his family and friends, while he expressed his unfaltering faith in the great truths he had taught and his uncomplaining submission to the will of that gracious providence which has a purpose even in the sparrow's fall. He desired further life only that he might carry on the work to which all his powers had been devoted.

As he had spoken by his living voice to myriads, so by his death he gave a more impressive lesson to the world. At the age of fifty-seven he was called up higher. "All the trumpets of Heaven sounded," and his work, which was not to be measured merely by years, was ended.

Now the great champion of the evangelistic Faith, the flaming zealot, the magnetic orator, the prolific author, the one man who more than any other affected the whole religious world, was laid to his final rest.

Peace to his honored ashes! May his rest be as sweet and satisfying as his life was laborious and crowned with suffering.

MRS. SUSIE SPURGEON

MR. C. H. SPURGEON

Tributes to Charles H. Spurgeon

From T. DE WITT TALMAGE

When twenty years ago Rev. Charles H. Spurgeon and I met in London, my salutation was, "I read your sermons"; and his answer was, "Everybody reads yours." From that day to this, at various times and in various ways, we have been in intercommunication.

But the volume of his earthly life is closed, and he has gone up to join the immortals. Among the first whom he picks out in Heaven will be the souls of the Jonathan Edwards and John Calvin stamp—the men who believe, and believe with all their might, souls of a tremendous evangelism. On earth we seek out those with whom we are in affinity, and so it will be in Heaven.

What a long battle with disease the English preacher had—the last seven months in agony! We had hoped he would conquer and again take pulpit and pen. But God knows best.

What a contrast between the honor in which his name is now held throughout Christendom and the caricature and abuse with which he was for many years assailed. He had kept these caricatures in a scrapbook and was in later years accustomed to show them to his friends.

The first picture I ever saw of him represented him as sliding down the railing of his pulpit, in the presence of his audience, to show how easy it was to go to Hell, then as climbing up the opposite rail of the pulpit to show how hard it was for a man to climb to Heaven. The most of the people at that time actually believed that he had taken those two postures, descending one rail and ascending the other.

Within a year I have seen a newspaper article implying that in early life he had assumed those attitudes.

Within a week the old story falsely ascribed to Mr. Beecher was ascribed to Mr. Spurgeon—that expression, on entering the pulpit, about a hot night, with a profane expletive. These old lies are passed on from age to age, now tacked onto one man and now tacked onto another.

Awhile after I had moved to Brooklyn, while walking along Schermerhorn Street with Mr. Beecher, he said, "Mr. Talmage, I am very glad you have come to Brooklyn. The misrepresentations and falsehoods told about me will now be divided up, and you will take half as your share."

But Mr. Spurgeon outlived his critics. In the long run every man comes to be taken for what he is worth. You can't puff him up, and you can't keep him down. As I told Mr. Martin Farquhar Tupper when he was last in this country and disposed to complain of some things said and written in regard to him, "Why, we in America never think much of a man until we have rubbed him down with a crash towel."

From WAYLAND HOYT
Pastor of First Baptist Church, Minneapolis

Mr. Spurgeon's chief characteristic was a firm reliance upon God, a faith that kept its eye steady and saw a bright outcome to the darkest experiences. He lived upon heavenly bounty and was so fully convinced that God would fulfill His promises that he never gave way to despondency.

Once when I asked him how he expected to accomplish a great undertaking he had in hand, he replied, "The Lord has never failed me yet, and why should I not trust Him now?"

This consciousness that God was with him and speaking through him made him the bold reformer, the earnest preacher, the grand organizer and noble man that he was.

From HENRY VAN DYKE

It is not possible to make a true estimate at the present moment of the work of Rev. Charles H. Spurgeon. It is too near to us; we lack perspective. It is too immense; we are so overwhelmed by the quantity of it that we are not in a position to put a right value upon its quality.

One thing we Americans are likely to forget, and that is its distinct character as a work in and for the city of London. It was adapted in every detail to the place in which it was performed. There was a great natural genius shown in this adaptation. It fitted London as a glove fits the hand, and this is one reason why it was so enormously useful.

I remember the late Canon Liddon speaking to me about this some years ago in the course of a long walk through the city. He counted Mr. Spurgeon's Tabernacle among the very greatest religious influences of the metropolis, because it drew together such vast multitudes under the power of common worship. It was an expression of human fellowship in aspiration and praise.

I think the future will increase our sense of the value of his work in this aspect. We shall also come to think more and more highly of the close connection which he made, by his example, between spiritual faith and practical benevolence. The Orphanage is the best of his sermons.

From JOHN KNOX ALLEN

In the death of Mr. Spurgeon there passes away one who was probably the greatest preacher of the century, perhaps of any century. Mr. Beecher is often spoken of in connection with him, but there is a difference. Mr. Beecher was a great orator. He had a vivid and powerful imagination; and as a prose poet, as an intellectual genius in the closer meaning of that term, he probably has had no peer in the pulpit in any age. But as a herald of the simple Gospel, as before all things a preacher, no one can compare with Mr. Spurgeon.

And in this way he equally deserves the name of genius. It is a great word to apply to anyone; but the man who did such great things and did them so easily, who could preach a sermon a day for long periods of time and a sermon too which would be listened to by multitudes; whose lines went out through all the earth and whose words to the end of the world; the man who could set in motion so many agencies for doing good and keep them going, was an elect man—did not merely achieve greatness but was born great.

His death is a loss to the church throughout the world; and were it not that the power which gave him to the world can easily give something more and better, it would be a loss that is irreparable.

From W. C. BITTING

It is too soon to make any final estimate of the man and minister, Charles Haddon Spurgeon. The world cannot pause in its grief to weigh. When the sense of loss has become less keen, then the various standards of judgment may be applied.

For the masses of Christians, his sermons had incomparable interest. They did not appeal so strongly to the cultured. He meant it so, perhaps. He dared to judge and condemn what he thought were doctrinal errors in his brethren; yet his censures were not of persons, but beliefs. He combined a remarkable tenacity of his own opinions with affection for those who differed most widely from him. This was true tolerance.

I will not soon forget the sermon he preached on his fifty-third birthday anniversary, just two days before the Queen's Jubilee—"Let the Children of Zion Rejoice in Their King." The soul of the man shone in it. He poured out himself in the opening services, and the discourse seemed rather like a revelation of his own gladness than an exhortation to 6,000 auditors. The man of faith, prayer, loyalty to Christ, joy, hope, was at his best.

He was like Jacob in prayer, a veritable Israel; like Abraham in faith; like Job in his suffering; now like John the Baptist, and now like John the apostle in his preaching; as steady as Micaiah before Ahab and Zedekiah in rebuking those whom he believed to be false prophets; like David in his superb religious emotions; like Paul in his fidelity to his Master; and like Jesus in humility and consecration. He was yet a man and imperfect, but less so than many of his detractors, who indeed are really few.

It will be long before the world knows another such. It takes centuries to produce one like him. The church universal has had a loss. She mourns. Millions of eyes moistened as they read of his death. To thousands of ears, no voice will ever sound so dear as his. All over the world hands that have grasped his have taken a new might to work for the Christ whom he exalted while humbling himself.

A true cardinal, a prince of the church; a name greater than all titles; a plain man more superb in unadorned manhood than if belettered by the world; a childlike Christian—Heaven's honors rested on him here. They are his everlasting joy now.

From WILLIAM T. SABINE
Pastor of the First Reformed Episcopal Church, New York

You ask a brief estimate of Mr. Spurgeon's life and work. Volumes would not do them justice. The world is his debtor.

Charles Haddon Spurgeon was called a Baptist, but he was one of those men too great to be claimed by any denomination. Millions of believers of every name were edified by his words and quickened by the example of his wonderful life.

Among his many admirable traits and at the root of them lay his clear apprehension of divine truth, his firm grasp of it, inflexible loyalty to it and incessant proclamation of it. He was a man of a whole Bible. From Genesis to Revelation it was to him "the true Word of the true God."

If he was conspicuous for anything, he was conspicuous for his unswerving allegiance to "the Word." His theology was as broad and as narrow as the Bible. With him a "thus saith the Lord" settled everything.

With a warm heart and a very clear head, a very busy hand and a supreme devotion to the Master he served, men may call him narrow if they please. God has set the seal of His divine approval, passing contradiction, on the work of the London Tabernacle pastor and called him to his reward. What a reward!

From JOHN L. SCUDDER
Pastor of the First Congregational Church,
Jersey City, New Jersey

When as a boy I entered Mr. Spurgeon's great Tabernacle and saw that vast concourse of people, I thought the famous preacher the most wonderful man living; and he was at that time. Although in this day he would be regarded as somewhat old-fashioned in his theology and narrow in his views, yet we must acknowledge him to be the most popular English preacher of this century.

His speech was simple, his manner direct, his earnestness unfeigned, his magnetism overwhelming. He was an ideal man for the middle classes, and by them he was universally beloved.

His church was one of the great sights of London and visited by travelers, especially on Sunday, as one of the principal points of interest.

His work can be summed up in the words: He loved Christ with all his heart, and he preached Christ with all his might. He kept the cross clearly in sight, pointed men to it, while he himself took a humble position behind it.

From CHARLES L. THOMPSON

Pastor of the Madison Avenue Presbyterian Church, New York

By general consent, the death of Mr. Spurgeon removes from earth one of the greatest preachers of all the ages. Whether we understand the secret of his power or not, the fact is past all question.

If called upon to group the chief elements of his pulpit greatness, I would say a strong mind, with all its forces at instant command, a marvelous knowledge of human nature, a heart-deep knowledge of the Bible, a spirit absolutely consecrated to Christ and the souls of men, and for the utterance of the Gospel such a voice as God has rarely given to mortal man.

His greatness as a preacher has somewhat obscured another side of his greatness which should not be forgotten. He had a genius for organizing. It is perhaps the rarest of all kinds of talent. By it he gave permanence to his work. The wonderful voice is silent, but much of his work organized in Christian institutions will go on.

On the whole, I believe more elements of religious power were combined in that man than in any other preacher of the sons of men. A vigorous and endlessly fertile brain, a great heart always breaking for the salvation of men, an executive hand to fasten his work, and a character so strong and Christlike it illuminated everything he did. Will we ever see his like again?

> Good-night, sweet prince,
> And flights of angels sing thee to thy rest.

From LYMAN ABBOTT

In "The Christian Union"

As a preacher, Mr. Spurgeon possessed the qualities most essential to success in the pulpit and is well worth the careful study of all preachers. He was not what men call an orator. Whether from deliberate choice, like Paul, or following the instincts of his nature, we know not; but he apparently deliberately laid aside all ambition to be eloquent—an ambition which has often proved destructive to pulpit power. He was one of the earliest to adopt that conversational and colloquial style of address which is more and more supplanting the former rhetorical style. If he sometimes fell below the dignity of public discourse, he never was guilty of rant.

As a student, he lived in the literature of the seventeenth century and derived from his study of it a singularly pure English. This English he used as the vehicle of convictions always sincerely entertained and earnestly presented. So, though he was sometimes conventional, he was never pretentious. He never marred his discourses by that fatal but common fault of religious discourse, cant.

He was a great student of the Bible and from it drew both the substance and the form of his discourses. He did not always understand the Bible as we do, but he always presented what he understood to be Bible teaching.

What is more important, from it he fed a nature which grew in spirituality as he grew in years. Even in so purely ethical a book as *John Ploughman's Talks,* underneath a practical wisdom as sententious as that of Poor Richard himself, gleams and glows a light of spiritual life which Benjamin Franklin wholly lacked, or at least never expressed.

The divisions of his sermons were sometimes ingenious rather than philosophical, sometimes artificial rather than truly artistic. His sometimes archaic method would not fit well in the hands of an imitator. But this ingenuity became a second nature in one who drew his literary as well as his theological inspiration so largely from an artificial age; hence his use of it was not truly artificial.

Moreover, all criticism of the form, whether of thought or of words, was disarmed by the genuineness of the life which filled and overflowed his words. That life was shown as notably in generous deeds and self-sacrificing service as in pulpit utterances; he was a great preacher because he was first of all a true man. His deeds and his words harmonized; he lived as he preached.

THE CHRISTIAN AT WORK

With the death of Charles Haddon Spurgeon a vast spiritual force has gone out not only in England but in the world. As St. Beuve said of Victor Cousin, he was not so much a person as a mighty, ever expanding, pervasive force!

He is not indeed, as some of his fulsome admirers maintain, to be ranked with Martin Luther; for he was very different in character from the unique German Reformer. Moreover, he had a far different sort of a battle to fight. He deserves rather to be compared with George Whitefield and John Wesley. He was more like the latter than the former, since he was a grand organizer as well as preacher.

His voice was wonderful. It swept in distinct, flexible, sweet, strong tones, molded into faultless articulation through the great tabernacle, reaching easily and apparently without the slightest effort six thousand hearers and riveting their entire attention from the first sentence. There was an indefinable quality in his voice, as is the case with all great orators, that made it captivating and thrilling. Perhaps it was his tremendous and irresistible personality that spoke through it. Whatever it was, it would conquer a vast multitude in an instant. This made him a peerless speaker.

To crown all, Mr. Spurgeon was a singularly unselfish and noble man in his personal character. He seemed not to know what worldliness was. His mode of life was frugal and unostentatious. Nor did he ever evince the slightest covetousness. Generous to a fault, he could not be induced to keep the fortunes laid freely at his feet. At his silver wedding his friends gave him $30,000; at his fiftieth year his congregation gave him $25,000; but both of these large sums were soon distributed by him to his various mission works. Such disinterested love illustrates the power of the Gospel. It will be long before this sinful world of ours will see his like again.

THE NEW YORK DAILY TRIBUNE

No preacher of modern times has enjoyed a wider publicity than the late Charles H. Spurgeon. The many volumes of his sermons and writings have gone out into all the world; and could all that has been written about him be collected, it would form a library of no mean size.

Yet there are many incidents untold and traits still undescribed. Every week, one and sometimes three sermons were printed and distributed all over the civilized world by the regular issue from Passmore &

Alabaster's printing office in Paternoster Row, London.

Monday morning was the only time he took for rest. He was speaking on Monday evening. If he went to preach elsewhere, it must be a fresh sermon. All were reported and printed.

On Thursday evening at the Metropolitan Tabernacle it was the same. On Friday afternoon he lectured to the students, and all through the week went on his continual and laborious authorship. Such things could only be possible to a man to whom, as he himself once incidentally and graphically described it, "sermons came floating in the air, so that he caught them on the wing and put them away in various corners of his brain to be used as occasion required."

His mode of preparation, which was scarcely ever begun for Sunday morning until Saturday evening, while the sermon for Sunday night was prepared on Sunday afternoon, was to sit down and think over some of the topics which had "come to him," and then to gather round him all the books which bore upon those topics and see which, to use his own expression, "laid hold of him the most tightly." Here are his own words upon the matter as spoken to the writer:

> I am frequently surrounded by a little host of texts, each clamoring for acceptance and saying, "Me, me, preach from me," so that I am often till ten o'clock before I make my final selection.

A Midnight Sermon

On one memorable occasion, however, all failed me. It was one of the strangest experiences I have known. Ten, eleven, twelve o'clock came, and still I had no topic for the following Sunday morning.

At last my wife came into the room, laid her hand on my shoulder and said, "Had you not better go to bed? Try what a few hours' sleep will do." I took her advice and retired.

About eight o'clock I sprang from the bed under the somewhat unpleasant consciousness of still being without a topic. On leaving the room she asked me where I was going. I replied, of course, into the study.

Noticing an amused smile upon her face, I asked her the cause. "You will find out when you get there," was the reply.

Going up to the table, what was my astonishment to find a text jotted down, a lot of notes scattered about in my own handwriting, of which I had no recollection whatever, and to feel a train of thought come back to me with the notes, which at once supplied me with a sermon.

A glimmering consciousness of the truth dawned upon me, but I hastened to her for an explanation. "About two o'clock this morning," she said, "you got up and went down to your study, and I followed you. You were apparently fast asleep. You seated yourself in your chair, gathered paper and pen, and began to write. I feared to disturb you, so I sat and waited. You thought and wrote for about one hour, then rose deliberately from your chair and went upstairs to bed again, and slept till you rose just now."

I preached that sermon, and it was certainly not inferior to my usual productions.

His Style of Oratory

Spurgeon's style of oratory was simple, forcible and, above everything, natural. In his younger days he was extremely dramatic, so much so as to give rise to many absurd stories, which he has taken the trouble personally to deny and disprove. One was the well-known anecdote about his showing how sinners went to Hell by sliding down the banisters of his pulpit. Without these absurd additions, however, his delivery was sufficiently histrionic and descriptive in action to make this no inconsiderable element in his remarkable success.

Preaching on one occasion from the subject of "Aaron staying the plague in the camp by standing between the living and the dead," he retired to the back of the large platform, almost out of sight of the audience; and then suddenly approaching, swinging an imaginary censer, he depicted the terrible earnestness of the High Priest with face and figure and language so as almost to overwhelm the throng gathered in the vast building.

The Old War-Horse

In these latter days his corpulence necessitated a more formal mode of delivery. But, like an old war-horse, he could not altogether forget the habits of the past. Under the inspiration of the moment he would sometimes start off as in days of yore, only to find that the time for such things had gone by, and rheumatic gout would bring him up "all standing," as a sailor would phrase it.

It is needless to say that such a speaker was not much encumbered with notes in the pulpit. The back of an old envelope, with the ragged edges trimmed off, bearing about six lines of writing, would sometimes remain as a memento of a discourse which had electrified six thousand people and which on the following morning would issue from the press to the four corners of the world, but more frequently he would go and leave "not a trace behind."

A Marvelous Voice

One of the great secrets of Spurgeon's power was his marvelous voice. He has been heard distinctly at the Crystal Palace, Sydenham, by 23,000 people; and in the Metropolitan Tabernacle he could whisper so as to be heard all over the building.

Another factor in his influence was his extreme naturalness. He seemed a man absolutely without disguise of any kind whatever; and the more frequently you came in contact with him, the more was this impression borne in upon you.

Upon the public platform, his eyes would flash at some story of private or public wrongdoing. He would lean forward, oblivious of everybody, with his soul in his face, listening to the story and, on its conclusion, start up and rushing forward would pour forth for some ten minutes or quarter of an hour a stream of indignant denunciation which not infrequently brought many of his audience to their feet, wild with enthusiastic endorsement of his sentiments.

This was not the mere trick of an orator. It was the nature of the man. Over a tale of sorrow he would weep so as to be unable to speak. Over a good joke he would laugh so as to be heard above all who were sitting with him on the platform.

In preaching, he was the same. You could not resist the conviction that, whoever in the audience doubted the truth of what he was saying, he himself believed it, every word. The nearer you got to him, the more you felt this.

A Hater of Shams

He had a hatred of shams of all kinds. He frequently said that nothing pleased him more than to put his foot through a false or needless code of etiquette.

For one of the students in his college to be in any way marked with the characteristics of the "clerical masher" was almost immediately fatal to the delinquent. A hard hand and a threadbare coat, accompanied by honesty and hard work on the part of the owner, were unfailing passports to his regard and esteem, and always to his help, if help were needed. But "needless spectacles," stiff, white cravat, black walking cane, formal broadcloth, clerical assumption and above all a frequent Sunday school miss seen on the man's left arm, first drew forth the most unsparing sarcasm and, if this failed, dismissal.

It was this characteristic of downright sincerity and thoroughness which made Spurgeon so universally loved and esteemed. Throughout the six millions of London his name is honored by all sorts and conditions of men, from cabmen to Cabinet Ministers.

Royal Hearers

Royalty visited the Tabernacle. Mr. Gladstone dined with him. A cabby, if he recognized him, would frequently refuse his fare, considering it an honor to have had him in his cab.

No death, since the death of Charles Dickens, will be more widely and truly mourned in England. Persons opposed to him in politics claimed his friendship; those differing from him in doctrine sent most generous contributions to his work; and he has letters from many of the crowned heads of Europe expressing thanks for the benefit derived from his sermons.

On one occasion he gave the substance of a letter he had just received from a royal personage on the Continent, attributing conversion to Christianity through reading his printed works and sermons and only asking that in the announcement the name might be suppressed for political reasons.

Not a Handsome Man

In height Spurgeon was about five feet six inches, and although never a handsome man in the conventional use of the term, he was in his youth possessed of that broad, powerful frame which is always attractive in a man from its indication of superior physical strength. The face, like the figure, was remarkable for strength rather than beauty of outline; but when lit up by the mind, was truly magnificent in its intensely spiritual expression.

In make and mental characteristics he bore no slight resemblance to the first Napoleon. There was the same pale, powerful face, the same physical conformation, the same inflexible determination of purpose, the same magnetic power over the hearts and minds of others. It may be added that there was in later years the same increasing corpulency also.

Once let Spurgeon's mind be made up that a certain thing was right, then the more opposition he encountered, the more determined he became to do just that thing. And he never once failed in anything he undertook. The first Napoleon was styled "The Little Corporal." Spurgeon by his students and deacons was called "The Governor." The statement, "The Governor is coming," made all stand at "attention."

His appearance toward the close of his life, even within ten or fifteen years of that period, was certainly anything but graceful. Each year he grew fatter. Incessant work and constant suffering distorted his features almost out of all semblance to their early comeliness.

Nothing but utter helplessness could keep him away from the fulfillment of an engagement. He would frequently struggle out of bed and come to a large meeting of his students, leaning upon his stick, one eye closed entirely, face and limbs swollen so as to make him almost unrecognizable, deliver a sermon or a lecture of an hour's duration with all his accustomed fire and force, then go home to lie utterly prostrated and almost at the point of death for two or three days, until the doctors brought him around again.

One of His Stories

A visitor to the Pastors' College, who dropped in casually to look around, might have come across a stout, burly individual in a long frock overcoat, a felt hat of the familiar American pattern punched in at the crown, with a stout stick over his shoulder or, if occasion required, used to limp with, and would probably take him for some English 'squire who had forgotten his top boots or for a well-to-do farmer come up like himself to look around the place.

That was Spurgeon. He never wore a clerical coat or hat in the pulpit or out of it, abhorred the title of "Reverend," and in all things aimed to be simply a man among men.

A brother stick to the one he usually carried was laughingly cherished by him at home, about which he delighted to tell the following story:

It is sometimes rather difficult to get along with deacons. Resist the Devil and he will flee from you; resist a deacon and he will fly at you.

When I first began to preach at New Park Street, the immense crowds made the heat so oppressive that I could scarcely preach. Many women were carried out fainting.

I asked that the windows be opened. The deacons, in the exercise of their high authority, objected. Next Sunday evening I ordered a man to open them before the commencement of service. They were ordered to be closed again. The following Sunday morning many of those windows were found mysteriously broken with wondrous regularity all around the building.

Great was the indignation and searching the investigation into this act of vandalism. It was never found out, though possibly suspected, as I made no great secret of my visit to the building, but this old stick was responsible for it. Possibly thinking that the same thing might occur again, the windows were left in future under my control.

Laughed at When on Horseback

It was while he lived at Clapham, before his removal to his last residence at Beulah Hill, Norwich, that Mr. Spurgeon was recommended to try horseback riding as a remedy for his excessive corpulency.

Fancy a man five feet six inches tall and fifty-two inches round on horseback for the first time. It was calculated to attract attention. And it did.

His approach to the gates was eagerly looked for by a large crowd of small boys, whose remarks were humorous, but not particularly flattering to his horsemanship. One well-wisher suggested that he should "get inside." The chorus of "Here he comes," "Here he comes" increased morning by morning until the procession became too triumphant even for Spurgeon's philosophy, and he relinquished equestrianism for his accustomed mode of progression.

His readiness and tact under the most trying circumstances never failed him. At the commencement of his career, when the opposition to his ministry was at its highest, all kinds of annoyances were poured upon him, which he always contrived to seize instantly and turn to good account. Sparrows were taken to the building at night and let loose, so as to fly at the gas and create a panic. He would always quote some passage of Scripture in his half-humorous fashion and say a few words about it which not only at once stopped all tumult but delighted and interested his hearers.

His Ready Wit and Resources

On one occasion he had been preaching about five minutes, when suddenly the gas went out and ten thousand people were plunged into total darkness. Some miscreant had got to the meter. The result might have been then what soon afterward really happened—a panic with great loss of life and limb. A few calm, reassuring words issued from his lips; then, without a moment's hesitation, he announced a fresh text—"I am the light of the world; he that believeth in me shall not walk in darkness, but shall have the light of life."

He spoke from the words, with a continual application of the surrounding circumstances to them. When the gas was at length lighted, no preacher could have desired a more attentive, absorbed audience. Then, casting aside his original text altogether, he spoke from the words, "Light is good," and so continued to the end of the service.

The anecdotes he could tell of the many circumstances in which this readiness had been absolutely necessary to him would fill a large volume. He was constantly coming in contact with religious cranks. So frequently was this the case that at the Tabernacle he was never alone. Every visitor passed under the searching gaze of deacons and personal friends before being admitted to his presence.

Yet on one occasion it was only his great tact which saved his life. When a man applied for conversation with him in the customary religious terms, he was permitted to enter the room.

In his usual affectionate manner Spurgeon placed a chair for him right opposite himself and began a conversation. And then, literally as well as figuratively, the "murder was out." The man had been commissioned by God to come and tell him that his work was now done and that he was the appointed minister who was to have the honor of sending him to his reward. Only by the exercise of care and tact did the great preacher escape the danger and get the man secured.

Far more sensational and startling incidents than this could be related, for nothing produces more fanatics, enthusiasts and madmen than religious mania; and at the time London was shaken to its center by the "Hell-fire preacher," all the religious cranks in England literally besieged him.

From J. M. BUCKLEY
In "The Christian Advocate"

The closing words of his last sermon were: "My time is ended, although I had much more to say. I can only pray the Lord to give you to believe in Him. If I should never again have the pleasure of speaking for my Lord upon the face of this earth, I should like to deliver, as my last confession of faith, this testimony: Nothing but faith can save this nineteenth century; nothing but faith can save England; nothing but faith can save the present unbelieving church; nothing but firm faith in the grand old doctrines of grace and in the ever-living and unchanging God can bring back to the church again a full tide of prosperity and make her to be the deliverer of the nations for Christ; nothing but faith in the Lord Jesus can save you or me. The Lord give you, my brothers, to believe to the utmost degree for His name's sake! Amen."

The words seem to have been prophetic.

An Unrivaled Voice

The elements of Mr. Spurgeon's character as a preacher were in most respects those common to good speakers but were possessed by him in an extraordinary degree. His voice had no equal for purposes of preaching to an immense congregation.

Early in his London career, when he first preached on a special occasion in the Crystal Palace to an audience of more than twenty thousand persons, Mrs. Spurgeon, who was present, became almost hysterical with fear lest he should not succeed in controlling them. He perceived her anxiety and tears and sent a messenger to ask her to please sit where he could not see her, being afraid that she would sympathetically affect him.

When he arose and began to speak, his voice reached the most distant hearer. The great multitude were quiet and absorbed until he finished. No other man known to the present generation could have done this; only the traditions of Whitefield's wonderful voice can be compared to Spurgeon's.

His personal appearance was unprepossessing, unless the expression of the eyes was caught or the face was lighted by a smile. A more homely man, in the ordinary meaning of the term, is seldom seen; irregular and coarse features, small, rather sunken eyes, protruding chin, bushy hair.

In his early days he was opposed and caricatured; but this did not embitter his spirit, nor did the almost idolatry of the worshipers at the

Tabernacle make him unduly vain; for he always gave to God the glory for all his work.

No one could hear him pray of late years without feeling that he relied humbly upon God.

Last Services Over His Remains

Mr. Spurgeon's death, as before stated, occurred at Mentone, France. The remains were immediately removed to London and on Monday, February 8, 1892, were deposited in the Metropolitan Tabernacle.

Early in the morning immense crowds were waiting for the doors to be opened, in order to obtain a last look on the illustrious dead. It became impossible to number the vast throng which passed by the casket, but it was estimated that in the first three hours more than thirteen thousand looked for the last time upon the face of the dead minister.

The last memorial service over the remains was held on Wednesday evening, February 10. The Metropolitan Tabernacle was crowded; and the services, which were not concluded until after midnight, were very solemn and impressive.

The next morning a majority of the shops in the vicinity of the Tabernacle were closed as a mark of respect to the dead minister, and the buildings very generally bore mourning emblems.

The funeral services opened at 11 o'clock. The members of Mr. Spurgeon's family, the Mayor of Croydon, several members of the House of Commons, Lady Burdett-Coutts and deputations from sixty religious bodies, were among those present.

After the singing of the last hymn that Mr. Spurgeon had announced before he was taken sick, "The sands of time are sinking," Dr. Pierson, the American minister who filled Mr. Spurgeon's pulpit during the latter's illness, made a most eloquent address. He dwelt at length upon Mr. Spurgeon's powerful influence. A cedar of Lebanon had fallen, he said, and the crash of its downfall had shocked the whole land. No such vast vacancy had been felt in the church for a century.

Dr. Pierson concluded his remarks by drawing parallels between the work done by Mr. Spurgeon and that performed by John Wesley. After the offering of prayers and the singing of hymns, Dr. Pierson pronounced the benediction.

The olive-wood coffin containing the remains was then taken from the catafalque, upon which it had rested since Monday night, and conveyed to the hearse in waiting at the main entrance of the tabernacle. As it was borne down the aisle, the entire congregation arose and joined in singing the hymn, "There is no night in Homeland."

After the mourners had entered carriages, the funeral procession started for Norwood Cemetery, where the remains are interred. There was an enormous number of coaches in the procession, and the entire route from the tabernacle to the cemetery was lined by an immense concourse of people.

Three mounted policemen preceded the hearse. On the coffin lay an open Bible. The sides of the hearse bore the text: "I have fought a good fight, I have finished my course, I have kept the faith." As the cortege moved slowly along, the spectators removed their hats and bowed their heads. The bells of St. Mary's and St. Mark's churches tolled solemnly as the funeral procession passed. The flags displayed along the route followed by the procession were all at half-mast.

Places of business between Kensington and Clapham were closed, and many of the houses had their blinds drawn. The children from the Stockwell Orphanage occupied a raised platform erected for their use at a point where a good view of the procession could be had. This platform was draped with black crape and other mourning emblems.

A large number of people took advantage of the deep feeling created by the noted divine's death, and they did a brisk trade in selling Mr. Spurgeon's portraits, biographies and mourning rosettes.

There was an immense crowd in Norwood Cemetery awaiting the arrival of the funeral procession. When the hearse entered the cemetery, all bared their heads. The coffin was taken from the hearse and borne reverently to the vault, in which it was deposited. This vault will be surmounted by a bronze statue of Mr. Spurgeon, and upon it will be placed bas-reliefs symbolic of the dead minister's benevolent works.

The only persons who were allowed in the cemetery were those who were furnished with tickets. The crowd began to assemble early in the morning; and long before the time set for the cortege to arrive, an enormous throng was stationed about the vault and in its vicinity.

The Rev. Archibald G. Brown, pastor of the East London Tabernacle, delivered the funeral oration at the cemetery. Dr. Pierson then offered a prayer, the language of which was touchingly eloquent.

The Rt. Rev. Randall Thomas Davidson, Bishop of Rochester, then pronounced the benediction. The services were very impressive, and many of the people who listened to them were moved to tears.

After the religious ceremonies had been concluded, the people present formed in line and slowly filed before the open vault and took their last look upon the coffin of the man whose loss is mourned by thousands in all parts of the world.

BOOK II

Sermons and Lectures
by C. H. Spurgeon

CHAPTER I

Hands Full of Honey

"And he [Samson] turned aside to see the carcase of the lion: and, behold, there was a swarm of bees and honey in the carcase of the lion. And he took thereof in his hands, and went on eating, and came to his father and mother, and he gave them, and they did eat: but he told not them that he had taken the honey out of the carcase of the lion."—Judg. 14:8, 9.

It was a singular circumstance that a man unarmed should have slain a lion in the prime of its vigor, yet more strange that a swarm of bees should have taken possession of the dried carcase and have filled it with their honey.

In that country, what with beasts, birds and insects and the dry heat, a dead body is soon cleansed from all corruption, and the bones are clean and white. Still the killing of the lion and the finding of the honey make up a remarkable story.

These singular circumstances became afterwards the subject of a riddle, but with that riddle we have no concern at this time. Samson himself is a riddle. He was not only a riddle-maker; he was himself an enigma very difficult to explain. With his personal character I have at this time little or nothing to do. We are not today resting at the house of "Gaius, mine host," where the pilgrims amused themselves with a dish of nuts after dinner; but we are on the march and must attend to the more important matter of refreshing and inspiriting those who are in our company.

Neither are we going to discuss difficulties. But as Samson took the honey without being stung, so would we gain instruction without debate.

We have in these days so much to do that we must make practical use of every incident that comes before us in the Word of God. My one design is to cheer the desponding and stir up all God's people to greater diligence in His service. I conceive that the text may legitimately be employed for this purpose. By the help of the divine Spirit, even after this lapse of time, we may find honey in the lion.

The particular part of the incident which is recorded in these two verses appears to have been passed over by those who have written upon Samson's life. I suppose it appeared to be too inconsiderable. They are taken up with his festive riddle, but they omit the far more natural and commendable fact of his bringing forth the honey in his hands and presenting it to his father and mother. This is the little scene to which I direct your glances.

It seems to me that the Israelitish hero, with a slain lion in the background, standing out in the open road with his hands laden with masses of honeycomb and dripping with honey, which he holds out to his parents, makes a fine picture worthy of the greatest artist.

And what a type we have here of our divine Lord and Master, Jesus, the Conqueror of Death and Hell. He has destroyed the lion that roared upon us and upon Him. He has shouted "victory" over all our foes. "It is finished" was His note of triumph; now He stands in the midst of His church with His hands full of sweetness and consolation, presenting them to those of whom He says, "These are my brother, and sister, and mother."

To each one of us who believe in Him, He gives the luscious food which He has prepared for us by the overthrow of our foes; He bids us come and eat that we may have our lives sweetened and our hearts filled with joy.

To me the comparison seems wonderfully apt and suggestive. I see our triumphant Lord laden with sweetness, holding it forth to all His brethren and inviting them to share in His joy.

But, beloved, it is written, "As he is, so are we in this world." All that are true Christians are, in a measure, like the Christ whose name they bear; and it is to His image that we are finally to be conformed. When He shall appear, we shall be like Him, for we shall see Him as He is; and meanwhile, in proportion as we see Him now, "we are changed into the same image, from glory to glory, even as by the Spirit of the Lord."

The Samson type may well serve as the symbol of every Christian in the world. The believer has been helped by divine grace in his spiritual conflicts, and he has known "the victory which overcometh the world, even our faith." He has thus been made more than a conqueror through Him that loved us, and now he stands in the midst of his fellowmen inviting them to Jesus. With the honey in his hands, which he continues still to feast upon, he displays the heavenly sweetness to all that are round about him, saying, "O taste and see that the Lord is good: blessed is the man that trusteth in him."

I have before now met with that popular artist Gustave Doré and suggested subjects to him. Had he survived among us and had another opportunity occurred, I would have pressed him to execute a statue of Samson handing out the honey—strength distributing sweetness— and it might have served as a perpetual reminder of what a Christian should be—a conqueror and a comforter, slaying lions and distributing honey.

The faithful servant of God wrestles with the powers of evil; but with far greater delight he speaks to his friends and companions, saying, 'Eat ye that which is good, and let your souls delight themselves in sweetness.' Set the statue before your mind's eye, and now let me speak about it.

Three touches may suffice. First, *the believer's life has its conflicts*; second, *the believer's life has its sweets*; third, *the believer's life leads him to communicate of those sweets to others*. Here is room for profitable meditation.

I. THE BELIEVER'S LIFE HAS ITS CONFLICTS

To become a Christian is to enlist for a soldier. To become a believer is to enter upon a pilgrimage. The road is often rough, the hills are steep, the valleys are dark. Giants block the way, and robbers lurk in corners.

The man who reckons that he can glide into Heaven without a struggle has made a great mistake. No cross, no crown; no sweat, no sweet; no conflict, no conquest.

These conflicts, if we take the case of Samson as our symbol, *begin early* in the life of the believer. While Samson was yet a child, the Spirit of the Lord moved him in the camps of Dan (see the last verse of chapter 13). As soon as he was on the verge of manhood, he must match himself with a lion.

God, who intended that His servant should smite the Philistines and check their proud oppression of His people, Israel, began early to train the hero for his life's conflict.

So, when Samson was going to seek a wife, he turned aside into the vineyards of Timnath, and a lion roared upon him. Yes, and the young believer, who as yet has not wrestled with the powers of darkness, will not be long before he hears the roar of the lion and finds himself in the presence of the great adversary.

Very soon we learn the value of the prayer, "Deliver us from the evil one!" Most of the Lord's servants have been men of war from their youth up. Without are fightings even when within there are no fears.

This early combat with the savage beast was intended by God to let him know his strength when under the influence of the Spirit and to train him for his future combats with Israel's enemies. He that is to smite the Philistines hip and thigh with a great slaughter until he has laid them heaps on heaps by his single prowess, must begin by rending a lion with his naked hands. He was to learn war in the same school as another and a greater hero, who afterwards said, "Thy servant slew both the lion and the bear: and this uncircumcised Philistine shall be as one of them."

Soldiers are made by war. You cannot train veterans or create victors except by battles. As in the wars of armies, so is it in spiritual contests: men must be trained for victory over evil by combat with it. Hence "it is good for a man that he bear the yoke in his youth"; for it will not gall his shoulders in after years.

It is assuredly a dangerous thing to be altogether free from trouble. In silken ease the soldier loses his prowess.

Look at Solomon, one of the greatest and wisest, yet, I might say, one of the least and most foolish of men. It was his fatal privilege to sit upon a throne of gold and sun himself in the brilliance of unclouded prosperity. Hence his heart soon went astray, and he fell from his high places.

Solomon in his early days had no trouble; for no war was then raging, and no enemy worth notice was then living. His life ran smoothly on, and he was lulled into a dreamy sleep, the sleep of the voluptuous. He had been happier far had he been, like his father, called from his earliest days to trial and conflict; for this might have taught him to stand fast upon the pinnacle of glory whereon the providence of God had placed him.

Learn, then, O young brother, that if, like Samson, you are to be a hero for Israel, you must early be inured to suffering and daring in some form or other. When you step aside and seek for meditation in the quiet of the vineyard, a young lion may roar upon you, even as in the earliest days of your Lord and Master's public service He was led into the wilderness to be tempted of the Devil.

These conflicts, dear friends, may often be *very terrible*. By a young lion is not meant a whelp, but a lion in the fulness of its early strength, not yet slackened in its pace or curbed in its fury by growing years. Fresh and furious, a young lion is the worst kind of beast that a man can meet with.

Let us expect as followers of Christ to meet with strong temptations, fierce persecutions and severe trials, which will lead to stern conflicts. Do not reckon, thou that art yet putting on thy harness, that thou shalt soon put it off or that, when thou puttest it off, it will be quite as bright as it is today. It will be dimmed with blood and dust and battered by many a blow. Perhaps thy foe may find a way to pierce it or at least to wound thee between its joints.

I would have every man begin to be a soldier of the cross, but I would at the same time have him count the cost, for it is no child's play. If he thinks it will be such, he will be grievously disappointed.

A young believer will, on a sudden, have a doubt suggested to him of which he never heard before; and it will roar upon him like a young lion; neither will he see all at once how to dispose of it. Or he may be placed in singular circumstances where his duty seems to run counter to the tenderest instincts of his nature; here, too, the young lion will roar upon him. Or one for whom he has an intense respect may treat him ill because he is a follower of Christ, and the affection and respect which he feels for this person may make his opposition the more grievous: in this also it is with him as when a lion roareth. Or he may suffer a painful bereavement or sustain a severe loss; or he may have a disease upon him with consequent pains and depressions, and these may cast the shadow of death upon his spirits; so that again a young lion roars upon him.

Brother, sister, let us reckon upon this and not be dismayed by it since in all this is the life of our spirit. By such lessons as these we are taught to do service for God, to sympathize with our fellow Christians and to value the help of our gracious Saviour. By all these we are weaned from earth and made to hunger for that eternal glory which is yet to be revealed, of which we may truly say, "No lion shall be there, nor any ravenous beast shall go up thereon."

These present evils are for our future good: their terror is for our teaching. Trials are sent us for much the same reason that the Canaanites were permitted to live in the Holy Land—that Israel might learn war and be equipped for battle against foreign foes.

These conflicts come early, and they are very terrible. Moreover, they happen to us *when we are least prepared for them.* Samson was not hunting for wild beasts; he was engaged on a much more tender business. He was walking in the vineyards of Timnath, thinking of anything but lions. And "behold," says the Scripture, "a young lion roared against him."

It was a remarkable and startling occurrence. He had left his father and mother and was quite alone; no one was within call to aid him in meeting his furious assailant.

Human sympathy is exceedingly precious, but there are points in our spiritual conflict in which we cannot expect to receive it. To each man there are passages in life too narrow for walking two abreast. Upon certain crags we must stand alone. As our constitutions differ, so our trials, which are suited to our constitutions, must differ also.

Each individual has a secret with which no friend can intermeddle; for every life has its mystery and its hid treasure. Do not be ashamed, young Christian, if you meet with temptations which appear to you to be quite singular: we have each one thought the same of his trials.

You imagine that no one suffers as you do, whereas no temptation hath happened unto you but such as is common to man, and God will with the temptation make a way of escape that you may be able to bear it. Yet for the time being you may have to enter into fellowship with your Lord when He trod the winepress alone, and of the people, there was none with Him.

Is not this for your good? Is not this the way to strength? What kind of piety is that which is dependent upon the friendship of man? What sort of religion is that which cannot stand alone? Beloved, you will have to die alone, and you need therefore grace to cheer you in solitude. The dear wife can attend you weeping to the river's brink, but into the chill stream she cannot go with you. And if you have not a religion which will sustain you in the solitudes of life, of what avail will it be to you in the grim lonesomeness of death?

Thus I reckon it to be a happy circumstance that you are called to solitary conflict that you may test your faith and see of what stuff your hope is made.

The contest was all the worse for Samson, that in addition to being quite alone, "there was nothing in his hand." This is the most remarkable point in the narrative. He had no sword or hunter's spear with which to wound the lordly savage. He had not even a stout staff with which to ward off his attack. Samson stood an unarmed, unarmored man in the presence of a raging beast.

So in our early temptations we are apt to think that we have no weapon for the war, and we do not know what to do. We are made to cry out, "I am unprepared! How can I meet this trial? I cannot grasp the enemy to wrestle with him. What am I to do?"

Herein will the splendor of faith and glory of God be made manifest, when you shall slay the lion; and yet it shall be said of you "that he had nothing in his hand"—nothing but that which the world sees not and values not.

Now, go one step further, for time forbids our lingering here. I invite you to remember that *it was by the Spirit of God that the victory was won.* We read, "And the Spirit of the Lord came mightily upon him, and he rent him as he would have rent a kid."

Let the Holy Spirit help us in our trouble, and we need neither company nor weapon; but without Him, what can we do?

Good Bishop Hall says:

> If that roaring lion, that goes about continually seeking whom he may devour, find us alone among the vineyards of the Philistines, where is our hope? Not in our heels; he is swifter than we: not in our weapons; we are naturally unarmed: not in our hands, which are weak and languishing: but in the Spirit of God, by whom we can do all things. If God fight in us, who can resist us? There is a stronger lion in us than that against us.

Our one necessity is to be endowed with power from on High: the power of the Holy Ghost. Helped by the Spirit of God, the believer's victory will be complete. The lion shall not be driven away but rent in pieces. Girt with the Spirit's power, our victory shall be as easy as it will be perfect. Samson rent the lion as though it were a little lamb or a kid of the goats.

Well said Paul, "I can do all things through Christ which strengtheneth me." Sin is soon overcome, temptations are readily refused, affliction is joyfully borne, persecution is gladly endured, when the Spirit of glory and of peace resteth upon us.

"With God all things are possible"; and as the believer is with God, it cometh to pass that all things are possible to him that believeth.

If we were surrounded by all the devils in Hell, we need not fear them for an instant if the Lord be on our side. We are mightier than all Hell's legions when the Spirit is mightily upon us. If we were to be beaten down by Satan until he had set his foot upon our breast, to press the very life out of us, yet if the Spirit of God helped us, we would reach out our hand and grasp the sword of the Spirit, which is the Word of God, and we would repeat the feat of Christian with Apollyon, when he gave the fiend such grievous wounds that he spread his dragon wings and flew away.

Wherefore fear not, ye tried ones, but trust in the Spirit of God; and your conflict shall speedily end in victory.

Sometimes our conflict is with past sin. We doubtfully inquire, "How can it be forgiven?" The temptation vanishes before a sight of the dying Redeemer.

Then inbred lust roars against us, and we overcome it through the blood of the Lamb, for "the blood of Jesus Christ his Son cleanseth us from all sin."

Sometimes a raging corruption or a strong habit wars upon us; then we conquer by the might of the sanctifying Spirit of God, who is with us and shall be in us evermore.

Or else it is the world which tempts, and our feet have almost gone; but we overcome the world through the victory of faith. And if all at once Satan raises against us the lust of the flesh, the lust of the eyes and the pride of life, we are still delivered; for the Lord is a wall of fire round about us.

The inward life bravely resists all sin; and God's help is given to believers to preserve them from all evil in the moment of urgent need, even as He helped His martyrs and confessors to speak the right word when called unprepared to confront their adversaries.

Care not, therefore, O thou truster in the Lord Jesus, how fierce thine enemy may be this day! As young David slew the lion and the bear and smote the Philistine too, even so shalt thou go from victory to victory. "Many are the afflictions of the righteous, but the Lord delivereth him out of them all." Wherefore, with a lionlike spirit, meet lions which seek to devour you.

II. THE BELIEVER'S LIFE HAS ITS SWEETS

We are not always killing lions; sometimes we are eating honey. Certain of us do both at a time; we kill lions, yet cease not to eat honey. Truly it has become so sweet a thing to enter into conflict for Christ's sake that it is a joy to contend earnestly for the Faith once delivered to the saints. The same Lord who hath bidden us, "Quit yourselves like men; be strong," has also said, "Rejoice in the Lord alway; and again I say, rejoice."

The believer's life has its sweets, and these are of the choicest: for what is sweeter than honey?

What is more joyful than the joy of a saint? What is more happy than the happiness of a believer? I will not condescend to make a comparison between our joy and the mirth of fools; I will go no further than a contrast.

Their mirth is as the crackling of thorns under a pot, which spit fire and make a noise and a flash, but there is no heat; and they are soon gone out. Nothing comes of it. The pot is long in boiling. But the Christian's delight is like a steady coal fire.

You have seen the grate full of coals all burning red, and the whole mass of coal has seemed to be one great glowing ruby. Everybody who has come into the room out of the cold has delighted to warm his hands, for it gives out a steady heat and warms the body even to its marrow.

Such are our joys. I would sooner possess the joy of Christ five minutes than I would revel in the mirth of fools for half a century. There is more bliss in the tear of repentance than in the laughter of gaiety. Our holy sorrows are sweeter than the worldling's joys. But, oh, when our joys grow full, divinely full, then are they unspeakably like those above, and Heaven begins below.

Did you never cry for joy? You say, perhaps, "Not since I was a child."

Nor have I; but I have always remained a child as far as divine joy is concerned. I could often cry for joy when I know whom I have believed and am persuaded that He is able to keep that which I have committed to Him.

Ours is a joy which will bear thinking over. You can dare to pry into the bottom of it and test its foundation. It is a joy which does not grow stale; you may keep it in your mouth by the year together, yet it never cloys; you may return to it again and again and again and find it still as fresh as ever. And the best of it is, there is no repentance after it. You are never sorry that you were so glad.

The world's gay folk are soon sick of their drink; but we are only sorry that we were not gladder still, for our gladness sanctifies. We are not denied any degree of joy to which we can possibly attain, for ours is a healthy, health-giving delight. Christ is the fulness of joy to His people, and we are bidden to enjoy Him to the full. Christians have their sweets, and those are as honey and the honeycomb, the best of the best.

Of these joys *there is plenty*. Samson found, as it were, a living spring of honey, since he discovered a swarm of bees. So abundant was the honey that he could take huge masses of the comb and carry it in his hands, and go away with it, bearing it to others.

In the love of Christ, in pardoned sin, in acceptance in the Beloved, in resting in God, in perfectly acquiescing in His will, in the hope of Heaven, there is such joy that none can measure it. We have such a living swarm of bees to make honey for us in the precious promises of God that there is more delight in store than any of us can possibly realize. There is infinitely more of Christ beyond our comprehension than we have as yet been able to comprehend.

How blessed to receive of His fullness, to be sweetened with His sweetness, yet to know that infinite goodness still remains!

Perhaps some of you have enjoyed so much of Christ that you could hardly bear any more; but your largest enjoyments are only as tiny shells filled by a single wave of the sea, while all the boundless ocean rolls far beyond your ken. We have exceeding great joy, yea, joy to spare.

Our Master's wedding feast is not so scantily furnished that we have to bring in another seat for an extra guest, or murmur to ourselves that we had better not invite at random lest we should be incommoded by too great a crowd. Nay, rather, the pillared halls of mercy in which the King doth make His feast are so vast that it will be our lifelong business to furnish them with guests, compelling more and more to come in, that His house may be filled and that His royal festival may make glad ten thousand times ten thousand hearts.

Dear friends, if you want to know what the elements of our joy are, I have already hinted at them, but I will for a moment enlarge thereon. *Our joys are often found in the former places of our conflicts.* We gather our honey out of the lions which have been slain for us or by us.

There is, first, our SIN. A horrible lion that! But it is a dead lion, for grace has much more abounded over abounding sin. O brothers, I have never heard of any dainty in all the catalog of human joys that could match a sense of pardoned sin. Full forgiveness! Free forgiveness! Eternal forgiveness! See, it sparkles like dew of Heaven. To know that God has blotted out my sin is knowledge rich with unutterable bliss. My soul has begun to hear the songs of seraphim when it has heard that note, "I have blotted out thy sins like a cloud, and as a thick cloud thine iniquities." Here is choice honey for you!

The next dead lion is conquered DESIRE. When a wish has arisen in the heart contrary to the mind of God and you have said, "Down with you! I will pray you down. You used to master me; I fell into a habit, and I was soon overcome by you; but I will not again yield to you. By God's grace I will conquer you"—I say, when at last you have obtained the victory, such a sweet contentment perfumes your heart that you are filled with joy unspeakable; you are devoutly grateful to have been helped of the Spirit of God to master your own spirit. Thus you have again eaten spiritual honey.

When you are able to feel in your own soul that you have overcome a strong temptation, the fiercer it was and the more terrible it was, the louder has been your song and the more joyful your thanksgiving. To go back to Mr. Bunyan again: when Christian had passed through the Valley of the Shadow of Death during the night and when he had come entirely out of it and the sun rose, you remember he looked back (pause). He was long in taking that look, I warrant you.

What thoughts he had while looking back! He could just discern that narrow track with the quagmire on one side and the deep ditch on the other. He could see the shades out of which the hobgoblins hooted and the fiery eyes glanced forth. He looked back by sunlight and thought within himself, "Ah me! What goodness has been with me! I have gone through all that, and yet I am unharmed!" What a happy survey it was to him!

Ah, the joy of having passed through temptation without having defiled one's garments! How must Shadrach, Meshach and Abednego have felt when they stepped out of the fiery furnace and were not even singed, neither had the smell of fire passed upon them. Happy men were they who had lived in the center of the seven-times-heated furnace where everything else was consumed. Here again is "a piece of an honeycomb."

We find honey again from another slain lion—namely, OUR TROUBLES after we have been enabled to endure them. This is the metal of which our joybells are cast. Out of the brass of our trials we make the trumpets of our triumph. He is not the happy man who has seen no trouble; but "blessed is he that endureth temptation, for when he is tried, he shall receive a crown of life that fadeth not away."

DEATH, too. Oh, the honey that is found in dead Death. Death is indeed dead. We triumph over him and are no more afraid of him than little children are of a dead lion. We pluck him by the beard and say to him, "O death, where is thy sting? O grave, where is thy victory?" We even look forward to the time of our departure with delight, when we shall leave this heavy clay and on spirit wings ascend unto our Father and our God.

You see, there is a rich store of honey for God's people, and we do not hesitate to eat it. Let others say as they will, we are a happy people— happy in Christ, happy in the Holy Spirit, happy in God our Father. So then, believers have their sweets.

III. THE BELIEVER'S LIFE LEADS HIM TO COMMUNICATE OF THESE SWEETS

As soon as we have tasted the honey of forgiven sin and perceived the bliss that God has laid up for His people in Christ Jesus, we feel it to be both our duty and privilege to communicate the good news to others. Here let my ideal statue stand in our midst: the strong man, conqueror of the lion, holding forth his hands full of honey to his parents. We are to be modeled according to this fashion.

And, first, we do this *immediately.* The moment a man is converted, if he would let himself alone, his instincts would lead him to tell his fellows. I know that the moment I came out of that little chapel where I found the Saviour, I wanted to pour out my tale of joy. I could have cried with Cennick—

> *Now will I tell to sinners round,*
> *What a dear Saviour I have found;*
> *I'll point to Thy redeeming blood,*
> *And say, "Behold the way to God!"*

I longed to tell how happy my soul was and what a deliverance I had obtained from the crushing burden of sin. I longed to see all others come and trust my Lord and live! I did not preach a sermon, but I think I could have told out all the Gospel at that first hour.

Did not you, my friend, feel much the same? Did not your tongue long to be telling of what the Lord had done for you? Perhaps you are one of those proper and retiring people who are greatly gifted at holding their tongues; therefore, you left the feet of Jesus in silence—silence which angels wondered at. Is that why you have held your tongue ever since? Perhaps if you had begun to speak, then you would have continued your testimony to this day.

I repeat my assertion that it is the instinct of every newborn soul to communicate the glad tidings which grace has proclaimed in his heart. Just as Samson had no sooner tasted of the honey than he carried a portion of it to his father and mother, so do we hasten to invite our neighbors to Christ.

My dear young friend, as soon as ever you know the joy of the Lord, open your mouth in a quiet, humble way and never allow yourself to be numbered with the deaf and dumb. Let no one stop you from unburdening your heart. Do not follow the bad example of those who have become dumb dogs because of their cowardice at the beginning.

The believer will do this *first to those who are nearest to him*. Samson took the honey to his father and mother who were not far away. With each of us the most natural action would be to tell a brother or a sister or a fellow workman or a bosom friend. It will be a great joy to see them eating the honey which is so pleasant to our own palate.

It is most natural in a parent at once to wish to tell his children of divine love—have you all done so? You pray for your children, but many of you would be the means of answering your own prayers if you would talk with them one by one. This may appear difficult, but once commenced, it will soon grow easy; and, indeed, if it be difficult, we should aspire to do it for that very reason. Should we not do many a difficult thing for Him who overcame all difficulties for us? At the least, do not deny to your own children the personal testimony of their father or mother to the surpassing power of grace and the unutterable sweetness of divine love. Tell it to those who are nearest to you.

The believer will do this as best he can. Samson, you see, brought the honey to his father and mother in a rough and ready style, going on eating it as he brought it.

If I wished to give honey to my father and mother, I should do it up rather daintily: I would at least put it in as respectable a dish as our kitchen could afford. But there were no plates and dishes out there in that Timnath vineyard, so his own hands were the only salvers upon which Samson could present the delicacy—"he took thereof in his hands, and came to his father and mother, and he gave them, and they did eat."

Perhaps you think, *If I am to speak to any person upon true religion, I should like to do it in poetry.* Better do it in prose, for perhaps they will take more notice of your verse than of your subject. Give them the honey *in your hands*; and if there is no dish, they cannot take notice of the dish.

"Ay, but I should like to do it very properly," says one; "it is a very important matter; I should like to speak most correctly." But my judgment is that, as you will not be likely to attain to correct speech all in a hurry and your friends may die while you are learning your grammar and your rhetoric, you had better tell them of Jesus according to your present ability.

Tell them there is life in a look at Jesus. Tell them the story simply, as one child talks to another. Carry the honey in your hands, though it drip all round. No hurt will come of the spilling; there are always little ones waiting for such drops.

If you were to make the Gospel drip about everywhere and sweeten all things, it would be no waste but a blessed gain to all around. Therefore, I say to you, tell of Jesus Christ as best you can, and never cease to do so while life lasts.

But then Samson did another thing, and every true believer should do it, too: he did not merely tell his parents about the honey, but *he took them some of it*. I do not read, "And he told his father and mother of the honey," but I read, "and he took thereof in his hands."

Nothing is so powerful as an exhibition of grace itself to others. Do not talk about it, but carry it in your hands.

"I cannot do that," says one. Yes, you can—by your life, your temper, your spirit, your whole bearing. If your hands serve God, if your heart serves God, if your face beams with joy in the service of God, you will carry grace wherever you go, and those who see you will perceive it. You will hardly have need to say, "Come and partake of grace"; for the grace of God in you will be its own invitation and attraction.

Let our lives be full of Christ, and we shall preach Christ. A holy life is the best of sermons. Soul winning is wrought by a winning life more surely than by winning words.

Take note, also, that Samson *did this with great modesty*.

We have plenty of people about nowadays who could not kill a mouse without publishing it in the Gospel Gazette, but Samson killed a lion and said nothing about it. He holds the honey in his hand for his father and mother—he shows them *that*; but we are specially informed that he told not his father nor his mother that he had taken it out of the carcase of the lion. The Holy Spirit finds modesty so rare that He takes care to record it.

In telling your own experience, be wisely cautious. Say much of what the Lord has done for you, but say little of what you have done for the Lord. You need not make much effort to be brief on that point, for I am afraid that there is not much of it, if all were told. Do not utter a self-glorifying sentence. Let us put Christ to the front, and the joy and blessedness that comes of faith in Him. And as for ourselves, we need not speak a word except to lament our sins and shortcomings.

The sum of what I have to say is this: if we have tasted any joy in Christ, if we have known any consolation of the Spirit, if faith has been to us a real power and if it has wrought in us peace and rest, let us communicate this blessed discovery to others. If you do not do so, mark you, you will have missed the very object for which God has blessed you.

I heard the other day of a Sunday school address in America which pleased me much. Speaking to the boys, the teacher said, "Boys, here's a watch; what is it for?"

The children answered, "To tell the time."

"Well," he said, "suppose my watch does not tell the time; what is it good for?"

"Good for nothing, sir."

Then he took out a pencil. "What is this pencil for?"

"It is to write with, sir."

"Suppose this pencil won't make a mark; what is it good for?"

"Good for nothing, sir."

Then he took out his pocketknife. "Boys, what is this for?"

They were American boys, and so they shouted, "To whittle with"— that is, to experiment on any substance that came in their way by cutting a notch in it.

"But," said he, "suppose it will not cut; what is the knife good for?"

"Good for nothing, sir."

Then the teacher asked, "What is the chief end of man?"

They replied, "To glorify God."

"But suppose a man does not glorify God; what is he good for?"

"Good for nothing, sir."

That brings out my point most clearly. There are many professors of whom I will not say that they are good for nothing, but methinks if they do not soon stir themselves up to glorify God by proclaiming the sweetness of God's love, it will go hard with them.

Remember how Jesus said of the savorless salt, "Henceforth it is good for nothing." What were you converted for? What were you forgiven for? What were you renewed for? What have you been preserved on earth for but to tell to others the glad tidings of salvation and so to glorify God? Do, then, go out with your hands full of the honey of divine love and hold it out to others.

You must assuredly do good by this; you cannot possibly do harm. Samson did not invite his father and mother to see the lion when he was alive and roaring—he might have done some hurt in that case by frightening them or exposing them to injury—but he settled the lion business himself; and when it came to honey, he knew that even his mother could not be troubled about *that*; therefore, he invited them both to share his gains.

When you get into a soul-conflict, do not publish your distress to all your friends, but fight manfully in God's name. But when you possess the joy of Christ and the love of the Spirit and grace is abundant in your soul, then tell the news to all around.

You cannot do any hurt by such a proceeding: grace does good, not harm, all its days. Even if you blunder over it, you will do no mischief. The Gospel spilled on the ground is not lost. Good, and only good, must come of making known salvation by Jesus Christ.

It will be much better for you to tell of the sweets of godliness than it will be to make riddles about the doctrine of it. Samson afterwards made a riddle about his lion and the honey, and that riddle ended in fighting and bloodshed.

We have known certain Christians spend their lives in making riddles about the honey and the lion, by asking tough doctrinal questions which even angels cannot answer: "Riddle me this," they say; and then it has ended in a fight, and brotherly love has been murdered in the fray.

It is much better to bring your hands full of honey to those who are needy and present it to them that they may eat of it, than it is to cavil and discuss.

No hurt can come of telling what the Lord has done for your soul, and it will keep you out of mischief. Therefore, I would stir up all Christians to continue from day to day exhibiting to needy sinners the blessedness of Christ, that unbelievers may come and eat thereof.

By doing this you will be blessing men far more than Samson could bless his parents; for our honey is honey unto eternity, our sweets are sweets that last to Heaven and are best enjoyed there. Call upon others to taste and see that the Lord is good, and you shall have therein much joy. You shall increase your own pleasure by seeing the pleasure of the Lord prospering in your hand.

What bliss awaits useful Christians when they enter into Heaven, for they shall be met there by many who have gone before them whom they were the means of turning to Christ.

I do often inwardly sing when I perceive that I can scarce go into any town or village but what somebody hunts me up to say to me, "Under God I owe my salvation to your sermons or to your books."

What will be the felicities of Heaven when we shall meet those who were turned to righteousness by our holding forth the Word of Life! Our Heaven will be seven heavens as we see them there.

If you have done nothing but exhibit in your lives the precious results of grace, you will have done well. If you have presented to your companions truths that were sweetness itself to you and tried to say in broken accents, "Oh, that you knew this peace!" it shall give you joy unspeakable to meet those in Glory who were attracted to Christ by such a simple means.

God make you all to be His witnesses in all the circles wherein you move.

CHAPTER II

Glory!

"Who hath called us unto his eternal glory."—I Pet. 5:10.

A fortnight ago, when I was only able to creep to the front of this platform, I spoke to you concerning the future of our mortal bodies. "We know that if our earthly house of this tabernacle were dissolved, we have a building of God, a house not made with hands, eternal in the heavens." On the next Sunday we went a step further. We did not preach so much about the resurrection of the body as upon the hope of glory for our entire nature, our text being, "Christ in you, the hope of glory."

Thus we have passed through the outer court and have trodden the hallowed floor of the Holy Place; now we are the more prepared to enter within the veil and to gaze awhile upon the glory which awaits us. We shall say a little—and oh, how little it will be—upon that glory of which we have so sure a prospect, that glory which is prepared for us in Christ Jesus, and of which He is the hope!

I pray that our eyes may be strengthened that we may see the heavenly light, and that our ears may be opened to hear sweet voices from the better land. As for me, I cannot say that I will speak of the glory, but I will try to stammer about it; for the best language to which a man can reach concerning glory must be a mere stammering.

Paul did but see a little of it for a short time, and he confessed that he heard things that it was not lawful for a man to utter; and I doubt not that he felt utterly nonplused as to describing what he had seen. Though a great master of language, yet for once he was overpowered; the grandeur of his theme made him silent. As for us, what can we do, where even Paul breaks down? Pray, dear friends, that the Spirit of glory may rest upon you, that He may open your eyes to see as much as can at present be seen of the heritage of the saints.

We are told that "eye hath not seen, nor ear heard, neither have entered into the heart of man, the things which God hath prepared for them that love him." Yet the eye has seen wonderful things. There are sunrises and sunsets, Alpine glories and ocean marvels which, once seen, cling to our memories throughout life. Yet even when nature is at her best, she cannot give us an idea of the supernatural glory which God has prepared for His people.

The ear has heard sweet harmonies. Have we not enjoyed music which has thrilled us? Have we not listened to speech which has seemed to make our hearts dance within us? Yet no melody of harp nor charm of oratory can ever raise us to a conception of the glory which God hath laid up for them that love Him.

As for the heart of man, what strange things have entered it! Men have exhibited fair fictions, woven in the loom of fancy, which have made the eyes to sparkle with their beauty and brightness; imagination has revelled and rioted in its own fantastic creations, roaming among islands of silver and mountains of gold or swimming in seas of wine and rivers of milk; but imagination has never been able to open the gate of pearl which shuts in the City of our God. No, it hath not yet entered the heart of man.

Yet the text goes on to say, "But he hath revealed it unto us by his Spirit." So Heaven is not an utterly unknown region, not altogether an inner brightness shut in with walls of impenetrable darkness. God hath revealed joys which He has prepared for His beloved; but mark you, even though they be revealed of the Spirit, yet it is no common unveiling, and the reason that it is made known at all is ascribed to the fact that "the Spirit searcheth all things, yea, the deep things of God."

So we see that the glory which awaits the saints is ranked among the deep things of God, and he that would speak thereof after the manner of the oracles of God must have much heavenly teaching.

It is easy to chatter according to human fancy; but if we would follow the sure teaching of the Word of God, we shall have need to be taught of the Holy Spirit, without whose anointing the deep things of God must be hidden from us. Pray that we may be under that teaching while we dwell upon this theme.

There are three questions which we will answer this morning. The first is, *What is the destiny of the saints?*—"Eternal glory," says the text. Second, *Wherein doth this glory consist?* I said we would answer the questions, but this is not to be answered this side the pearly gates. Third, *What should be the influence of this prospect upon our hearts?* What manner of people ought we to be whose destiny is eternal glory? How should we live who are to live forever in the glory of the Most High?

I. WHAT THEN IS THE DESTINY OF THE SAINTS?

Our text tells us that God has "called us unto his *eternal glory.*"

"Glory!" Does not the very word astound you? "Glory!" Surely that belongs to God alone! Yet the Scripture says "glory," and glory it must mean, for it never exaggerates.

Think of glory for us who have deserved eternal shame! Glory for us poor creatures who are often ashamed of ourselves! Yes, I look at my Book again, and it actually says "glory"—nothing less than glory. Therefore, so must it be.

Now, since this seems so amazing and astonishing a thing, I would so speak with you that not a relic of incredulity may remain in your hearts concerning it. I would ask you to follow me while we look through the Bible, not quoting every passage which speaks of glory, but mentioning a few of the leading ones.

This glory has been promised. What said David? In Psalm 73:24 we meet with these remarkable words: "Thou shalt guide me with thy counsel, and afterward receive me to glory."

In the original Hebrew there is a trace of David's recollection of Enoch's being translated; and, though the royal psalmist did not expect to be caught away without dying, yet he did expect that after he had followed the guidance of the Lord here below, the great Father would stoop and raise up His child to be with Himself forever. He expected to be received into glory. Even in those dim days, when as yet the light of the Gospel was but in its dawn, this prophet and king was able to say, "Thou shalt afterward receive me to glory."

Did he not mean the same thing when in Psalm 84:11 he said, "The Lord will give grace and glory: no good thing will he withhold from them that walk uprightly"? Not only no good thing under the name of grace will God withhold from the upright, but no good thing under the head of glory.

No good of Heaven shall be kept from the saints; no reserve is even set upon the throne of the great King, for our Lord Jesus has graciously promised, "To him that overcometh will I grant to sit with me in my throne, even as I also overcame, and am set down with my Father in his throne."

"No good thing"—not even amongst the infinitely good things of Heaven—will God "withhold from them that walk uprightly."

If David had this persuasion, much more may we walk in the light of the Gospel. Since our Lord Jesus hath suffered and entered into His glory, and we know that we shall be with Him where He is, we are confident that our rest shall be glorious.

Brethren, it is *to this glory that we have been called.* The people of God having been predestinated, have been called with an effectual calling—called so that they have obeyed the call and have run after Him who has drawn them.

Now, our text says that He has "called us unto his eternal glory by Christ Jesus." We are called to repentance, called to faith, called to holiness, called to perseverance, all this that we may afterwards attain unto glory.

We have another Scripture of like import in I Thessalonians 2:12: "Who hath called you unto his kingdom and glory."

We are called unto His kingdom according to our Lord's word, "Fear not, little flock; for it is your Father's good pleasure to give you the kingdom." We are called to be kings, called to wear a crown of life that fadeth not away, called to reign with Christ in His glory.

If the Lord had not meant us to have the glory, He would not have called us unto it, for His calling is no mockery. He would not by His Spirit have fetched us out from the world and separated us unto Himself if He had not intended to keep us from falling and preserve us eternally.

Believer, you are called to glory; do not question the certainty of that to which God has called you.

And we are not only called to it, brethren, but *glory is especially joined with justification.* Let me quote Romans 8:30: "Moreover whom he did predestinate, them he also called: and whom he called, them he also justified: and whom he justified, them he also glorified."

These various mercies are threaded together like pearls upon a string:

there is no breaking the thread, no separating the precious things. They are put in their order by God Himself, and they are kept there by His eternal and irreversible decree. If you are justified by the righteousness of Christ, you shall be glorified through Christ Jesus, for thus hath God purposed, and so must it be.

Do you not remember how salvation itself is linked with glory? Paul, in II Timothy 2:10, speaks of "the salvation which is in Christ Jesus with eternal glory." The two things are riveted together and cannot be separated.

The saved ones must partake of the glory of God, for for *this are they being prepared every day*. In the 9th of Romans, where Paul speaks about the predestinating will of God, he says in verse 23: "...the vessels of mercy, which he had afore prepared unto glory." This is the process which commenced in regeneration and is going on in us every day in the work of sanctification.

We cannot be glorified so long as sin remains in us; we must first be pardoned, renewed and sanctified; then we are fitted to be glorified. By communion with our Lord Jesus, we are made like to Him, as saith the apostle in II Corinthians 3:18: "But we all, with open face beholding as in a glass the glory of the Lord, are changed into the same image from glory to glory, even as by the Spirit of the Lord." It is very wonderful how by the wisdom of God everything is made to work this way.

Look at the blessed text in II Corinthians 4:17, where Paul says, "For our light affliction, which is but for a moment, worketh for us a far more exceeding and eternal weight of glory"; where he represents that all that we can suffer, whether of body or of mind, is producing for us such a mass of glory that he is quite unable to describe it, and so he uses hyperbolic language in saying, "a far more exceeding and eternal weight of glory."

O blessed men, whose very losses are their gains, whose sorrows produce their joys, whose griefs are big with Heaven! Well may we be content to suffer, if so it be, that all things are working together for our good and are helping to pile up the excess of our future glory.

It seems we are called to glory and we are being prepared for it; thus is it not also a sweet thought that *our present fellowship with Christ is the guarantee of it?*

In Romans 8:17 it is said, "If so be that we suffer with him, that we may be also glorified together." Going to prison with Christ will bring us into the palace with Christ. Smarting with Christ will bring us into reigning with Christ. Being ridiculed, slandered and despised for Christ's sake will bring us to be sharers of His honor and glory and immortality.

Who would not be with Christ in His humiliation if this be the guarantee that we shall be with Him in His glory? Remember those dear words of the Lord Jesus, "Ye are they which have continued with me in my temptations. And I appoint unto you a kingdom, as my Father hath appointed unto me."

Let us shoulder the cross, for it leads to the crown. "No cross, no crown"; but he that has shared the battle shall partake in the victory.

I am not yet done, for there is a text, Hebrews 2:10, which is well worthy of our consideration: *we are to be brought to glory.*

It is said of our Lord that it "became him, for whom are all things, and by whom are all things, in bringing many sons unto glory, to make the captain of their salvation perfect through sufferings." Beloved, we are called to glory, we are being prepared for it, and we shall be brought to it.

We might despair of ever getting into the glory land if we had not One to bring us there, for the pilgrim's road is rough and beset with many foes; but the "Captain of our salvation," a greater than Bunyan's Greatheart, is conducting the pilgrim band through all the treacherous way, and He will bring the "many sons"—where?—"*unto glory*"; nowhere short of that shall be their *ultimatum.*

Glory, glory shall surely follow upon grace; for Christ the Lord, who has come into His glory, has entered into covenant engagements that He will bring all the "many sons" to be with Him.

Mark this, and then I will quote no more Scriptures: *this glory will be for our entire manhood,* for our body as well as for our soul.

You know that text in the famous resurrection chapter—I Corinthians 15:43. Paul speaks of the body as being "sown in dishonour," but he adds, "It is raised in glory." Then in Philippians 3:21 he says of our divine Lord at His coming, "Who shall change our vile body, that it may be fashioned like unto his glorious body, according to the working whereby he is able even to subdue all things unto himself."

What a wonderful change that will be for this frail, feeble, suffering body! In some respects it is not vile, for it is a wonderful product of divine skill and power and goodness; but inasmuch as it hampers our spiritual nature by its appetites and infirmities, it may be called a "vile body."

It is an unhandy body for a spirit: it fits a soul well enough, but a spirit wants something more ethereal, less earthbound, more full of life than this poor flesh and blood and bone can ever be.

Well, the body is to be changed. What alteration will it undergo? It will be rendered perfect. The body of a child will be fully developed, and the dwarf will attain to full stature. The blind shall not be sightless in Heaven, neither shall the lame be halt, nor shall the palsied tremble. The deaf shall hear, and the dumb shall sing God's praises.

We shall carry none of our deficiencies or infirmities to Heaven. As good Mr. Ready-to-Halt did not carry his crutches there, neither shall any of us need a staff to lean upon. There we shall not know an aching brow or a weak knee or a failing eye. "The inhabitant shall no more say, I am sick."

And it shall be an impassive body, a body that will be incapable of any kind of suffering. No palpitating heart, no sinking spirit, no aching limbs, no lethargic soul shall worry us there. No, we shall be perfectly delivered from every evil of that kind.

Moreover, it shall be an immortal body. Our risen bodies shall not be capable of decay, much less of death. There are no graves in Glory. Blessed are the dead that die in the Lord, for their bodies shall rise, never to know death and corruption a second time. No smell or taint of corruption shall remain upon those whom Jesus shall call from the tomb. The risen body shall be greatly increased in power: it is "sown in weakness," says the Scripture, but it is "raised in power."

I suppose there will be a wonderful agility about our renovated frame. Probably it will be able to move as swiftly as the lightning flash, for so do angels pass from place to place, and we shall in this, as in many things else, be as the angels of God. Anyhow, it will be a "glorious body" and it will be "raised in glory," so that the whole of our manhood shall participate of that wonderful depth of bliss which is summed up in the word—"glory."

Thus I think I have set before you much of what the Word of God saith upon this matter.

May the Holy Spirit help me while I try very hesitatingly and stammeringly to answer the inquiry,

II. WHEREIN DOTH THIS DESTINY CONSIST?

Do you know how much I expect to do? It will be but little. You remember what the Lord did for Moses when the man of God prayed— "I beseech thee, shew me thy glory"! All that the Lord Himself did for Moses was to say, "Thou shalt see my back parts: but my face shall not be seen."

How little, then, can we hope to speak of this glory! Its back parts are too bright for us: as for the face of that glory, it shall not be seen by any of us here below, though by and by we shall behold it.

I suppose if one who had been in glory could come straight down from Heaven and occupy this platform, he would find that his discoveries could not be communicated because of the insufficiency of language to express such a weight of meaning.

The saints' destiny is *glory*. What is glory, brethren? What is it, I mean, among the sons of men? It is generally understood to be fame, a great repute, the sound of trumpets, the noise of applause, the sweets of approbation among the crowd and in high places.

The Queen of Sheba came from afar to see the glory of Solomon. What was that glory, brethren? It was the glory of a rare wisdom excelling all others; it was the glory of immense riches expended upon all manner of magnificence and splendor. As for this last glory the Lord says of it that a lily of the field had more of it than Solomon; at least "Solomon in all his glory was not arrayed like one of these."

Yet that is what men mean by glory—rank, position, power, conquest—things that make the ears of men to tingle when they hear of them—things extraordinary and rare. All this is but a dim shadow of what God means by glory, yet out of the shadow we may obtain a little inkling of what the substance must be.

God's people shall be wise, and even famous, for they shall "shine as the stars for ever and ever." God's people shall be rich; the very streets of their abode are paved with gold exceeding rich and rare. God's people shall be singularly honored; there shall be a glory about them unrivaled, for they shall be known as a peculiar people, a royal priesthood, a race of beings lifted up to reveal their Maker's character beyond all the rest of His works.

I reckon that glory to a saint means, first of all, *purified character.*
The brightest glory that really can come to anyone is the glory of character. Thus God's glory among men is His goodness, His mercy, His
justice, His truth.

But shall such poor creatures as we are ever have perfect characters?
Yes, we shall one day be perfectly holy. God's Holy Spirit, when He
has finished His work, will leave in us no trace of sin: no temptation
shall be able to touch us, there will be in us no relics of our past and
fallen state. Oh, will not that be blessed?

I was going to say it is all the glory I want—the glory of being perfect
in character, never sinning, never judging unjustly, never thinking a
vain thought, never wandering away from the perfect law of God, never
vexed again with sin which has so long been my worst enemy.

One day we shall be glorious because the Devil himself will not be
able to detect a fault in us, and those eyes of God, which burn like
fire and read the inmost secrets of the soul, will not be able to detect
anything blameworthy in us. Such shall be the character of the saints
that they shall be meet to consort with Christ Himself, fit company
for that thrice holy Being before whom angels veil their faces. This
is glory!

Next, I understand by "glory" *our perfected manhood.* When God
made Adam, he was a far superior being to any of us. Man's place in
creation was very remarkable. The psalmist says:

*"For thou hast made him a little lower than the angels, and hast crowned
him with glory and honour. Thou madest him to have dominion over the
works of thy hands; thou hast put all things under his feet: all sheep and
oxen, yea, and the beasts of the field; the fowl of the air, and the fish of
the sea, and whatsoever passeth through the paths of the seas."*

No king among men in these days could rival Adam in the Garden
of Eden. He was indeed monarch of all that he surveyed. From the
lordly lion down to the tiniest insect, all living creatures paid him
willing homage.

Can we ever rise to this last honor? Brethren, listen, "It doth not
yet appear what we shall be: but we know that, when [Christ] shall
appear, we shall be like him; for we shall see him as he is." Is there
any limit to the growth of the mind of a man? Can we tell what he
may reach?

We read of Solomon that God gave him largeness of heart as the sand of the sea. God will give to His people glory that will include in it more largeness of heart than Solomon ever knew. Then shall we know even as we are known by God. Now we see, but it is "through a glass darkly," but then we shall see "face to face."

You have met with men of great intellect, and you have looked up to them: but assuredly the smallest babe in Christ, when he shall reach Heaven, shall have a greater intellect than the most profound philosopher who has ever astounded mankind by his discoveries.

We shall not always be as we are today, contracted and hampered because of our little knowledge, our slender faculties and our dull perceptions. Our ignorance and prejudice shall vanish. What a man will become we can scarcely tell when he is remade in the image of God and made like unto our divine Lord who is "the firstborn among many brethren."

Here we are but in embryo. Our minds are but the seeds, or the bulbs, out of which shall come the flower and glory of a nobler manhood. Your body is to be developed into something infinitely brighter and better than the bodies of men here below.

And as for the soul—we cannot guess to what an elevation it shall be raised in Christ Jesus. There is room for the largest expectation here, as we conjecture what will be the full accomplishment of the vast intent of eternal love, an intent which has involved the sacrifice of the only begotten Son of God. That can be no mean design which has been carried on at the expense of the best that Heaven itself possessed.

Further, by "glory" and coming to glory, I think we must understand *complete victory*. Dwelling in the age of the Romans, men said to themselves as they read the Scriptures, "What does the apostle mean by 'glory'?" They could scarcely help connecting it with conquest and the return of the warrior in triumph.

Men called it glory in those days when valiant warriors returned from fields of blood with captives and spoil. Then did the heroes ride through the streets of Rome, enjoying a triumph voted them by the senate. Then for the while the men of war were covered with glory, and all the city was glorious because of them.

As Christians, we hate the word *glory* when it is linked with wholesale murder and girt in garments rolled in blood; yet there is a kind

of fighting to which you and I are called, for we are soldiers of the
cross. And if we fight valiantly under our great Captain, rout every
sin and are found faithful even unto death, then we shall enter glory
and receive the honor which belongs to men who have fought a good
fight and have kept the faith. It will be no small glory to obtain the
crown of life which fadeth not away.

Is not this a full glory if we only place these three things together:
a purified character, a perfected nature, a complete victory?

An invaluable ingredient in true glory is *the divine approval.* "Glory"
among men means approbation.

It is a man's glory when he is honored of his Queen and she hangs
a medal on his breast or when his name is mentioned in the high court
of Parliament and he is ennobled for what he has done. If men speak
of our actions with approval, it is called fame and glory.

Oh, but one drop of the approbation of God has more glory in it
than a sea full of human praise! And the Lord will reward His own
with this holy favor. He will say, "Well done, good and faithful servant," and Christ before the universe will say, "Come, ye blessed of
my Father." Oh, what glory that will be!

They were despised and rejected of men; they "wandered about in
sheepskins and goatskins, destitute, afflicted, tormented"; but now God
approves them and they take seats among the peers of Heaven, made
noble by the approbation of the Judge of all. This is glory with an
emphasis—substantial glory. One approving glance from the eye of
Jesus, one accepting word from the mouth of the Father, will be glory
enough for any one of us, and this we shall have if we follow the Lamb
whithersoever He goeth.

But this is not all. Children of God will have *the glory of reflecting
the glory of God.*

When any of God's unfallen creatures shall wish to see the greatness of God's goodness, mercy and love, they that dwell in Heaven
will point out a glorified saint. Whenever any spirit from far-off regions
desires to know what is meant by faithfulness and grace, some angel
will reply, "Go and talk with those who have been redeemed from
among men."

I believe that you and I will spend much of eternity in making known
to principalities and powers the unsearchable riches of the grace of

God. We shall be mirrors reflecting God, and in us shall His glory be revealed.

There may be myriads of races of pure and holy beings of whom we have never heard as yet, and these may come to the New Jerusalem as to the great metropolis of Jehovah's universe. And when they come there, they will gaze upon the saints as the highest instances of divine grace, wisdom, power and love.

It will be their highest pleasure to hear how eternal mercy dealt with us unworthy ones. How we shall delight to rehearse to them the fact of the Father's eternal purpose, the story of the incarnate God—the God that loved and died, and the love of the blessed Spirit who sought us in the days of our sin and brought us to the cross foot, renewing us in the spirit of our minds and making us to be sons of God.

O brothers and sisters, this shall be our glory, that God shall shine through us to the astonishment of all.

Yet I think glory includes somewhat more than this. In certain cases a man's *glory lies in his relationships*.

If any of the royal family should come to your houses, you would receive them with respect; yes, and even as they went along the street they would be spied out, and passersby would say, "That is the prince!" They would honor the son of our good Queen.

But royal descent is a poor business compared with being allied to the King of Kings. Many angels are exceeding bright, but they are only servants to wait upon the sons. I believe that there will be a kind of awe upon the angels at the sight of men. When they see us in our glory, they will rejoice to know our near relation to their Lord and to fulfill their own destiny as ministering spirits appointed to minister to the heirs of salvation.

No pride will be possible to the perfected, but we shall then realize the exalted position to which, by our new birth and the divine adoption, we have been raised. "Behold, what manner of love the Father hath bestowed upon us, that we should be called the sons of God." Sons of God! Sons of the Lord God Almighty! Oh, what glory this will be!

Then there will be connected with this the fact that *we shall be connected with Jesus in everything*. For do not you see, brethren, it was because of our fall that Christ came here to save men; when He wrought out a perfect righteousness, it was all for us; when He died, it was all for us; and when He rose again, it was all for us? What is more, we lived in Christ, we died in Him, we were buried in Him and rose in Him, and we shall ascend into Heaven to reign with Him.

All our glory is by Christ Jesus, and in all the glory of Christ Jesus we have a share. We are members of His body; we are one with Him.

I say, the creatures that God has made, when they shall come to worship in the New Jerusalem, will stand and gaze at glorified men, and with bated breath will say one to another, "These are the beings whose nature the Son of God assumed! These are the chosen creatures whom the Prince of Heaven bought with His own blood."

They will stand astonished at the divine glory which will be manifested in beings emancipated from sin and Hell and made heirs of God, joint-heirs with Jesus Christ.

Will not even angels be surprised and awed as they look on the church and say to one another, "This is the bride, the Lamb's wife!" They will marvel how the Lord of glory should come to this poor earth to seek a spouse and that He should enter into eternal union with such a people.

"Glory, glory dwelleth in Immanuel's land!" Now we are getting near to the center of it. I feel inclined, like Moses, to put off my shoes from my feet, for the place whereon we stand is holy ground, now that we are getting to see poor bushes like ourselves aglow with the indwelling God and changed from glory unto glory.

Yet this is not all, for there in Heaven *we shall dwell in the immediate presence of God.* We shall dwell with Him in nearest and dearest fellowship! All the felicity of the Most High will be our felicity. The blessedness of the triune Jehovah shall be our blessedness forever and ever.

Did you notice that our text says, "He hath called us unto *his* glory"? This outshines everything. The glory which the saints will have is the same glory which God possesses and such as He alone can bestow.

Listen to this text: "Whom he justified, them *he* also glorified." He glorifies them, then!

I know what it is to glorify God, and so do you; but when we poor creatures glorify God it is in a poor way, for we cannot add anything to Him. But what must it be for God Himself to glorify a man! The glory which you are to have forever, my dear, believing brother, is a glory which God Himself will put upon you.

Peter, as a Hebrew, perhaps uses a Hebraism when he says "his glory." It may be that he means the best of glory that can be, even as the Jews were wont to say—"The trees of God," when they meant the greatest trees, or "the mountains of God," when they intended the highest mountains. So by the glory of God, Peter may mean the richest, fullest glory that can be.

In the original, the word *glory* has about it the idea of "weight," at which the Apostle Paul hints when he speaks of a "weight of glory." This is the only glory that has weight in it; all else is light as a feather.

Take all the glories of this world, and they are outweighed by the small dust of the balance. Place them here in the hollow of my hand, all of them: a child may blow them away as thistledown.

God's glory has weight; it is solid, true, real, and he that gets it possesses no mere name or dream or tinsel, but he has that which will abide the rust of ages and the fire of judgment.

The glory of God! How shall I describe it! I must set before you a strange scriptural picture.

Mordecai must be made glorious for his fidelity to his king, and singular is the honor which his monarch ordains for him. This was the royal order:

"Let the royal apparel be brought which the king useth to wear, and the horse that the king rideth upon, and the crown royal which is set upon his head: And let this apparel and horse be delivered to the hand of one of the king's most noble princes, that they may array the man withal whom the king delighteth to honour, and bring him on horseback through the street of the city, and proclaim before him, Thus shall it be done to the man whom the king delighteth to honour."

Can you not imagine the surprise of the Jew when robe and ring were put upon him, and when he found himself placed upon the king's horse?

This may serve as a figure of that which will happen to us: we shall be glorified with the glory of God. The best robe, the best of Heaven's array, shall be appointed unto us, and we shall dwell in the house of the Lord forever.

Highest of all our glory will be *the enjoyment of God Himself*. He will be our exceeding joy. This bliss will swallow up every other, the blessedness of God. "The Lord is my portion," saith my soul. "Whom have I in heaven but thee? and there is none upon earth that I desire beside thee." Our God shall be our glory.

Yet bear with me. I have left out a word again: the text has it, "Unto his *eternal* glory." Ay, but that is the gem of the ring. The glory which God has in reserve for His chosen will never come to an end: it will stay with us, and we shall stay with it forever.

It will always be glory, too. Its brightness will never become dim. We shall never be tired of it or sated with it. After ten thousand thousand millions of years in Heaven our happiness shall be as fresh as when it first began.

Those are no fading laurels which surround immortal brows. Eternal glory knows no diminution.

Can you imagine a man being born at the same time that Adam was created and living all these thousands of years as king like Solomon, having all he could desire? His would seem to be a glorious life. But if at the end of seven thousand years that man must needs die, what has it profited him? His glory is all over now; its fires have died out in ashes.

But you and I, when we once enter Glory, shall receive what we can neither lose nor leave. Eternity! Eternity! This is the sweetness of all our future bliss.

Rejoice, ye saintly ones! Take your harps down from the willows, any of you who are mourning; and if you never sang before, yet sing this morning, 'God has called us unto His eternal glory,' and this is to be our portion world without end.

I can only find time for a few words upon the concluding head:

III. WHAT INFLUENCE SHOULD ALL THIS HAVE UPON OUR HEARTS?

I think, first, it ought to excite *desire* in many here present that you might attain unto glory by Christ Jesus.

Satan, when he took our blessed Lord to the top of an exceeding high mountain, tempted Him to worship him by offering Him the kingdoms of the world and all the glories thereof.

Satan is very clever, and I will at this time take a leaf out of his book. Will you not fall down and worship the Lord Jesus when He can give you the kingdom of God and all the glory thereof, and all this, not in pretense, but in reality? If there was any force in the temptation to worship Satan for the sake of the glory of this world, how much more reason is there for urging you to worship the Son of God that you may obtain His salvation with eternal glory!

I pray the Holy Ghost to drop a hot desire into many a poor sinner's breast this morning that you may cry, "If this glory is to be had, I will have it. And I will have it in God's way, for I will believe in Jesus, I will repent, I will come to God and so obtain His promise."

Second, this ought to move us to the feeling of *fear*. If there be such a glory as this, let us tremble lest by any means we should come short of it.

O my dear hearers, especially you that are my fellow members, brother church officers and workers associated with me, what a dreadful thing it will be if any one of us should come short of this glory! Oh, if there were no Hell, it would be Hell enough to miss of Heaven! If there were no pit that is bottomless nor worm undying nor fire unquenchable, it would be boundless misery to have a shadow of a fear of not reaching to God's eternal glory.

Let us therefore pass the time of our sojourning here in fear, and let us watch unto prayer and strive to enter in at the strait gate. God grant we may be found of Him at last to praise and honor!

If we are right, how this ought to move us to *gratitude*. Think of this! We are to enjoy "his eternal glory"! What a contrast to our deserts! Shame and everlasting contempt are our righteous due apart from Christ.

If we were to receive according to our merits, we should be driven from His presence and from the glory of His power. Verily, He hath not dealt with us after our sins nor rewarded us according to our iniquities; for, after all our transgressions, He has still reserved us for glory and reserved glory for us. What love and zeal should burn in our bosoms because of this!

Last of all, it should move us to a dauntless *courage*. If this glory is to be had, do we not feel like the heroes in Bunyan's picture?

Before the dreamer there stood a fair palace. He saw persons walking upon the top of it, clad in light and singing. Around the door stood armed men to keep back those who would enter. Then a brave man came up to one who had a writer's ink-horn by his side and said, "Set down my name." Straightway the warrior drew his sword and fought with all his might until he had cut his way to the door; then he entered. They within were heard to sing—

> Come in, come in,
> Eternal glory thou shalt win.

Will you not draw your swords this morning and fight against sin till you have overcome it? Do you not desire to win Christ and to be found in Him? Oh, let us now begin to feel a passion for eternal glory; and then in the strength of the Spirit and in the name of Jesus, let us press forward till we reach it.

Even on earth we may taste enough of this glory to fill us with delight. The glory which I have described to you dawns on earth, though it only comes to its noontide in Heaven. The glory of sanctified character, the glory of victory over sin, the glory of relationship to God, the glory of union with Christ—these are all to be tasted in a measure here below. These glories send their beams down even to these valleys and lowlands. Oh, to enjoy them today and thus to have earnests and foretastes of glory!

If we have them, let us go singing on until we reach the place where God's eternal glory shall surround us. Amen.

CHAPTER III

The Luther Sermon at Exeter Hall

"For in Jesus Christ neither circumcision availeth any thing, nor uncircumcision; but faith which worketh by love."—Gal. 5:6.

Paul makes a clean sweep of that trust in the externals of religion, which is the common temptation of all time. Circumcision was a great thing with the Jew, and oftentimes he trusted in it; but Paul declares that it availeth nothing. There might be others who were glad that they were not Jews, but Paul declares that their uncircumcision availeth no more than its opposite.

Certain matters connected with godliness are external, yet they are useful in their places: especially is that the case with baptism, the Lord's supper, assembling of ourselves together, reading of the Word and public prayer and praise. These are proper and profitable; but none must be made in any measure or degree the ground of our hope of salvation, for this text sweeps them all away and plainly describes them as availing nothing if they are made to be the foundations of our trust.

In Luther's day, superstitious confidence in external observances had overlaid faith in the Gospel; ceremonies had multiplied excessively, and the plain and simple way of salvation was obscured. There was need of some sturdy soul who, seeing the truth himself, should show it to others. When God raised up Martin Luther, who was born four centuries ago, he bore emphatic testimony against salvation by outward forms and by the power of priestcraft, affirming that salvation is by faith and that the church of God is a company of priests, every believer being a priest unto God.

If Luther had not affirmed it, the doctrine would have been just as true, for the distinction between clergy and laity has no excuse in

Scripture, which calls the saints, "God's *kleros*"—God's clergy or heritage.

Again we read, "Ye are a royal priesthood." Every man that believes in the Lord Jesus Christ is anointed to exercise the Christian priesthood; therefore, he need not put his trust in another, seeing the supposed priest is no more than any other man.

Each man must be accountable for himself before God. Each one must read and search the Scriptures for himself, must believe for himself and, when saved, must offer up himself as a living sacrifice unto God by Jesus Christ, who is the only High Priest of our profession.

So much for the negative side of the text, which is full of warning to this ritualistic age.

The chief testimony of our great reformer was to the justification of a sinner in the sight of God by faith in Jesus Christ and by that alone. He could fitly have taken this for his motto: "In Jesus Christ neither circumcision availeth any thing, nor uncircumcision; but faith which worketh by love."

While in the Augustinian monastery at Wittenberg, troubled and perturbed in mind, he read there in an old Latin Bible this text, "The just shall live by faith"—a new idea to him. But by its means spiritual light entered his soul in some degree. But such were the prejudices of his upbringing and such the darkness of his surroundings that he still hoped to find salvation by outward performances.

Luther therefore fasted long, till he was found swooning from hunger. He was exceedingly zealous for salvation by works.

At last he made a pilgrimage to Rome, hoping to find there everything that was holy and helpful. Disappointed in his search, yet he found more than he looked for.

On the pretended staircase of Pilate, while in the act of climbing it upon his knees, the Wittenberg text again sounded in his ear like a thunderclap: "The just shall live by faith."

Up he started and descended those stairs, never to grovel upon them again. The chain was broken, the soul was free. Luther had found the light; henceforth it became his life's business to flash that light upon the nations, crying evermore, "The just shall live by faith."

The best commemoration which I can make of this man is to preach the doctrine which he held so dear. You who are not saved can best assist me by believing the doctrine and proving its truth in your own cases. May the Holy Ghost cause it to be so in hundreds of instances. Let us inquire,

I. WHAT IS THIS FAITH?

We are always talking about it, but what is it? Whenever I try to explain it, I am afraid lest I should confuse rather than expound.

Story of Bunyan

There is a story told concerning John Bunyan's *Pilgrim's Progress*. Good Thomas Scott, the commentator, wrote notes to it. He thought *Pilgrim's Progress* a difficult book, and he would make it clear.

A pious cottager in his parish who had the book was reading it when her minister called. He said to her, "Oh, I see you are reading Bunyan's *Pilgrim's Progress*. Do you understand it?" She answered innocently enough, "Oh, yes, sir, I understand Mr. Bunyan very well, and I hope that one day I shall be able to understand your explanations."

I am afraid lest you should say when I have done, "I understand what faith is, as I find it in the Bible, and one day, perhaps, I may be able to understand the preacher's explanation of it."

Warned by this, I will speak as plainly as I can.

First, it is to be remembered that faith is not a mere creed holding. It is very proper to say, "I believe in God the Father Almighty, Maker of Heaven and earth," and so forth; you may repeat all that and be no "believer" in the scriptural sense of that term. Though the creed be true, it may not be true to you.

It would have been the same to you if the opposite had been true, for you put the truth away like a paper in a pigeonhole and it has no effect upon you. "A very proper doctrine," you say, "a very proper doctrine," and so you put it to sleep. It does not influence your heart nor affect your life.

Do not imagine that the professing an orthodox creed is the same thing as faith in Christ. A truthful creed is desirable for many reasons; but if it be a dead, inoperative thing, it cannot bring salvation. Faith is belief of the truth, but it is more.

Important Distinction

Again, faith is not the mere belief that there is a God, though that we must have; for we cannot come to God except we "believe that he is, and that he is a rewarder of them that diligently seek him." We are to believe *in* God—that He is good, blessed, true, right and therefore to be trusted, confided in and praised. Whatever He may do, whatever He may say, God is not to be suspected but believed in.

You know what it is to believe in a man, do you not—to believe in a man so that you follow him, confide in him and accept his advice? In that same way faith believes in God—not only believes that He is, but finds rest in His character, His Son, His promise, His covenant, His Word and everything about Him. Faith livingly and lovingly trusts in her God about everything.

Especially must we believe in what God has revealed in Scripture—that it is verily and indeed a sure and infallible testimony to be received without question. We accept the Father's witness concerning Jesus and take heed thereto "as unto a light that shineth in a dark place."

Faith has specially to believe in Him who is the sum and substance of all this revelation, even Jesus Christ, who became God in human flesh that He might redeem our fallen nature from all the evils of sin and raise it to eternal felicity.

We believe *in* Christ, *on* Christ and *upon* Christ, accepting Him—because of the record which God has given to us concerning His Son, that He is the propitiation for our sins. We accept God's unspeakable Gift and receive Jesus as our all in all.

If I wanted to describe saving faith in one word, I should say that it is *trust*. It is so believing God and so believing in Christ that we trust ourselves and our eternal destinies in the hands of a reconciled God.

In the second place, we will consider

II. WHY FAITH IS SELECTED AS THE WAY OF SALVATION

I would remind you that if we could not answer this question it would not matter. Since the Lord has appointed believing as the way of grace, it is not ours to challenge His choice. Beggars must not be choosers. Let us trust, if so the Lord ordains.

No Help for Past Defects

But we can answer this question in a measure. First, it is clear that *no other way is possible.* It is not possible for us to be saved by our own merits, for we have broken the Law already, and future obedience, being already due, cannot make up for past defects.

> *Could my tears forever flow,*
> *Could my zeal no respite know,*
> *All for sin could not atone:*
> *Thou must save, and Thou alone.*

The road of good works is blocked up by our past sins, and it is sure to be further blocked up by future sins; therefore, we ought to rejoice that God has commended to us the open road of faith.

God has chosen the way of faith *that salvation might be by grace.* If we had to do anything in order to save ourselves, we should be sure to impute a measure of virtue to our own doings or feelings or prayers or almsgivings, thus detracting from the pure grace of God.

But salvation comes from God as a pure favor—an act of undeserved generosity and benevolence. The Lord will, therefore, only put it into the hand of faith since faith arrogates nothing to herself. Faith, in fact, disowns all idea of merit, and the Lord of grace therefore elects to place the treasure of His love in the hand of faith.

Pride Crucified

Again, it is of faith *that there may be no boasting.* If our salvation be of our doings or feelings, we are sure to boast; but if it be of faith, we cannot glory in self. "Where is boasting then? It is excluded. By what law? of works? Nay: but by the law of faith." Faith is humble and ascribes all praise to God. Faith is truthful and confesses her obligation to the sovereign grace of God.

I bless the Lord that He has chosen this way of faith because *it is so suitable for poor sinners.* Some among us tonight would never have been saved if salvation had only been prepared for the good and righteous.

Suppose you were in the last article of death; what good works could you do? Yonder dying thief found it a happy thing that by faith he could trust the crucified One and before set of sun, could be with Him in Paradise.

Faith is a way suitable for sinners, especially for sinners who are soon to die. In some sense we are all in that condition. Some of us peradventure are especially so, for what man among us knows that he will see tomorrow's dawn?

I bless God again that the way of salvation is by faith because *it is a way open to the most unlearned.*

What fine theology we get nowadays—deep thinking they call it. The men go down so deep into their subjects and so stir the mud at the bottom that you cannot see them and they cannot see themselves. I apprehend that teachers of a certain school do not themselves know what they are talking about.

Now, if salvation were only to be learned by reading through huge folios, what would become of multitudes of poor souls in Bow and Bethnal Green and Seven Dials? If the Gospel had consisted of a mass of learning, how could the unlearned be saved?

But now we can go to each one of them and say, "Jesus died."

> There is life in a look at the crucified One;
> There is life at this moment for thee.

III. LUTHER'S LIFE

I am going to finish in a way suitable to this Luther memorial. You have heard a great deal about Luther's preaching salvation by faith alone; now let us turn to Luther's life and see what Luther himself meant by it. What kind of faith did Luther himself exhibit by which he was justified?

First, faith led him to *an open avowal of what he believed.* Luther did not mean to go up to Heaven by the back stairs, as many young men hope to do. You wish to be Christians on the sly, so as to escape the offense of the cross. Luther did not refuse to confess Christ and take up his cross and follow Him. He knew that he who with his heart believeth must also with his mouth make confession, and he did so right nobly.

He began teaching and preaching the truth which had enlightened his own soul. One of his sermons displeased Duke George of Saxony; but as it saved a lady of high rank, Luther did not fret. He was not the man to conceal truth because it was dangerous to avow it. It cost him something to stand up boldly for a pure and simple Gospel, but he believed the testimony he gave was worth much more than it cost.

The river of life is as free as any river that flows to the sea, and all the world may stoop down and drink. Luther wished the people to have free access to the Bible. He was not always excessively polite in his speech; he was too earnest for that. He spoke from the heart, he was all on fire, and his words were heated sevenfold. He did not conceal his convictions. He nailed his theses to the church door where all might read them.

When astronomers require a new constellation in the heavens, let it be "the hammer and nails." O you who make no profession, let this man's outspoken faith rebuke you!

His *dauntless valor for truth* caused him to be greatly hated in his own day with a ferocity which has not yet died out. It has always been so and always will be so. Light has no fellowship with darkness; oil and water will not unite; there is no concord between Christ and Belial. Yet Luther would not sacrifice his convictions for the sake of the applause of men. Feeling that he was right, he went ahead and did not stop to count the consequences. Ridicule, malice, even the dark dungeon, could not turn him aside nor daunt his holy courage.

Young men, I do not know what your ambition may be, but I hope you do not wish to be in this world mere chips in the porridge, giving forth no flavor whatever. My ambition does not run in that line. I know that, if I have no intense haters, I can have no intense lovers; and I am prepared to have both.

When right-hearted men see honest love of truth in a man, they cry, "He is our brother. Let him be our champion." When the wrong-hearted reply, "Down with him!" we thank them for the unconscious homage which they thus pay to decision of character.

No child of God should court the world's approbation. Certainly Luther did not. He pleased God, and that was enough for him.

His faith was of this kind also—that it moved him to *a hearty reverence for what he believed to be Holy Scripture.* I am sorry that he was not always wise in his judgment of what the Bible contains, yet to him Scripture was the last court of appeal. If any had convinced Luther of error out of that Book, he would gladly have retracted. But that was not their plan; they simply said, "He is a heretic; condemn him or make him retract."

To this he never yielded for an instant. Alas, in this age numbers of men are setting up to be their own inspired writers. I have been told that every man who is his own lawyer has a fool for his client. And I am inclined to think that, when any man sets up to be his own saviour and his own revelation, much the same thing occurs. That conceited idea is in the air at this present: every man is excogitating his own Bible.

Not so Luther. He loved the sacred Book! He fought by its help. It was his battle-axe and weapon of war. A text of Scripture fired his soul; but the words of tradition he rejected.

He would not yield to Melancthon or Zwingle or Calvin or whoever it might be, however learned or pious. He took his own personal faith to the Scripture and, according to his light, followed the Word of the Lord. May many a Luther be in this place!

The next thing I note was *the intense activity of his faith.* Luther did not believe in God doing his own work, so as to lie by in idleness himself. Not a bit of it.

A disciple once said to Mahomet, "I am going to turn my camel loose and trust in providence." "No," said Mahomet, "trust in providence, but tie up your camel carefully." This resembled Oliver Cromwell's Puritan precept, "Trust in God, but keep your powder dry." Luther believed above most men in keeping his powder dry. How he worked! By pen, by mouth, by hand; he was energetic almost beyond belief.

He seemed a many-handed man. He did works which would have taxed the strength of hundreds of smaller men. He worked as if everything depended upon his own activity; then he fell back in holy trust upon God as though he had done nothing. This is the kind of faith which saves a man both in this life and in that which is to come.

Again, *Luther's faith abounded in prayer.* What supplications they were! Those who heard them tell us of his tears, his wrestlings, his holy arguments. He would go into his closet heavy at heart and remain there an hour or two, then come forth singing, "I have conquered, I have conquered." "Ah," said he one day, "I have so much to do today that I cannot get through it with less than three hours' prayer." I thought he was going to say, "I cannot afford to give even a quarter of an hour to prayer"; but he increased his prayer as he increased his labor.

This is the faith that saves—a faith that lays hold on God and prevails with Him in private supplication.

Dukes Could Not Stop Him

His was a faith that *delivered him entirely from the fear of man.* Duke George is going to stop him. "Is he?" said Luther. "If it were to rain Duke Georges, I would go." He is exhorted not to go to Worms, for he will be in danger. If there were as many devils in Worms as there are tiles on the housetops, he would be there. And he was there, as you all know, playing the man for the Gospel and for his God.

He committed himself to no man, but kept his faith in God pure and unmingled. Dukes, emperors, doctors, electors were all as nothing to Luther when they stood against the Lord. Be it so with us also.

His was a faith that made him risk all for the truth. There seemed no hope of his ever coming back from Worms alive. He was pretty sure to be burned like John Huss; and the wonder is that he escaped. His very daring brought him safety from peril. He expressed his regret that the crown of martyrdom would, in all probability, be missed by him; but the faith which is prepared to die for Jesus was within him.

He who in such a case saves his life shall lose it, but he that loses his life for Christ's sake shall find it unto life eternal.

Religion in a Glass Case

This was the faith that made Luther a man among men and *saved him from priestly affectation.* I do not know whether you admire what is thought to be very superior religion. It is a thing of beauty, but not of use. It ought always to be kept in a glass case. It is made up for drawing rooms and religious meetings, but would be out of place in a shop or on a farm.

Now, Luther's religion was with him at home at the table, as well as in the pulpit. His religion was part and parcel of his common life; and that life was free, open, bold and unrestrained.

It is easy to find fault with him from the superfine standpoint, for he lived in an honest unguardedness. My admiration kindles as I think of the hearty openness of the man. I do not wonder that even ungodly Germans revere him, for he is all a German and all a man. When he speaks, he does not take his words out of his mouth to look at them and to ask Melancthon whether they will do, but he hits hard. He has spoken a dozen sentences before he has thought whether they are polished or not.

Indeed, he is utterly indifferent to criticism. He speaks what he thinks and feels. He is at his ease, for he feels at home: is he not everywhere in his great Father's house? Has he not a pure and simple intent to speak the truth and do the right?

Luther's Homelife

I like Luther with a wife and children. I like to see him with his family and a Christmas tree, making music with little Johnny Luther on his knee. I love to hear him sing a little hymn with the children and tell his pretty boy about the horses in Heaven with golden bridles and silver saddles. Faith had not taken away his manhood but sanctified it to noblest uses. Luther did not live and move as if he were a mere cleric, but as a brother to our common humanity.

After all, brethren, you must know that the greatest divines have to eat bread and butter like other people. They shut their eyes before they sleep, and they open them in the morning, just like other folks. This is matter of fact, though some stilted gentlemen might like us to doubt it. They feel and think like other men. Why should they seem as if they did not? Is it not a good thing to eat and drink to the glory of God and show people that common things can be sanctified by the Word of God and prayer?

What if we do not wear canonicals? The best vestments in the world are thorough devotion to the Lord's work. If a man lives aright, he makes every garment a vestment, every meal a sacrament, every house a temple. All our hours are canonical, all our days holy days, every breath incense, every pulse music for the Most High.

Luther's Charity

They tell us that Luther ignored good works. It is true he would not allow good works to be spoken of as the means of salvation; but of those who professed faith in Jesus, he demanded holy lives.

Luther abounded in prayer and charity. What an almsgiver he was! I fear he did not at all times duly regard the principles of the Charity Organization Society. As he goes along, if there are beggars he empties his pockets for them. Two hundred crowns have just come in; and though he has a family about him, he cries, "Two hundred crowns! God is giving me my portion in this life." "Here," says he to a poor brother minister, "take half. And where are the poor? Fetch them in. I must be rid of this!"

I am afraid that his Catherine was forced at times to shake her head at him; for, in truth, he was not always the most economical husband that might be. In almsgiving, he was second to none, and in all the duties of life he rose far beyond the level of his age.

Like all other men, he had his faults; but as his enemies harp on that string and go far beyond the truth, I need not dwell upon his failings. I wish that the detractors of Luther were half as good as he. All the glory of his grand career be unto the Lord alone.

Last, Luther's faith was a faith that *helped him under struggles that are seldom spoken of.*

I suppose that never man had greater soul-conflict than he. He was a man of heights and depths. Sometimes he went up to Heaven and sang his hallelujahs; then he went down again into the abyss with his "misereres."

Great, vigorous man that he was, he had a bad liver. He was grievously afflicted in body in ways which I need not mention, which sometimes laid him aside for months together, being so racked and tortured that he longed to die. His pains were extreme, and we wonder how he endured them so well.

But ever between the attacks of illness, Luther was up again preaching the Word of God. Those desperate struggles with the Devil would have crushed him but for his faith. The Devil seems to have been constantly assailing him, and he was constantly assailing the Devil. In that tremendous duel, he fell back upon his Lord and, trusting in Omnipotence, put Satan to rout.

Young men, I pray that a Luther may spring up from your ranks. How gladly would the faithful welcome him! I, who am more a follower of Calvin than of Luther, and much more a follower of Jesus than of either of them, would be charmed to see another Luther upon this earth.

God bless you, brethren, for Christ's sake. Amen.

CHAPTER IV

The Best War Cry

"The Lord his God is with him, and the shout of a king is among them."—Num. 23:21.

It was a singular spectacle to see the king of Moab and his lords climbing to the tops of the craggy rocks, accompanied by that strange being, the Eastern prophet Balaam. They are seeking to look upon Israel with the evil eye and flash down curses upon her tents in the plain beneath.

You see them gazing down from the mountains upon the encampment in the wilderness below, like vultures from aloft spy out their prey. They watch with keen and cruel eyes. Cunning and malice are in their countenances. How Balak longs to crush the nation which he fears! They are secretly endeavoring by spell and enchantment to bring evil upon the people whom Jehovah has chosen and led into the wilderness.

You see them offering their seven bullocks and seven rams upon the seven altars which they have set upon Pisgah's rocks. Balaam retires to wait until the afflatus shall come upon him and he shall be able to prophesy. In all probability Moses knew nothing about this at the time; certainly the people below knew nothing of the foul conspiracy.

There lay the tribes in the valley, unaware that mischief was brewing and quite unable to meet the dark design even if they had been aware of it. What a mercy it was for them that they were guarded by a Watcher and a Holy One whose eyes can never slumber. How true it is—"I the Lord do keep it; I will water it every moment: lest any hurt it, I will keep it night and day."

The Lord's eyes are fixed upon Balaam the hireling and Balak the son of Zippor. In vain do they weave the enchantment and work the divination. They shall be utterly ashamed and confounded. They were baffled in their machinations and utterly defeated in their schemes, and that for one single reason: it is written, "JEHOVAH SHAMMAH—the Lord is there."

God's presence in the midst of His people is as a wall of fire round about them and a glory in their midst. The Lord is their light and their salvation; whom shall they fear?

Crafty Intrigues

At this present time God has a people, a remnant according to the election of grace, who still dwell like sheep in the midst of wolves. When, as a part of the Lord's church, we look at our surroundings, we see much that might cause us alarm; for never, either day or night, is Satan quiet. Like a roaring lion, he goeth about seeking whom he may devour. He plots in secret his crafty devices. If it were possible, he would deceive even the very elect.

This prince of darkness has on earth many most diligent servants, compassing sea and land to make proselytes, laying out all their strength and using all their craft and cunning if by any means they may destroy the kingdom of God and blot out the truth from under Heaven.

It is saddest of all to see certain men who know the truth in some degree, as Balaam did, entering into league with the adversary against the true Israel. These combine their arts and use all possible means that the Gospel of the grace of God and the church that holds it, may utterly be destroyed. If the church be not destroyed, it will be no thanks to her enemies; for they would swallow her up quick.

When we look upon the signs of the times, our hearts grow heavy. Iniquity abounds. The love of many waxes cold. Many false spirits have gone abroad into the earth. And some whom we looked upon as helpers are proving themselves to be of another order. What then? Are we dismayed? By no means, for that same God who was in the midst of the church in the wilderness is in the church of these last days.

The Immortal Church

Again shall her adversaries be defeated. Still will He defend her, for the Lord has built His church upon a rock, and the gates of Hell shall not prevail against her. The reason of her safety is this:

God in the midst of her doth dwell,
Nothing shall her remove;

> *The Lord to her a helper shall,*
> *And that right early, prove.*

Our text declares the grand safeguard of the church of God, ensuring her against every peril known and unknown, earthly or satanic: "Jehovah his God is with him, and the shout of a king is among them."

May the Holy Spirit help me while I try to speak first upon *God's presence with His people*; second, upon *the results of that presence*; third, upon *how, by the grace of God, that presence may be preserved continually amongst us.*

First, let me speak a little upon

I. GOD'S PRESENCE AMONG HIS PEOPLE

It is an extraordinary presence, for God's ordinary and usual presence is everywhere. Whither shall we flee from His presence? He is in the highest heaven and in the lowest hell. The hand of the Lord is upon the high hills, and His power is in all deep places.

A Peculiar Presence

This knowledge is too high and wonderful for us, yet everywhere is God. In Him we live and move and have our being. Still there is a peculiar presence, for God was among His people in the wilderness as He was not among the Moabites and the Edomites their foes. And God is in His church as He is not in the world.

It is a peculiar promise of the covenant that God will dwell with His people and walk among them. By the gift of the Holy Spirit, the Lord is with us and in us at this hour. He saith of His church, "Here will I dwell, for I have desired it." This is much more than God's being about us. It includes the favor of God towards us, His consideration of us, His working with us. An active nearness to bless is the presence of which we speak.

Here we may say with great reverence that God is with His people *in the entireness of His nature*. The Father is with us, for the Father Himself loveth us. "Like as a father pitieth his children, so the Lord pitieth them that fear him."

He is near to us, supplying our needs, guiding our steps, helping us in time and tutoring us for eternity. God is where His children are, hearing every groan of their sorrow, marking every tear of their distress.

The Father is in the midst of His family, acting a father's part towards them. "Lord, thou hast been our dwelling-place in all generations." He is never far from any into whose breasts He has put the Spirit of adoption whereby we cry, "Abba, Father!"

Come, ye children of God, rejoice in this: your heavenly Father has come unto you and abides with you.

We have also the presence of the divine Son of God. Said He not to His apostles, "Lo, I am with you alway, even unto the end of the world"? Have we not this for our joy whenever we come together, that we meet in His name and that He still says, "Peace be unto you" and manifests Himself unto us as He doth not unto the world?

Many of you know most delightfully what it is to have fellowship with God, for "truly our fellowship is with the Father, and with his Son, Jesus Christ": this fellowship were not ours if we were not made nigh by His precious blood. Very near are we to the heart of Christ. He dwells with us—yea, He is one with us.

Peculiarly this presence relates to the Holy Ghost. It is He who represents the Lord Jesus who has gone from us. We have a double portion of Christ's Spirit because we see Him now that He is taken up; even as Elisha had a double portion of Elijah's spirit, according to the prophet's saying, "If thou see me when I am taken from thee, it shall be so unto thee"—that is, a double portion of my spirit shall rest upon thee.

It was expedient that our Lord and Master should go, that the Spirit might be given. That Spirit once outpoured at Pentecost has never been withdrawn. He is still in the midst of this dispensation, working, guiding, quickening, comforting, exercising all the blessed office of the Paraclete and being for us and in us God's Advocate, pleading for the truth and for us.

The Glory of the Church

Yes, dear friends, the Father, the Son and the Holy Spirit are in the midst of the true church of God when that church is in a right and healthy state. If the triune God be gone away from the church, then her banners must trail in the dust, for her warriors have lost their strength.

This is the glory of the church of God—to have the grace of the Lord Jesus Christ, the love of God the Father and the communion of the Holy Ghost to be her never-failing benediction. What a glory to have Father, Son and Holy Spirit manifesting the Godhead in the midst of our assemblies and blessing each one of us.

For God to dwell with us—what *a condescending presence* this is! And will God in very truth dwell among men? If the Heaven of heavens cannot contain Him, will He abide among His people? He will! He will! Glory be to His name! 'Know ye not that your bodies are the temples of the Holy Ghost?' God dwelleth in us.

Wonderful word! Who can fathom the depth of this grace! The mystery of the incarnation is equaled by the mystery of the indwelling. That God the Holy Ghost shall dwell in our bodies is as extraordinary as that God the Son should inhabit that body which was born of the blessed virgin.

Strange, strange is this, that the Creator should dwell in His creatures, that the Infinite should tabernacle in finite beings. Yet so it is, for He has said, "Certainly I will be with thee."

What *an awe* this imparts to every true church of God! You may go in and out of certain assemblies, and you may say, "Here we have beauty! Here we have adornment, musical, ecclesiastical, architectural, oratorical and the like!" But to my mind there is no worship like that which proceeds from a man when he feels—the Lord is here. What a hush comes over the soul! Here is the place for the bated breath, the unsandaled foot, the prostrate spirit. Now are we on holy ground.

When the Lord descends in the majesty of His infinite love to deal with the hearts of men, then it is with us as it was in Solomon's Temple when the priests could not stand to minister by reason of the glory that filled the place. Man is set aside, for God is there.

In such a case the most fluent think it better to be silent; for there is at times more expressiveness in absolute silence than in the fittest words. "How dreadful is this place! This is none other but the house of God, and this is the gate of heaven." For why? Because Jacob had said, "Surely the Lord is in this place."

We regard the lowliest assemblies of the most illiterate people with solemn reverence if God be there; we regard the largest assemblies of the wealthiest and most renowned with utter indifference if God be not there.

The one *necessary* of the church is, the Lord God must be in the midst of her, or she is nothing. If God be there, peace will be within her walls and prosperity within her palaces. If the Lord be not there, woe unto the men that speak in His name; for they shall cry in bitterness, "Who hath believed our report?" Woe unto the waiting people, for they shall go away empty! Woe unto the sinners in a forsaken Zion because for them comes no salvation!

The presence of God makes the church to be a joyful, happy, solemn place. This brings glory to His name and peace to His people. But without it, all faces are pale, all hearts are heavy.

Brethren, this presence of God is *clearly discerned* by the gracious, though others may not know it. Yet methinks even the ungracious in a measure perceive it. Coming into the assembly, they are struck with a secret something, they know not what; and if they do not immediately join in the worship of the present God, yet a deep impression is made upon them beyond any that could be caused by the sound of human speech or by the grandeur of outward show. They feel awed and retire abashed.

The Great Enemy

Certainly the Devil knows where God is—none better than he. He hates the camp of which Jehovah is the leader. Against it he doubles his enmity, multiplies his plots and exercises all his power. He knows where his kingdom finds its bravest assailants; therefore, he attacks their headquarters, even as did Balaam and Balak of old.

Let us look at Balaam for a moment. May we never run in the way of Balaam for a reward, but let us stand in his way for a moment that he may be our beacon.

This man had sold himself for gold; and though he knew God and spoke under inspiration, yet he knew Him not in his heart but was willing to curse God's people for hire. He was thwarted in his design because God was there.

It is worth our while to see what kind of a God Jehovah is in Balaam's estimation. He describes our God in verse 19—"God is not a man, that he should lie; neither the son of man, that he should repent: hath he said, and shall he not do it? or hath he spoken, and shall he not make it good?"

Balaam perceived that the God who was in the midst of His people is not a changeable God, not a false god, not one who promises and forgets or promises and eats His words or promises what He cannot and will not perform.

The Sure Promises

The God of Israel is faithful and true, immutable, unchanging. Every one of His promises shall be fulfilled. None of His words shall fall to the ground. "Hath he said, and shall he not do it? hath he spoken, and shall it not come to pass?"

What a joy it is to have such a God as this among us—a promise-making and a promise-keeping God; a God at work for His people, as He has declared He would be; a God comforting and cheering His people and fulfilling in their experience that which His Word had led them to expect. This God is our God forever and ever; He shall be our Guide even unto death.

My dear friends, we sometimes hear men talk of the failure of the church. We are afraid that some churches do fail. Wherever failure occurs, the bottom of it is the absence of the Lord of hosts, for He cannot fail.

Speaking of the district in which he lives, I heard one say:

> We are a religious people. Almost all attend a place of worship, but I am bound to add that of spiritual life we have few traces. One church has given up its prayer meetings; another feels that its entertainments are more important than its worship; and another is notorious for worldliness.

This is a testimony as terrible as it is common.

Dead Christians

The worst thing that can be said of any Christian community is this: "Thou hast a name that thou livest, and art dead." "Thou art neither cold nor hot." Our Lord Jesus says, "I would thou wert cold or hot. So then because thou art lukewarm, and neither cold nor hot, I will spew thee out of my mouth."

A church without life and zeal makes Christ sick; He cannot bear it. He can put up with downright godlessness sooner than with a profession of religion out of which the life and the power are gone, since it has cooled down into lukewarmness.

This, then, we should pray for continually—the presence of God in the midst of His people.

> *Great Shepherd of Thine Israel*
> *Who didst between the cherubs dwell*
> *And ledd'st the tribes, Thy chosen sheep,*
> *Safe through the desert and the deep,*
> *Thy church is in the desert now;*
> *Shine from on high, and guide us through;*
> *Turn us to Thee, Thy love restore;*
> *We shall be saved, and sigh no more.*

To whet your desire for this, let me pass on to the second head of my subject, which is briefly to describe

II. THE RESULTS OF THIS DIVINE PRESENCE

Some of these results are *mentioned in the context.* One of the first is *leading*—"God brought them out of Egypt" (vs. 22). The best critics give us another rendering: "God is bringing them out of Egypt."

When God is in the midst of His people, He is leading them, so that we may cheerfully sing that song, "He leadeth me; He leadeth me," and go on with David to word it, "He leadeth me beside the still waters."

We want no other leader in the church when we have God; for His eye and arm will guide His people.

I am always afraid of having human rules in a church and equally fearful of being governed by human precedents. I am afraid of power being vested in one or two or twenty men; the power must be in the Lord Himself. That church which has God in the midst of it rules itself and goes right without any other guidance but that which comes of the Holy Spirit's working. Such a church keeps together without aiming at uniformity and goes on to victory even though it makes no noise.

That movement is right which is led by God, and that is sure to be all wrong which is led in the best possible way if God be absent. Organization is all very good, but I sometimes feel inclined to join with Zwingle in the battle when he said, "In the name of the Holy Trinity let all loose": for when everybody is free, if God be present, everybody is bound to do the right. When each man moves according to the divine instinct in him, there will be little need of regulations. All is order where God rules.

Just as the atoms of matter obey the present power of God, so do separate believers obey the one great impelling influence.

Oh, for God to be in the church to lead it; then it shall be rightly guided. Do not fall in love with this particular system or that, my brother; do not cry up this scheme of working or that! Get the Spirit of God, and almost any shape that spiritual life takes will be a form of energy suitable for the particular emergency.

God never leads His people wrongly. It is for them to follow the fiery, cloudy pillar. Though it lead them through the sea, they shall traverse it dry-shod. Though it lead them through a desert, they shall be fed. Though it bring them into a thirsty land, they shall drink to the full of water from the rock. We must have the Lord with us to guide us into our promised rest.

The next blessing is *strength*. "He hath as it were the strength of an unicorn" (vs. 22). It is generally agreed that the creature here meant is an extinct species of urus or ox, most nearly represented by the buffalo of the present period. This gives us the sentence, "He hath as it were the strength of a buffalo."

When God is in a church, what rugged strength, what massive force, what irresistible energy is sure to be there!

And how untameable is the living force! You cannot yoke this buffalo to everybody's plough: it has its own free way of living, and it acts after its own style.

When the Lord is with a church, her power is not in numbers, though very speedily she will increase. Her power is not wealth, though God will take care that the money comes when it is needed. Her power lies in God, and that power becomes irresistible, untameable, unconquerable. Force and energy are with the Lord.

I do fear that what many bodies of Christian people need is this force.

Examine yonder religious body. It is huge, but it lacks muscle. It is a fine-looking organization; but soul, sinew and backbone are wanting. Where God is, there is sure to be life-force.

When the Spirit of God descended upon the first saints, they began to speak with wondrous power; and though they were persecuted, they were not subdued. No bit could be put into their mouths to hold them in, for they went everywhere preaching the Word.

Of the true Israel it shall be said—His strength is as the strength of the buffalo: it cannot be controlled or conquered.

The next result is *safety*. "Surely there is no enchantment against Jacob, neither is there any divination against Israel." The presence of God quietly baffles all the attempts of the evil one.

I have noticed in this church, where we have had God's presence in a great measure, that all around us people have gone off to this opinion and to the other fancy; yet our members as a rule have stood firm.

Skepticism, Witchcraft to Be Ignored

Persons say to me, "Do you not sometimes answer the skepticisms of the day?" I answer, No. They do not come in my way. "Do not modern opinions trouble your church?" They have not done so. Why? Because God is there, and spiritual life in vigorous exercise does not fall a victim to disease.

A gracious atmosphere does not agree with modern doubt. When people fall into that evil, they go where the thing is indulged, or at least where it is combated; where in some way or other they can develop their love of novelty and foster the notion of their own wisdom. Infidelity, Socinianism and modern thought can make no headway where the Spirit is at work. Enchantment does not lie against Israel, and divination does not touch Jacob.

If a church will keep to truth, keep to God and do its own work, it can live like a lamb in the midst of wolves without being torn in pieces.

Have God with you, and not only the evil of doctrinal error but every other shall be kept far from you. There was even when Christ was in the church a Judas in the midst of it; and even in the apostles' days there were some that went out from them because they were not of them; for if they had been of them, doubtless they would have continued with them; hence, we may not expect to be without false brethren.

But the true safety of the church is not a creed, not an enactment for expelling those who violate the creed; the presence of God alone can protect His people against the cunning assaults of their foes.

Upon these words, ". . . there is no enchantment against Jacob, no divination against Israel," suffer a few sentences. There are still a few foolish people in the world who believe in witchcraft and spells; but ye, beloved, if you love the Lord, throw such nonsense to the winds. Do you not hear people talk about this being lucky and that unlucky? This notion is heathenish and unchristian. Never utter such nonsense.

But even if there were such things as witchcraft and divination, if this house were full of devils and the air swarmed with invisible spirits of an evil sort, yet if we be the people of God, surely there is no enchantment against us. Divination cannot touch a child of God: the evil one is chained. Wherefore be of good courage: if God be for us, who can be against us?

Signs and Wonders

Further than that, God gives to His people the next blessing, that is of His so *working among them* as to make them a wonder and cause outsiders to raise inquiries about them.

"According to this time it shall be said of Jacob and of Israel, What hath God wrought?" Is not that a singular thing? Here is Balaam with his seven altars, seven bullocks and seven rams. Here is Balak. They are all going to compass some dreadful evil against Israel.

The prophet is a man of great skill in the occult arts; and what does God say? In effect, 'From this hour in which you try to curse them, I will bless them more than ever, until I will make them and their enemies say, "What hath God wrought?"'

Brethren, there is another question, "What hath Israel wrought?" I am glad that Israel's work is not my subject just now because I should make a very wretched sermon out of it. We have better music in the words, "What hath God wrought?" Let me tell not what *I* have done, but what God has done; not what human nature is, but what God's nature is and what the grace of God will work in the midst of His people.

If God be with us, we shall be signs and wonders until those about us shall say, "What is this that God is doing?" Yes, in you, poor Jacob, wrestling, halting on your thigh, men shall see marvels and cry, "What hath God wrought?" Much more shall it be so with you, my brother Israel, you who have prevailed and won the blessing; you are as a prince with God, and you shall make men inquire, "What hath God wrought?"

When God is with His people, He will give them *power of a destructive kind.* Do not be frightened. Here is the text for it: "Behold, the people shall rise up as a great lion, and lift up himself as a young lion"—

that is, as a lion in the fullness of his vigor—"he shall not lie down until he eat of the prey, and drink the blood of the slain."

When He is in it, God has put into His church a most wonderful destructive power as against spiritual wickedness.

A healthy church kills error and tears in pieces evil.

Not so very long ago our nation tolerated slavery in our colonies. Philanthropists endeavored to destroy slavery, but when was it utterly abolished? When Wilberforce roused the church of God and when the church of God addressed herself to the conflict, she tore the evil thing to pieces.

I have been amused with what Wilberforce said the day after they passed the Act of Emancipation. He merrily said to a friend when it was all done, "Is there not something else we can abolish?"

That was said playfully, but it shows the spirit of the church of God. She lives in conflict and victory. Her mission is to destroy everything bad in the land.

See the fierce devil of intemperance, how it devours men! Earnest men have been laboring against it, and they have done something for which we are grateful; but if ever intemperance is put down, it will be when the entire church of God shall arouse herself to protest against it. When the strong lion rises up, the giant of drunkenness shall fall before him. "He shall not lie down until he eat of the prey, and drink the blood of the slain."

I augur for the world the best results from a fully aroused church. If God be in her, there is no evil which she cannot overcome. This crowded London of ours sometimes appalls me. The iniquity which reigns and rages in the lower districts, the general indifference and the growing atheism of the people—these are something terrible. But let not the people of God be dismayed. If the Lord be in the midst of us, we shall do with this as our sires have done with other evils— rise up in strength and not lie down till the evil is destroyed. The destructions, mark you, of God's people are not the destructions of men and women; they consist in the overthrow of sin, the tearing in pieces of systems of iniquity. This it is which God shall help His church to do, He being in the midst of her.

Once more: the results of God's presence are to be seen, not only in the context, but in other matters which we have personally experienced and hope to experience more fully still. Note them.

When God is in a church, there is a *holy awe* upon the hearts of His people; there is also childlike trustfulness, hopefulness, consequent courage and joy.

When the Lord is in the midst of His people, the ordinances of His house are exceeding sweet. Baptism and the Lord's Supper become divinely painted pictures of our burial in Christ and of our life through Him. The preaching of the Word drops as dew and distils as the rain. The meetings for prayer are fresh and fervent. We feel it such a happy thing to be there, we want to stay in them hour after hour. The very house wherein we meet grows beautiful to us; we love the place where our Lord is wont to meet with us.

Then work for Christ is easy, nay, delightful. God's people never want urging on; they are eager for the fray when the Lord is with them. Then, too, suffering for Christ becomes pleasant, yea, any kind of suffering is easily borne.

> I can do all things, or can bear
> All sufferings, if my Lord be there:
> Sweet pleasures mingle with the pains,
> While His left hand my head sustains.

Prayer grows abundant all over the church, both in private and in public. Then life is made vigorous; the feeblest becomes as David, and David like the angel of the Lord. Then love is fervent, unity is unbroken, truth is esteemed, and the living of truth in the life is sought after by all the people of God.

Then the church enlarges the bounds of her tent, for she breaks forth on the right hand and on the left. Then her seed inherits the Gentiles, and the desolate places are inhabited.

Then God gives unto her the holy energy with which she vanquishes nations. When God is with her, she becomes like a sheaf of fire in the midst of the stubble and consumes her adversaries round about. "Fair as the moon, clear as the sun, and terrible as an army with banners" is a church which has God in her midst.

The King's Battle Cry

But now notice one thing in my text, and with that I close this description. Where God is, we are told, *"The shout of a king is among them."*

What is the shout of a king? When great commanders are known to have come into a camp, what a thrill of joy it causes among their trusty warriors! When the soldiers have been much dejected, it has been whispered in their tents,

> The king has come to marshal us,
> All in his armor dressed,

and from that moment every man is cheered up.

At the sight of the king as he comes riding into the camp the host raises a great shout. What means it? It is a shout of loyal love—they are glad to welcome their leader.

So it is when we sing, "The King Himself comes near"; we are all as glad as glad can be. Those who cannot come out to see their Prince because they are lying on their sickbeds in hospitals, clap their hands, while even the little children in their mothers' arms join in the general joy. "The King is come," say they, and His presence kindles their enthusiasm till they make the hills ring again.

Cromwell and Heroes

You know how the stern Ironsides felt when Cromwell came along. Every man was a hero when he led the way. They were ready for any adventure, no matter how difficult, as long as their great chief was there.

That enthusiasm which was inspired by Alexander and by Napoleon and by other great commanders is the earthly image of the spiritual fervor felt by the church when the Lord Jesus is in her midst.

What next? When the King comes and they have received Him with enthusiasm, He cries, "Now is the hour of battle." At once a shout goes up from His warriors who are eager for the fight.

When a clan of Highlanders was led to the battle by their chief, he had only to show them the enemy, and with one tremendous shout they leaped upon them like lions.

It is so with the people of God. When God is with us, then are we strong, resolute, determined. The charge of the servants of God is as the rush of a hurricane against a bowing wall and a tottering fence. In God is our confidence of victory. With God present, no man's heart fails him, no doubt enters the host. "Be strong, and quit yourselves like men" is the word passed round; for their King's eye makes them brave, and the presence of His majesty secures them triumph.

The Great Need

My brethren, let us cry to God, entreating Him to be among us. This it is that you want in your Sunday schools, in your mission halls, in your street preaching, in your tract distributing. It is this that I want beyond everything when I have to speak to you in this vast house. If I could hear the sound of my Master's feet behind me, I would speak though I were lying upon the borders of the grave; but if God be gone, I am bereft of power. What is the use of words without the Spirit? We might as well mutter to the whistling winds as preach to men without the Lord. O God, if Thou be with us, then the shout of a King is among us; but without Thee, we pine away.

Third, let us look at a very important point, and a very practical one, too.

III. THE SECURING AND PRESERVING OF THE PRESENCE OF GOD WITH THE CHURCH

This is a matter that would require several sermons to discuss it fully; but I notice that there is *something even in the confirmation of a church* to secure this.

God is very tolerant, and He bears with many mistakes in His servants and yet blesses them. But depend upon it: unless a church is formed at the very outset upon scriptural principles and in God's own way, sooner or later all the mistakes of her constitution will turn out to be sources of weakness.

Christ loves to dwell in a house which is built according to His own plans, and not according to the whims and fancies of men. The church ought not set up as her authority the decrees of men, either living or dead. Her ruler is Christ. Associations formed otherwise than according to Scripture must fail in the long run. I wish Christians would believe this. Chillingworth said, "The Bible, and the Bible alone, is the religion of Protestants." That is not true.

Certain Protestants have tacked many other things to the Bible, and they are suffering as the result of their folly; for they cannot keep their church from becoming formal. They have admitted a little unhealthy leaven, and it will leaven the whole lump. The dry rot in one part of the house will spread throughout the whole fabric sooner or later. Let us be careful to build on the foundation of Christ; then let every man take heed how he build thereon; for even if the foundation is good, yet if he build with hay and stubble, the fire will cause him grievous loss.

But next, God will only dwell with a church which is *full of life*. The living God will not inhabit a dead church. Hence the necessity of having really regenerated people as members of the church. We cannot secure this in every case with all our watching; tares will grow among the wheat. But if the admission of unregenerate men is usual and there are no restrictions, then the Lord will be grieved and leave us.

God dwelleth not in temples made with hands; He has nothing to do with bricks and mortar; He dwells in living souls. Remember that text: "God is not the God of the dead, but of the living," and it bears this sense among others, that He is not the God of a church made up of unconverted people.

Oh, that we may all live unto God, and may that life be past all question.

That being supposed, we next notice that to have God among us we must be *full of faith*. Unbelief gives forth such a noxious vapor that Jesus Himself could not stop where it was. His strength was paralyzed; 'He could not do mighty works there because of their unbelief.'

Faith creates an atmosphere in which the Spirit of God can work. Meanwhile, the Spirit of God Himself creates that faith so that it is all of His own working from first to last.

Brothers, sisters, do you believe your God? Do you believe up to the hilt? Alas! too many only believe a little. But do you believe His every word? Do you believe His grandest promises? Is He a real God to you, making His words into facts every day of your lives? If so, then the Lord is among us as in the holy place. Faith builds a pavilion in which her King delights to sit enthroned.

With that must come *prayer*. Prayer is the breath of faith. I do not believe God will ever be long with a church that does not pray. I feel certain that when meetings for prayer, when family prayer, when private prayer, when any form of prayer comes to be at a discount, the Lord will leave the people to learn their weakness.

Want of prayer cuts the sinews of the church for practical working. She is lame, feeble, impotent, if prayer be gone.

If anything be the matter with the lungs, we fear consumption. Prayer meetings are the lungs of the church, and anything the matter there means consumption to the church or, at best, a gradual decline, attended with general debility.

O my brothers, if we want to have God with us, pass the watchword round, "Let us pray." Let us pray after the fashion of the widow who was importunate and would not be repulsed. Remember, it is written, "Men ought always to pray, and not to faint." Where prayer is fervent, God is present.

Supposing there is this faith and prayer: we shall also need *holiness of life*. You know what Balaam did when he found he could not curse the people? Satanic was his advice. He bade the king of Moab seduce the men of Israel by the women of Moab that were fair to look upon. These were to fascinate them by their beauty, then to invite them to their idolatrous rites, which rites were orgies of lust. He hoped that the lewdness of the people would grieve the Lord and cause Him to leave them; then Moab could smite them. Sadly, he succeeded.

If it had not been for Phineas, who in holy wrath drove his javelin right through a man and woman in the very act of sin, sparing none in the vehemence of his zeal, Israel had been quite undone.

So in a church. The Devil will work hard to lead one into licentiousness, another into drunkenness, a third into dishonesty, and others into worldliness. If he can only get the goodly Babylonish garment and the wedge of gold buried in an Achan's tent, then Israel will be chased before her adversaries.

God cannot dwell in an unclean church. A holy God abhors the very garments spotted by the flesh. Be ye holy as Christ is holy. Do not take up with this German-silver electrotype holiness, which is so much boasted of nowadays.

Do not be deluded into self-righteousness, but seek after real holiness; and if you do find it, you will never boast about it: your life will speak, but your lips will never dare to say, "See how holy I am." Real holiness dwells with humility and makes men aspire after that which yet lies beyond them. Be holy, upright, just, straight, true, pure, chaste, devout. God, send us this behavior; then we shall keep Him among us as long as we live.

Last, when we have reached to that, let us have *practical consecration*. God will not dwell in a house which does not belong to Him.

The first thing with any one of us is to answer this question: Dost thou give thyself up to Christ, body, soul and spirit, to live and to die for Him? Wilt thou give Him all that thou hast of talent and ability, substance, time and life itself?

Where there is a church made up of consecrated people, there God will remain. There He will make a heaven below. There the shout of a King shall be heard. There His strength shall be revealed. There His glory shall be seen even as it is beheld on High. The Lord send us this, for Jesus' sake. Amen and amen.

CHAPTER V

The Blind Eye and Deaf Ear

(A Lecture to Students)

Having often said in this room that a minister ought to have one blind eye and one deaf ear, I have excited the curiosity of several brethren who have requested an explanation. It appears to them—as it does also to me—that the keener eyes and ears we have, the better.

Well, gentlemen, since the text is somewhat mysterious, you shall have the exegesis of it.

A part of my meaning is expressed in plain language by Solomon in the book of Ecclesiastes (7:21): "Also take no heed unto all words that are spoken; lest thou hear thy servant curse thee." The margin says, "Give not thy heart to all words that are spoken"—do not take them to heart or let them weigh with you; do not notice them or act as if you heard them. You cannot stop people's tongues; therefore, the best thing is to stop your own ears and never mind what is spoken.

There is a world of idle chitchat abroad, and he who takes note of it will have enough to do. He will find that even those who live with him are not always singing his praises and that, when he has displeased his most faithful servants, they have, in the heat of the moment, spoken fierce words which it would be better for him not to have heard.

Who has not, under temporary irritation, said that of another which he has afterwards regretted? It is the part of the generous to treat passionate words as if they had never been uttered. When a man is in an angry mood, it is wise to walk away from him and leave off strife before it be meddled with. If we are compelled to hear hasty language, we must endeavor to obliterate it from the memory and say with David, "But I, as a deaf man, heard not. I was as a man that heareth not, and in whose mouth are no reproofs."

Tacitus describes a wise man as saying to one that railed at him, "You are lord of your tongue, but I am also master of my ears"—you may say what you please, but I will hear what I choose.

We cannot shut our ears as we do our eyes, for we have no ear lids; yet, as we read of him that "stoppeth his ears from hearing of blood," it is, no doubt, possible to seal the portal of the ear so that nothing contraband shall enter.

We would say of the general gossip of the village and of the unadvised words of angry friends—do not hear them; or if you must hear them, do not lay them to heart, for you also have talked idly and angrily in your day and would even now be in an awkward position if you were called to account for every word that you have spoken, even about your dearest friend.

Thus Solomon argued as he closed the passage which we have quoted, "For oftentimes also thine own heart knoweth that thou thyself likewise hast cursed others."

Be Deaf and Blind to Past Differences

In enlarging upon my text, let me say, first, when you commence your ministry, make up your mind to begin with a clean sheet. *Be deaf and blind to the longstanding differences which may survive in the church.* As soon as you enter upon your pastorate, you may be waited upon by persons who are anxious to secure your adhesion to their side in a family quarrel or church dispute. Be deaf and blind to these people. Assure them that bygones must be bygones with you, that as you have not inherited your predecessor's cupboard, you do not mean to eat his cold meat. If any flagrant injustice has been done, be diligent to set it right; but if it be a mere feud, bid the quarrelsome party cease from it and tell him once for all that you will have nothing to do with it.

The answer of Gallio will almost suit you:

"If it were a matter of wrong or wicked lewdness, O ye Jews, reason would that I should bear with you: But if it be a question of words and names, and of your law, look ye to it; for I will be no judge of such matters."

When I came to New Park Street Chapel as a young man from the country and was chosen pastor, I was speedily interviewed by a good man who had left the church, having, as he said, been "treated shamefully." He mentioned the names of half a dozen persons, all prominent members of the church, who had behaved in a very unchristian manner to him. He, poor innocent sufferer, had been a model of patience and holiness.

I learned his character at once from what he said about others (a mode of judging which has never misled me) and made up my mind how to act. I told him that the church had been in a sadly unsettled state and that the only way out of the snarl was for everyone to forget the past and begin again.

He said that the lapse of years did not alter facts. I replied that it would alter a man's view of them if in that time he had become a wiser and better man. However, I added, that all the past had gone away with my predecessors, that he must follow them to their new spheres and settle matters with *them,* for I would not touch the affair with a pair of tongs. He waxed somewhat warm, but I allowed him to radiate until he was cool again.

We shook hands and parted. He was a good man, but constructed upon an uncomfortable principle, so that he came across the path of others in a very awkward manner at times. If I had gone into his narrative and examined his case, there would have been no end to the strife.

I am quite certain that, for my own success and for the prosperity of the church, I took the wisest course by applying my blind eye to all disputes which dated previously to my advent.

Be Not Bribed by Flattery

It is the extreme of unwisdom for a young man fresh from college or from another charge to suffer himself to be earwigged by a clique and to be bribed by kindness and flattery to become a partisan and so to ruin himself with one-half of his people.

Know nothing of parties and cliques, but be the pastor of all the flock and care for all alike. Blessed are the peacemakers. And one sure way of peacemaking is to let the fire of contention alone. Neither fan it, nor stir it, nor add fuel to it, but let it go out of itself. Begin your ministry with one blind eye and one deaf ear.

Regarding Church Finances

I should recommend the use of the same faculty, or want of faculty, with regard to finance in the matter of your own salary. There are some occasions, especially in raising a new church, when you may have no deacon who is qualified to manage that department; therefore, you may feel called upon to undertake it yourselves. In such a case, you are not to be censured—you ought even to be commended.

Many a time also the work would come to an end altogether if the preacher did not act as his own deacon and find supplies both temporal and spiritual by his own exertions. To these exceptional cases I have nothing to say but that I admire the struggling worker and deeply sympathize with him, for he is overweighted and is apt to be a less successful soldier for his Lord because he is entangled with the affairs of this life.

In churches which are well established and can afford a decent maintenance, the minister will do well to supervise all things, but interfere with nothing.

If deacons cannot be trusted, they ought not to be deacons at all. But if they are worthy of their office, they are worthy of our confidence. I know that instances occur in which they are sadly incompetent, yet they must be borne with, and in such a state of things the pastor must open the eye which otherwise would have remained blind.

Rather than the management of church funds should become a scandal, we must resolutely interfere; but if there is no urgent call for us to do so, we had better believe in the division of labor and let deacons do their own work.

We have the same right as other officers to deal with financial matters if we please, but it will be our wisdom as much as possible to let them alone, if others will manage them for us.

When the purse is bare, the wife sickly, and the children numerous, the preacher *must* speak if the church does not properly provide for him; but to be constantly bringing before the people requests for an increase of income is not wise. When a minister is poorly remunerated and he feels he is worth more and the church could give him more, he ought kindly, boldly and firmly communicate with the deacons first. If they do not take it up, he should then mention it to the brethren in a sensible, businesslike way, not as craving a charity, but as putting it to their sense of honor that the "labourer is worthy of his hire."

Let one say outright what he thinks, for there is nothing to be ashamed of; but there would be much more cause for shame if he dishonored himself and the cause of God by plunging into debt: let him therefore speak to the point in a proper spirit to the proper persons and there end the matter. Do not resort to secret complaining.

Faith in God should tone down our concern about temporalities and enable us to practice what we preach, namely—"Take no thought, saying, What shall we eat? or, What shall we drink? or, Wherewithal shall we be clothed?. . . for your heavenly Father knoweth that ye have need of all these things."

Some who have pretended to live by faith have had a very shrewd way of drawing out donations by turns of the indirect corkscrew; but you will either ask plainly, like men, or you will leave it to the Christian feeling of your people and turn to the items and modes of church finance a blind eye and a deaf ear.

Be Blind and Deaf to Gossip

The blind eye and the deaf ear will come in exceedingly well in connection with the gossips of the place. Every church, every village and family, is plagued with certain Mrs. Grundys who drink tea and talk vitriol. They are never quiet, but buzz around to the great annoyance of those who are devout and practical. No one needs to look far for perpetual motion; he has only to watch their tongues.

At tea meetings, Dorcas meetings and other gatherings, they practice vivisection upon the characters of their neighbors; and they are eager to try their knives upon the minister, the minister's wife, the minister's children, the minister's wife's hat, the dress of the minister's daughter, and how many new ribbons she has worn for the last six months, and so on *ad infinitum.*

There are also certain persons who are never so happy as when they are "grieved to the heart" to have to tell the minister that Mr. A. is a snake in the grass, that he is quite mistaken in thinking so well of Messrs. B. and C., and that they have heard quite "promiscuously" that Mr. D. and his wife are badly matched.

Then follows a long string about Mrs. E., who says that she and Mrs. F. overheard Mrs. G. say to Mrs. H. that Mrs. J. should say that Mr. K. and Miss L. were going to move from the chapel and hear Mr. M., and all because of what old N. said to young O. about that Miss P.

Never listen to such people. Do as Nelson did when he put his blind eye to the telescope and declared that he did not see the signal, there-fore would go on with the battle.

Let the creatures buzz—and do not even hear them, unless indeed they buzz so much concerning one person that the matter threatens to be serious; then it will be well to bring them to terms and talk in sober earnestness to them. Assure them that you are obliged to have facts definitely before you, that your memory is not very tenacious, that you have many things to think of, that you are always afraid of making any mistake in such matters and that, if they would be good enough to write down what they have to say, the case would be more fully before you and you could give more time to its consideration.

Mrs. Grundy will not do that; she has a great objection to making clear and definite statements; she prefers talking at random.

I heartily wish that by any process we could put down gossip, but I suppose it will never be done so long as the human race continues what it is; for James tells us that "every kind of beasts, and of birds, and of serpents, and of things in the sea, is tamed, and hath been tamed of mankind: but the tongue can no man tame; it is an unruly evil, full of deadly poison."

What can't be cured must be endured, and the best way of enduring it is not to listen to it.

Over one of our old castles a former owner has inscribed these lines—

THEY SAY.
WHAT DO THEY SAY?
LET THEM SAY.

Thin-skinned persons should learn this motto by heart. The talk of the village is never worthy of notice. Never take any interest in it except to mourn over the malice and heartlessness of which it is too often the indicator.

In his "Plain Preaching," Mayow very forcibly says:

If you were to see a woman killing a farmer's ducks and geese for the sake of having one of the feathers, you would see a person acting as we do when we speak evil of anyone for the sake of the pleasure we feel in evil speaking. For the pleasure we feel is not worth a single feather, and the pain we give is often greater than a man feels at the loss of his property.

Insert a remark of this kind now and then in a sermon, when there is no special gossip abroad. It may be of some benefit to the more sensible; I quite despair of the rest.

Above all, never join in talebearing yourself. Beg your wife to abstain from it also. Some men are too talkative by half. They remind me of the young man who was sent to Socrates to learn oratory. On being introduced to the philosopher, he talked so incessantly that Socrates asked for double fees. "Why charge me double?" said the young fellow. "Because," said the orator, "I must teach you two sciences: the one, how to hold your tongue, and the other, how to speak."

The first science is the more difficult, but aim at proficiency in it, or you will suffer greatly and create trouble without end.

Avoid Suspicion

Avoid with your whole soul that spirit of suspicion which sours some men's lives. And *to all things from which you might harshly draw an unkind inference, turn a blind eye and a deaf ear.* Suspicion makes a man a torment to himself and a spy towards others. Once begin to suspect, and causes for distrust will multiply around you, and your very suspiciousness will create the major part of them. Many a friend has been transformed into an enemy by being suspected.

Do not, therefore, look about you with the eyes of mistrust, nor listen as an eavesdropper with the quick ear of fear. To go about the congregation ferreting out disaffection like a gamekeeper after rabbits is a mean employment and is generally rewarded most sorrowfully.

Lord Bacon wisely advises "the provident stay of inquiry of that which we would be loath to find." When nothing is to be discovered which will help us to love others, we had better cease from the inquiry; for we may drag to light that which may be the commencement of years of contention.

I am not, of course, referring to cases requiring discipline, which must be thoroughly investigated and boldly dealt with; but I have upon my mind mere personal matters where the main sufferer is yourself. Here it is always best not to know, nor wish to know, what is being said about you, either by friends or foes.

Those who praise us are probably as much mistaken as those who abuse us, and the one may be regarded as a set off to the other, if indeed it be worthwhile taking any account at all of man's judgment.

If we have the approbation of our God, certified by a placid con-science, we can afford to be indifferent to the opinions of our fellow-men, whether they commend or condemn. If we cannot reach this point, we are babes and not men.

Some are childishly anxious to know their friend's opinion of them; but if it contains the smallest element of dissent or censure, they regard him as an enemy forthwith.

Surely we are not popes, and do not wish our hearers to regard us as infallible! We have known men become quite enraged at a perfectly fair and reasonable remark and regard an honest friend as an oppo-nent who delighted to find fault. This misrepresentation on the one side has soon produced heat on the other, and strife has ensued.

How much better is gentle forbearance! You must be able to bear criticism, or you are not fit to be at the head of a congregation. You must let the critic go without reckoning him among your deadly foes, or you will prove yourself a mere weakling.

It is wisest always to show double kindness where you have been severely handled by one who thought it his duty to do so, for he is probably an honest man and worth winning. He who in your early days hardly thinks you fit for the pastorate may yet become your firm-est defender if he sees that you grow in grace, advance in qualification for the work. Do not, therefore, regard him as a foe for truthfully expressing his doubts. Does not your own heart confess that his fears were not altogether groundless? Turn your deaf ear to what you judge to be his harsh criticism and endeavor to preach better.

Persons from love of change, from pique, from advance in their tastes and other causes, may become uneasy under our ministry, and it is well for us to know nothing about it. Perceiving the danger, we must not betray our discovery, but bestir ourselves to improve our sermons, hop-ing that the good people will be better fed and forget their dissatisfac-tion. If they are truly gracious persons, the incipient evil will pass away, and no real discontent will arise; or if it does, you must not provoke it by suspecting it.

Where I have known that there existed a measure of disaffection to myself, I have not recognized it, unless it has been forced upon me; but have, on the contrary, acted towards the opposing person with all the more courtesy and friendliness, and I have never heard any more of the matter.

If I had treated the good man as an opponent, he would have done his best to take the part assigned him and carry it out to his own credit; but I felt that he was a Christian and had a right to dislike me if he thought fit and that if he did so I ought not to think unkindly of him. Therefore, I treated him as one who was a friend to my Lord, if not to me, gave him some work to do which implied confidence in him, made him feel at home, and by degrees won him to be an attached friend as well as a fellow-worker.

The best of people are sometimes out at elbows and say unkind things. *We* should be glad if our friends could quite forget what we said when we were peevish and irritable, and it will be Christlike to act towards others in this matter as we would wish them to do towards us.

Never make a brother remember that he once uttered a hard speech in reference to yourself. If you see him in a happier mood, do not mention the former painful occasion. If he be a man of right spirit, he will in the future be unwilling to vex a pastor who has treated him so generously. If he be a mere boor, it is a pity to hold any argument with him. Therefore, the past had better go by default.

It would be better to be deceived a hundred times than to live a life of suspicion. It is intolerable. The miser who traverses his chamber at midnight and hears a burglar in every falling leaf is not more wretched than the minister who believes that plots are hatching against him and that reports to his disadvantage are being spread.

I remember a brother who believed that he was being poisoned. He was persuaded that even the seat he sat upon and the clothes he wore had, by some subtle chemistry, become saturated with death. His life was one perpetual scare.

Such is the existence of a minister when he mistrusts all around him. Nor is suspicion merely a source of disquietude; it is a moral evil and injures the character of the man who harbors it.

Suspicion in kings creates tyranny, in husbands jealousy, and in ministers bitterness, such bitterness as in spirit dissolves all the ties of the pastoral relation, eating like a corrosive acid into the very soul of the office and making it a curse rather than a blessing.

When once this terrible evil has curdled all the milk of human kindness in a man's bosom, he becomes more fit for the detective force than for the ministry. Like a spider, he begins to cast out his lines and fashions a web of tremulous threads, all of which lead up to himself and warn him of the least touch of even the tiniest midge.

There he sits in the center, a mass of sensation, all nerves and raw wounds, excitable and excited, a self-immolated martyr drawing the blazing fagots about him, and apparently anxious to be burned.

The most faithful friend is unsafe under such conditions. The most careful avoidance of offense will not secure immunity from mistrust but will probably be construed into cunning and cowardice.

Society is almost as much in danger from a suspecting man as from a mad dog, for he snaps on all sides without reason and scatters right and left the foam of his madness.

It is vain to reason with the victim of this folly, for with perverse ingenuity he turns every argument the wrong way and makes your plea for confidence another reason for mistrust.

It is sad that he cannot see the iniquity of his groundless censure of others, especially of those who have been his best friends and the firmest upholders of the cause of Christ.

> I would not wrong
> Virtue so tried by the least shade of doubt;
> Undue suspicion is more abject baseness
> Even than the guilt suspected.

No one ought be made an offender for a word; but when suspicion rules, even silence becomes a crime. Brethren, shun this vice by renouncing the love of self. Judge it to be a small matter what men think or say of you, caring only for their treatment of your Lord.

If you are naturally sensitive, do not indulge the weakness nor allow others to play upon it. Would it not be a great degradation of your office if you were to keep an army of spies in your pay to collect information as to all that your people said of you? And yet it amounts to this if you allow certain busybodies to bring you all the gossip of the place.

Drive the creatures away. Abhor those mischief-making, tattling handmaidens of strife. Those who will fetch will carry, and no doubt the gossips go from your house and report every observation which falls from your lips—with plenty of garnishing of their own.

Remember that, as the receiver is as bad as the thief, so the hearer of scandal is a sharer in the guilt of it. If there were no listening ears, there would be no talebearing tongues. While you are a buyer of ill wares, the demand will create the supply, and the factories of falsehood will be working full-time.

No one wishes to become a creator of lies, yet he who hears slanderers with pleasure and believes them with readiness will hatch many a brood into active life.

Solomon says, "A whisperer separateth chief friends" (Prov. 16:28). Insinuations are thrown out and jealousies aroused till "mutual coolness ensues, and neither can understand why; each wonders what can possibly be the cause. Thus the firmest, the longest, the warmest and most confiding attachments, the sources of life's sweetest joys, are broken up perhaps forever."

This is work worthy of the arch-fiend himself, but it could never be done if men lived out of the atmosphere of suspicion.

As it is, the world is full of sorrow through this cause, a sorrow as sharp as it is superfluous. This is grievous indeed. Campbell eloquently remarks:

> The ruins of old friendships are a more melancholy spectacle to me than those of desolated palaces. They exhibit the heart, which was once lighted up with joy, all damp and deserted and haunted by those birds of ill-omen that nestle in ruins.

O suspicion, what desolations thou hast made in the earth!

Learn to disbelieve those who have no faith in their brethren. Suspect those who would lead you to suspect others. A resolute unbelief in all the scandalmongers will do much to repress their mischievous energies.

In his Cripplegate Lecture, Matthew Poole says:

> Common fame hath lost its reputation long since, and I do not know anything which it hath done in our day to regain it; therefore, it ought not to be credited. How few reports there are of any kind which, when they come to be examined, we do not find to be false! For my part, I reckon, if I believe one report in twenty, I make a very liberal allowance.
>
> Especially distrust reproaches and evil reports, because these spread fastest, as being grateful to most persons who suppose their own reputation to be never so well grounded as when it is built upon the ruins of other men's.

Because the persons who would render you mistrustful of your friends are a sorry set, and because suspicion is in itself a wretched and torment-ing vice, resolve to turn towards the whole business your blind eye and your deaf ear.

Never Hear What Was Not Meant for You

Need I say a word or two about the wisdom of never hearing what was not meant for you. The eavesdropper is a mean person, very little if anything better than the common informer; and he who says he over-heard may be considered to have heard over and above what he should have done.

Jeremy Taylor wisely and justly observes:

> Never listen at the door or window; for besides that it contains in it a danger and a snare, it is also invading my neighbor's privacy and a lay-ing that open which he therefore encloses that it might not be open.

It is a well-worn proverb that listeners seldom hear any good of them-selves. Listening is a sort of larceny, but the goods stolen are never a pleasure to the thief. Information obtained by clandestine means must, in all but extreme cases, be more injury than benefit to a cause.

The magistrate may judge it expedient to obtain evidence by such means, but I cannot imagine a case in which a minister should do so. Ours is a mission of grace and peace. We are not prosecutors who search out condemnatory evidence, but friends whose love would cover a mul-titude of offenses.

The peeping eyes of Canaan, the son of Ham, shall never be in our employ; we prefer the pious delicacy of Shem and Japheth, who went backward and covered the shame which the child of evil had published with glee.

Be Blind and Deaf to Criticism and Praise

To opinions and remarks about yourself turn also as a general rule the blind eye and the deaf ear. Public men must expect public criticism; and as the public cannot be regarded as infallible, public men may expect to be criticized in a way which is neither fair nor pleasant.

To all honest and just remarks we are bound to give due measure of heed; but to the bitter verdict of prejudice, the frivolous faultfind-ing of men of fashion, the stupid utterances of the ignorant, and the fierce denunciations of opponents, we may very safely turn a deaf ear.

We cannot expect those to approve of us whom we condemn by our testimony against their favorite sins; their commendation would show that we had missed our mark.

We naturally look to be approved by our own people, the members of our churches and the adherents of our congregations. When they make observations which show that they are not very great admirers, we may be tempted to discouragement if not to anger. Herein lies a snare.

When I was about to leave my village charge for London, one of the old men prayed that I might be "delivered from the bleating of the sheep." For the life of me I could not imagine what he meant, but the riddle is plain now, and I have learned to offer the prayer myself.

Too much consideration of what is said by our people—whether it be in praise or in depreciation—is not good for us. If we dwell on high with "that great Shepherd of the sheep," we shall care little for all the confused bleatings around us. But if we become "carnal, and walk as men," we shall have little rest if we listen to this, that and the other which every poor sheep may bleat about us.

Perhaps it is quite true that you were uncommonly dull last Sunday, but there was no need that Mrs. Clack should come and tell you that Deacon Jones thought so. It is more than probable that, having been out in the country all the previous week, your preaching was very like milk and water; but there can be no necessity for your going around among the people to discover whether they noticed it or not. Is it not enough that your conscience is uneasy upon the point? Endeavor to improve for the future, but do not want to hear all that every Jack, Tom and Mary may have to say about it.

On the other hand, you were on the high horse in your last sermon and finished with quite a flourish of trumpets: you feel considerable anxiety to know what impression you produced.

Repress your curiosity: it will do you no good to inquire. If the people should happen to agree with your verdict, it will only feed your pitiful vanity. If they think otherwise, your fishing for their praise will injure you in their esteem.

In any case, it is all about yourself, and this is a poor theme to be anxious about. Play the man, and do not demean yourself by seeking compliments like little children when dressed in new clothes, who say,

"See my pretty frock." Have you not by this time discovered that flattery is as injurious as it is pleasant? It softens the mind and makes you more sensitive to slander.

In proportion as praise pleases you, censure will pain you.

Besides, it is a crime to be taken off from your great object of glorifying the Lord Jesus by petty considerations as to your little self. And if there were no other reason, this ought to weigh much with you.

Pride is a deadly sin and will grow without your borrowing the parish water cart to quicken it. Forget expressions which feed your vanity. And if you find yourself relishing the unwholesome morsels, confess the sin with deep humiliation.

Payson showed that he was strong in the Lord when he wrote to his mother:

> You must not, certainly, my dear mother, say one word which even looks like an intimation that you think me advancing in grace. I cannot bear it. All the people here, whether friends or enemies, conspire to ruin me. Satan and my own heart, of course, will lend a hand; and if you join, too, I fear all the cold water which Christ can throw upon my pride will not prevent its breaking out into a destructive flame.
>
> As certainly as anybody flatters and caresses me, my heavenly Father has to whip me: and an unspeakable mercy it is that He condescends to do it.
>
> I can, it is true, easily muster a hundred reasons why I should not be proud; but pride will not mind reason nor anything else but a good drubbing. Even at this moment I feel it tingling in my fingers' ends and seeking to guide my pen.

Knowing something myself of those secret whippings which our good Father administers to His servants when He sees them unduly exalted, I heartily add my own solemn warnings against your pampering the flesh by listening to the praises of the kindest friends you have. They are injudicious, so beware of them.

A sensible friend who will unsparingly criticize you from week to week will be a far greater blessing to you than a thousand undiscriminating admirers if you have sense enough to bear his treatment and grace enough to be thankful for it.

When I was preaching at the Surrey Gardens, an unknown censor of great ability used to send me a weekly list of my mispronunciations and other slips of speech. That he never signed his name was my only cause of complaint against him, for he left me in a debt which I could not acknowledge.

I take this opportunity of confessing my obligations to him, for with genial temper and an evident desire to benefit me, he marked down most relentlessly everything which he supposed me to have said incorrectly. Concerning some of these corrections, he was in error himself; but for the most part, he was right, and his remarks enabled me to perceive and avoid many mistakes.

I looked for his weekly memoranda with much interest, and I trust I am all the better for them. If I had repeated a sentence two or three Sundays before, he would say, "See same expression in such a sermon," mentioning number and page. He remarked on one occasion that I too often quoted the line, "Nothing in my hands I bring," and added, "We are sufficiently informed of the vacuity of your hands." He demanded my authority for calling a man *covechus*; and so on.

Possibly some young men might have been discouraged, if not irritated, by such severe criticisms; but they would have been very foolish, for in resenting such correction they would have been throwing away a valuable aid to progress.

No money can purchase outspoken honest judgment; and when we can get it for nothing, let us utilize it to the fullest extent. The worst of it is that, of those who offer their judgments, few are qualified to form them; and we shall be pestered with foolish, impertinent remarks unless we turn to them all the blind eye and the deaf ear.

In the case of false reports against yourself, for the most part use the deaf ear. Unfortunately, liars are not yet extinct; and, like Richard Baxter and John Bunyan, you may be accused of crimes which your soul abhors.

Be not staggered thereby, for this trial has befallen the very best of men. Even your Lord did not escape the envenomed tongue of falsehood. In almost all cases it is the wisest course to let such things die a natural death.

A great lie, if unnoticed, is like a big fish out of water: it dashes and plunges and beats itself to death in a short time. To answer it is to supply it with its element and help it to a longer life.

Falsehoods usually carry their own refutation somewhere about them and sting themselves to death. Some lies especially have a peculiar smell, which betrays their rottenness to every honest nose. If you are disturbed by them, the object of their invention is partly answered; but your silent endurance disappoints malice and gives you a partial victory which God in His care of you will soon turn into a complete deliverance.

Your blameless life will be your best defense, and those who have seen it will not allow you to be condemned so readily as your slanderers expect. Only abstain from fighting your own battles. In nine cases out of ten your accusers will gain nothing by their malevolence but chagrin for themselves and contempt from others. To prosecute the slanderer is very seldom wise.

I remember a beloved servant of Christ who in his youth was very sensitive and, being falsely accused, proceeded against the person at law. An apology was offered. It withdrew every iota of the charge and was most ample, but the good man insisted upon its being printed in the newspapers.

The result convinced him of his own unwisdom. Multitudes, who would otherwise have never heard of the libel, asked what it meant and made comments thereon, generally concluding with the sage remark that he must have done something imprudent to provoke such an accusation.

He was heard to say that so long as he lived, he would never resort to such a method again, for he felt that the public apology had done him more harm than the slander itself.

Standing as we do in a position which makes us choice targets for the Devil and his allies, our best course is to defend our innocence by our silence and leave our reputation with God.

Enemies Must Sometimes Be Answered

Yet there are exceptions to this general rule. When distinct, definite, public charges are made against a man, he is bound to answer them and answer them in the clearest and most open manner. To decline all investigation is in such a case practically to plead guilty. And whatever may be the mode of putting it, the general public ordinarily regard a refusal to reply as a proof of guilt.

Under mere worry and annoyance, it is by far the best to be altogether passive; but when the matter assumes more serious proportions and our accuser defies us to a defense, we are bound to meet his charges with honest statements of fact.

In every instance counsel should be sought of the Lord as to how to deal with slanderous tongues; and in the issue, innocence will be vindicated and falsehood convicted.

Some ministers have been broken in spirit, driven from their position, even injured in character by taking notice of village scandal.

I know a fine young man, for whom I predicted a career of usefulness, who fell into great trouble because he at first allowed it to be a trouble and then worked hard to make it so. He came to me and complained that he had a great grievance.

It was a grievance, but from beginning to end it was all about what some half-dozen women had said about his procedure after the death of his wife. It was originally too small a thing to deal with. A Mrs. Q. had said that she should not wonder if the minister married the servant then living in his house. Another represented her as saying that he ought to marry her. Then a third, with a malicious ingenuity, found a deeper meaning in the words and construed them into a charge.

Worst of all, the dear sensitive preacher must needs trace the matter out and accuse a score or two of people of spreading libels against him, even threaten some of them with legal proceedings.

If he could have prayed over it in secret or even have whistled over it, no harm would have come of the tittle-tattle. But this dear brother could not treat the slander wisely, for he had not what I earnestly recommend to you, namely, a blind eye and a deaf ear.

Be Blind and Deaf Relative to Other Churches and Pastors

Once more, my brethren, the blind eye and the deaf ear will be useful to you *in relation to other churches and their pastors.*

I am always delighted when a brother in meddling with other people's business burns his fingers. Why did he not attend to his own concerns and not episcopize in another's diocese?

I am frequently requested by members of churches to meddle in their home disputes; but unless they come to me with authority, officially appointing me to be umpire, I decline.

Alexander Cruden gave himself the name of "the Corrector." I have never envied him the title. It would need a peculiar inspiration to enable a man to settle all the controversies of our churches, and as a rule those who are least qualified are the most eager to attempt it.

For the most part, interference, however well intentioned, is a failure. Internal dissensions in our churches are very like quarrels between man and wife: when the case comes to such a pass that they must fight it out, the interposing party will be the victim of their common fury.

No one but Mr. Verdant Green will interfere in a domestic battle, for the man of course resents it, and the lady, though suffering from many a blow, will say, "You leave my husband alone; he has a right to beat me if he likes."

However great the mutual animosity of conjugal combatants, it seems to be forgotten in resentment against intruders.

So, amongst the very independent denomination of Baptists, the person outside the church who interferes in any manner is sure to get the worst of it.

Do not consider yourself to be the bishop of all the neighboring churches, but be satisfied with looking after Lystra or Derbe or Thessalonica or whichever church may have been allotted to your care, and leave Philippi and Ephesus in the hands of their own pastors. Do not encourage disaffected persons in finding fault with their minister or in bringing you news of evil in other congregations.

When you meet your brother ministers, do not be in a hurry to advise them. They know their duty quite as well as you know yours, and your judgment upon their course of action is probably founded upon partial information supplied from prejudiced sources.

Do not grieve your neighbor by your meddlesomeness. We have all enough to do at home, and it is prudent to keep out of all disputes which do not belong to us.

We are recommended by one of the world's proverbs to wash our dirty linen at home. I will add another line to it and advise that we do not call on our neighbors while their linen is in the suds. This is due to our friends and will best promote peace.

"He that passeth by, and meddleth with strife belonging not to him, is like one that taketh a dog by the ears"—he is very apt to be bitten, and few will pity him. Bridges wisely observes:

Our blessed Master has read us a lesson of godly wisdom. He healed the contentions in His own family, but when called to meddle with strife belonging not to Him, He gave answer, "Who made me a judge or a divider over you?"

Self-constituted judges win but little respect; if they were more fit to censure, they would be less inclined to do so.

Many a trifling difference within a church has been fanned into a great flame by ministers outside who had no idea of the mischief they were causing. They gave verdicts upon *ex parte* statements, and so egged on opposing persons who felt safe when they could say that the neighboring ministers quite agreed with them.

My counsel is that we join the "Know-nothings," and never say a word upon a matter till we have heard both sides. Moreover, that we do our best to avoid hearing either one side or the other if the matter does not concern us.

Is not this a sufficient explanation of my declaration that I have one blind eye and one deaf ear and that they are the best eye and ear I have?

CHAPTER VI

C. H. Spurgeon's Last Sermon

The closing words of the last sermon Mr. Spurgeon preached to his congregation in London are given elsewhere in this volume. The following is the last sermon he ever preached. It has a pathetic interest from the fact that with this discourse his lips were sealed. He delivered two addresses to the friends assembled at Mentone—one on the last evening of 1891 by way of retrospect, and the other on the first morning of the new year by way of prospect. He delivered both addresses sitting, and the following is his New Year's discourse:

Passing at this hour over the threshold of the New Year, we look forward, and what do we see? Could we procure a telescope which would enable us to see to the end of the year, should we be wise to use it? I think not. We know nothing of the events which lie before us—of life or death to ourselves or to our friends or of changes of position or of sickness or health. What a mercy that these things are hidden from us!

If we foresaw our best blessings, they would lose their freshness and sweetness while we impatiently waited for them. Anticipation would sour into weariness, and familiarity would breed contempt. If we could foresee our troubles, we should worry ourselves about them long before they came, and in that fretfulness we should miss the joy of our present blessings. Great mercy has hung up a veil between us and the future; there let it hang.

Still, all is not concealed. Some things we clearly see. I say "we," but I mean those whose eyes have been opened; for it is not everyone who can see in the truest sense.

A lady said to Mr. Turner, "I have often looked upon that prospect, but I have never seen what you have put into your picture." The great artist simply replied, "Don't you wish you could see it?"

Looking into the future with the eye of faith, believers can see much that is hidden from those who have no faith. Let me tell you in a few words what I see as I look into the new year.

I see a highway cast up by the foreknowledge and predestination of God. Nothing of the future is left to chance. Not the falling of a sparrow nor the losing of a hair is left to haphazard, but all the events of life are arranged and appointed. Not only is every turn in the road marked in the divine map, but every stone on the road and every drop of morning dew or evening mist that falls upon the grass which grows at the roadside.

We are not to cross a trackless desert; the Lord has ordained our path in His infallible wisdom and infinite love. "The steps of a good man are ordered by the Lord; and he delighteth in his way."

I see, next, a Guide provided as our companion along the way. To Him we gladly say, "Thou shalt guide me with thy counsel." He is waiting to go with us through every portion of the road. "The Lord, he it is that doth go before thee; he will be with thee; he will not fail thee." We are not left to pass through life as though it were a lone wilderness, a place of dragons and owls; for Jesus says, "I will not leave you comfortless; I will come to you."

Though we should lose father and mother and the dearest friends, there is One who wears our nature who will never quit our side. One like unto the Son of Man is still treading the lifeways of believing hearts, and each true believer cometh up from the wilderness, leaning upon the Beloved.

We feel the presence of the Lord Jesus even now, in this room, where two or three are gathered in His name; and I trust we shall feel it through all the months of the year, whether it be the time of the singing of birds or the season of ripe fruits or the dark months when the clods are frozen into iron.

In this Riviera we ought the more readily to realize our Lord's presence because the country is so like "Thy land, O Immanuel!" Here is the land of oil, olive and of figs and of the clusters of Eshcol. By such a blue sea He walked, and up such rocky hills He climbed. But whether here or elsewhere, let us look for Him to abide with us, to make this year truly to be "a year of our Lord."

Beside the way and the Guide, I perceive very clearly, by the eye of faith, *strength for the journey provided.* Throughout the whole distance of the year, we shall find halting places where we may rest and take refreshment, then go on our way singing, "He restoreth my soul."

We shall have strength enough, but none to spare; and that strength will come when it is needed and not before. When saints imagine that they have strength to spare, they turn sinners and are apt to have their locks shorn by the Philistines. The Lord of the way will find the pilgrims with sufficient spending money for the road, but He may not think it wise to burden them with superfluous funds.

God all-sufficient will not fail those who trust Him. When we come to the place for shouldering the burden, we shall reach the place for receiving the strength. If it pleases the Lord to multiply our troubles from one to ten, He will increase our strength in the same proportion. To each believer the Lord still says, "As thy days, so shall thy strength be."

You do not feel that you have the grace to die with; what of that? You are not yet dying. While you have yet to deal with the business and duty of life, look to God for the grace which these require; when life is ebbing out and your only thought is about landing on the eternal shore, then look to God your Saviour for dying grace in dying moments.

We may expect an inrush of divine strength when human strength is failing and a daily impartation of energy as daily need requires. Our lamps shall be trimmed as long as they shall need to burn. Let not our present weakness tempt us to limit the Holy One of Israel.

There is a hospice on every pass over the Alps of life, a bridge across every river of trial which crosses our way to the Celestial City. Holy angels are as numerous to guard us as fallen ones to tempt us. We shall never have a need for which our gracious Father has furnished no supply.

I see most plainly a Power overruling all things which occur in the way we tread. I see an alembic in which all things are transformed. "All things work together for good to them that love God, to them who are the called according to his purpose."

I see a wonder-working hand which turns for us the swords of disease into the ploughshares of correction and the spears of trial into the pruning hooks of discipline. By this divine skill bitters are made sweet and poisons turned to medicines. "Nothing shall by any means harm you" is a promise too strong for feeble faith, but full assurance finds it true. Since God is for us, who can be against us?

What a joy to see Jehovah Himself as our banner and God Himself with us as our Captain! Forward, then, into the New Year, "for there shall no evil befall you."

One thing more—and this is brightness itself: this year we trust we shall see God glorified by us and in us. If we realize our chief end, we reach our highest enjoyment. It is the delight of the renewed heart to think that God can get glory out of such poor creatures as we are.

"God is light." We cannot add to His brightness, but we may act as reflectors which, though they have no light of their own, yet, when the sun shines upon them, reflect His beams and send them where, without such reflection, they might not have come. When the Lord shines upon us, we will cast that light upon dark places and make those who sit in the shadow of death to rejoice in Jesus our Lord.

We hope that God has been in some measure glorified in some of us during the past year, but we trust He will be glorified by us far more in the year which now begins. We will be content to glorify God either actively or passively. We would have it so happen that, when our life's history is written, whoever reads it will not think of us as "self-made men," but as the handiwork of God, in whom His grace is magnified. Not in us may men see the clay, but the Potter's hand.

They said of one, "He is a fine preacher," but of another, "We never notice how he preaches, but we feel that God is great." We wish our whole life to be a sacrifice, an altar of incense continually smoking with sweet perfume to the Most High.

Oh, to be borne through the year on the wings of praise to God! To mount from year to year and raise at each ascent a loftier and yet lowlier song unto the God of our life! The vista of a praiseful life will never close, but continue throughout eternity. From psalm to psalm, from hallelujah to hallelujah, we will ascend the hill of the Lord, until we come into the holiest of all where, with veiled faces, we will bow before the Divine Majesty in the bliss of endless adoration.

Throughout this year may the Lord be with you! Amen.

BOOK III

John Ploughman's Talk
and Pictures

A HANDSAW IS A GOOD THING,
BUT NOT TO SHAVE WITH

Our friend will cut more than he will eat, and shave off something more than hair, then he will blame the saw. His brains don't lie in his beard, nor yet in the skull above it, or he would see that his saw will only make sores.

There's sense in choosing your tools, for a pig's tail will never make a good arrow, nor will his ear make a silk purse. You can't catch rabbits with drums, nor pigeons with plums. A good thing is not good out of its place.

It is much the same with lads and girls. You can't put all boys to one trade, nor send all girls to the same service. One chap will make a London clerk, and another will do better to plow and sow, reap and mow, and be a farmer's boy.

It's no use forcing them; a snail will never run a race, nor a mouse drive a wagon.

> *Send a boy to the well against his will,*
> *The pitcher will break and the water spill.*

With unwilling hounds it is hard to hunt hares. To go against nature and inclination is to row against wind and tide. They say you may praise a fool till you make him useful: I don't know so much about that, but I do know that if I get a bad knife I generally cut my finger, and a blunt axe is more trouble than profit.

No, let me shave with a razor if I shave at all, and do my work with the best tools I can get.

The Wrong Occupation

Never set a man to work he is not fit for, for he will never do it well.

They say that if pigs fly, they always go with their tails forward; awkward workmen are much the same. Nobody expects cows to catch crows, or hens to wear hats.

There's reason in roasting eggs, and there should be reason in choosing servants. Don't put a round peg into a square hole, nor wind up your watch with a corkscrew, nor set a tenderhearted man to whip wife-beaters, nor a bear to be a relieving officer, nor a publican to judge of the licensing laws. Get the right man in the right place, then all goes as smooth as skates on ice; but the wrong man puts all awry, as the sow did when she folded the linen.

It is a temptation to many to trust them with money. Don't put them to take care of it if you ever wish to see it again. Never set a cat to watch cream, nor a pig to gather peaches, for if the cream and the peaches go a-missing, you will have yourself to thank for it. It is a sin to put people where they are likely to sin. If you believe the old saying, When you set a beggar on horseback he will ride to the Devil, don't let him have a horse of yours.

Be Your Own Errand Boy

If you want a thing well done, do it yourself, and pick your tools.

It is true that a man must row with such oars as he has, but he should not use the boathook for a paddle. Take not the tongs to poke the fire, nor the poker to put on the coals. A newspaper on Sundays is as much out of place as a warming-pan on the first of August, or a fan on a snowy day: the Bible suits Sunday a deal better.

He who tries to make money by betting uses a wrong tool and is sure to cut his fingers. As well hope to grow golden pippins on the bottom of the sea as to make gain among gamblers if you are an honest man. Hard work and thrifty habits are the right razor; gambling is a handsaw.

Killing Flies With Sledgehammers

Some things want doing gently, and telling a man of his faults is one of them. You would not fetch a hatchet to break open an egg, nor kill a fly on your boy's forehead with a sledgehammer, and so you must not try to mend your neighbor's little fault by blowing him up sky high. Never fire off a musket to kill a midge, and don't raise a hue and cry about the half of nothing.

Do not throw away a saw because it is not a razor, for it will serve your turn another day and cut your hambone if it won't shave off your stubble. A whetstone, though it cannot cut, may sharpen a knife that will. A match gives little light itself, but it may light a candle to brighten up the room.

Use each thing and each man according to common sense, and you will be uncommonly sensible. You don't milk horses nor ride cows, and by the same rule you must make of every man what he is meant for, and the farm will be as right as a trivet.

Everything has its use, but no one thing is good for all purposes. The baby said, "The cat crew, and the cock rocked the cradle," but old folks knew better: the cat is best at mousing and the cock at rousing. That's for that, as salt is for herrings and sugar for gooseberries and Nan for Nicholas. Don't choose your tools by their looks, for that's best which does best. A silver trowel lays very few bricks.

Pretty Tools but Poor

You cannot curry a horse with a tortoise-shell comb, or fell oaks with a penknife or open oysters with a gold toothpick. *Fine* is not so good as *fit* when work is to be done. A good workman will get on pretty well with a poor tool, and a brave soldier never lacks a weapon; still, the best is good enough for me, and John Ploughman does not care to use a clumsy tool because it looks pretty.

Better ride on an ass that carries you than on a steed which throws you; it is far better to work with an old-fashioned spade which suits your hand than with a newfangled invention you don't understand.

In trying to do good to your fellowmen, the Gospel is out of sight the best instrument to work with. The new doctrine which they call "modern thought" is nothing better than a handsaw, and it won't work a bit.

This fine new nothing of a gospel would not save a mouse, nor move the soul of a tomtit; but the glorious Gospel of Jesus Christ is suited to man's need and by God's grace does its work famously. Let every preacher and teacher keep to it, for they will never find a better. Try to win men with its loving words and precious promises, and there's no fear of labor in vain.

Some praise the balm of Gilead or man's morality; many try the Roman salve or the oil of Babylon; and others use a cunning ointment mixed by learned philosophers; but for his own soul's wounds, and for the hurts of others, John Ploughman knows but one cure, and that is given gratis by the Good Physician to all who ask for it. A humble faith in Christ Jesus will soon bring you this sovereign remedy. Use no other, for no other is of use.

HE LIVES UNDER THE SIGN OF THE CAT'S FOOT

I'M YOUR MATCH   I SCRATCH.

The question was once asked, "When should a man marry?" The merry answer was that for young men it is too soon, and for old men it is too late.

This is all very fine, but it will not wash. Both the wisdom and the folly of men seem banded together to make a mock of this doctrine. Men are such fools that they must and will marry, even if they marry fools. It is wise to marry when we can marry wisely, and then the sooner the better.

How many show their sense in choosing a partner it is not for me to say, but I fear that in many cases love is blind and makes a very blind choice. I don't suppose some people would ever get married at all if love had its wits about it.

It is a mystery how certain parties ever found partners; truly there's no accounting for tastes. However, as they make their bed they must lie on it, and as they tie the knot, they must be tied by it.

If a man catches a tartar, or lets a tartar catch him, he must take his dose of tartaric acid and make as few ugly faces as he can. If a three-legged stool comes flying through the air, he must be thankful for such a plain token of love from the woman of his choice, and the best thing he can do is to sit down on it and wait for the next little article.

Twenty of One and a Score of the Other

When it is said of a man, "He lives under the sign of the cat's foot," he must try and please his pussy, that she may not scratch him more than such cats generally do.

A good husband will generally have a good wife, or make a bad wife better. Bad Jack makes a great noise about bad Jill, but there's generally twenty of one where there's a score of the other.

They say a burden of one's own choosing is never felt to be heavy; but I don't know, some men are loaded with mischief as soon as they have a wife to carry. Yet

> A good woman is worth, if she were sold,
> The fairest crown that's made of gold.

She is a pleasure, a treasure and a joy without measure.

A good wife and health are a man's best wealth; and he who is in such a case should envy no man's place. Even when a woman is a little tart, it is better than if she had no spirit and made her house into a dirt pie. A shrew is better than a slut, though one can be quite miserable enough with either. If she is a good housewife and looks well after the children, one may put up with a Caudle lecture now and then, though a cordial lecture would be a deal better.

A husband is in a pickle indeed if he gets tied up to a regular scold. He might as well be skinned and set up to his neck in a tub of brine.

Did you ever hear the scold's song? Read it, you young folks who think of committing matrimony, and think twice before you get married once.

> *When in the morn I ope mine eyes*
> *To entertain the day,*
> *Before my husband e'en can rise,*
> *I scold him—then I pray.*

> *When I at table take my place,*
> *Whatever be the meat,*
> *I first do scold—and then say grace,*
> *If so disposed to eat.*

> *Too fat, too lean, too hot, too cold,*
> *I always do complain;*
> *Too raw, too roast, too young, too old—*
> *Faults I will find or feign.*

> *Let it be flesh, or fowl, or fish,*
> *It never shall be said*
> *But I'll find fault with meat or dish,*
> *With master or with maid.*

> *But when I go to bed at night*
> *I heartily do weep,*
> *That I must part with my delight—*
> *I cannot scold and sleep.*

> *However, this doth mitigate*
> *And much abate my sorrow,*
> *That though tonight it be too late,*
> *I'll early scold tomorrow.*

When the husband is not a man, it is not to be wondered at if the wife wears the top boots: the mare may well be the best horse when the other horse is a donkey. Well may a woman feel that she is lord and master when she has to earn the living for the family, as is sometimes the case. She ought not to be the head, but if she has all the brains, what is she to do?

Shiftless Husbands

What poor dawdles many men would be without their wives! As poor softy Simpkins says, "If Bill's wife becomes a widow, who will cut the pudding up for him, and will there be a pudding at all?"

It is grand when the wife knows her place and keeps it, and they both pull together in everything. Then she is a helpmeet indeed and makes the house a home.

Old friend Tusser says,

> When husband is absent let housewife be chief,
> And look to their labor who live from their sheaf;
> The housewife's so named for she keepeth the house,
> And must tend on her profit as cat on a mouse.

He is very pat upon it that much of household affairs must rest on the wife, and he writes:

> Both out, not allow,
> Keep home, housewife thou.

Like the old man and woman in the toy which shows the weather, one must be sure to be in if the other goes out. When the king is abroad, the queen must reign at home; when he returns to his throne, he is bound to look upon her as his crown and prize her above gold and jewels. He should feel, "If there's only one good wife in the whole world, I've got her."

John Ploughman has long thought just that of his own wife, and after five and twenty years he is more sure of it than ever. He never bets, but he would not mind wagering a farthing cake that there is not a better woman on the surface of the globe than his own, very own beloved.

A Taste of Tongue

Happy is the man who is happy in his wife. Let him love her as he loves himself, and a little better, for she is his better half.

> Thank God that hath so blest thee,
> And sit down, John, and rest thee.

There is one case in which I don't wonder if the wife does put her mate under the cat's foot, and that is when he slinks off to the public and wastes his wages. Even then love and gentleness is the best way of getting him home. But really, some topers have no feeling and laugh at kindness; therefore, nobody can be surprised if the poor wife bristles up and gives her lord and master a taste of tongue.

Nothing tries married love more than the pothouse. Wages wasted, wife neglected, children in rags. If she gives it him hot and strong, who can blame her? Pitch into him, good woman, and make him ashamed of himself, if you can. No wonder you lead a cat-and-dog life while he is such a sorry dog.

Still, you might as well go home and set him a better example, for two blacks will never make a white. And if you put him in hot water he's sure to get some spirits to mix with it.

A GOOD WORD FOR WIVES

We pulled up the horses at the sign of the "Good Woman."
As there is good entertainment for man, if not for beast,
under that sign, we will make a stay of it and dip our pen into
some of that superfine ink which has no galls in it. When he writes
on so fair a subject, John Ploughman must be on his best behavior.

It is astonishing how many old sayings there are against wives:
you may find nineteen to the dozen of them.

The men years ago showed the rough side of their tongues
whenever they spoke of their spouses. Some of these sayings are
downright shocking; as for instance, that very wicked one,
"Every man has two good days with his wife—the day he marries
her and the day he buries her"; and that other, "He that loseth
his wife and a farthing, has a great loss of the farthing."

Quaint Old Ballad

I recollect an old ballad that Gaffer Brooks used to sing about
a man's being better hung than married; it shows how common
it was to abuse the married life. It is almost too bad to print it,
but here it is as near as I remember it:

> *There was a victim in a cart,*
> *One day for to be hanged,*
> *And his reprieve was granted,*
> *And the cart made for to stand.*

> *"Come, marry a wife and save your life,"*
> *The judge aloud did cry;*
> *"Oh, why should I corrupt my life?"*
> *The victim did reply.*

> *"For here's a crowd of every sort,*
> *And why should I prevent their sport?*
> *The bargain's bad in every part,*
> *The wife's the worst—drive on the cart."*

Now this rubbish does not prove that the women are bad, but

that their husbands are good for nothing, or else they would not make up such abominable slanders about their partners.

The rottenest bough cracks first, and it looks as if the male side of the house was the worse of the two, for it certainly has made up the most grumbling proverbs.

Angelic Women

There have, no doubt, been some shockingly bad wives in the world who have been provoking enough to make a man say:

If a woman were as little as she is good,
A peashell would make her a gown and a hood.

But how many thousands have there been of true helpmeets worth far more than their weight in gold!

There is only one Job's wife mentioned in the Bible and one Jezebel, but there are no end of Sarahs and Rebekahs. I am of Solomon's mind, that, as a rule he that findeth a wife findeth a good thing. If there's one bad shilling taken at the grocer's, all the neighbors hear of it, but of the hundreds of good ones, report says nothing. A good woman makes no noise, and no noise is made about her, but a shrew is noted all over the parish.

Taking them for all in all, they are most angelical creatures and a great deal too good for half the husbands.

It is much to the women's credit that there are very few old sayings against husbands, although in this case sauce for the goose would make capital sauce for the gander; and the mare has as good reasons for kicking as the horse has.

They must be very forbearing, or they would have given the men a Roland for every Oliver. Pretty dears, they may be rather quick in their talk, but is it not the nature of bells and belles to have tongues that swing easy?

Henpecked Husbands

They cannot be so very bad after all, or they would have had their revenge for the many cruel things which are said against them. And if they are a bit masterful, their husbands cannot be such very great victims, or they would surely have sense enough to hold their tongues about it.

Men don't care to have it known when they are thoroughly well henpecked, and I feel pretty certain that the old sayings are nothing but chaff, for if they were true, men would never dare to own it.

A true wife is her husband's better half, his lump of delight, his flower of beauty, his guardian angel, his heart's treasure. He says to her: "I shall in thee most happy be. In thee, my choice, I do rejoice. In thee I find content of mind. God's appointment is my contentment."

In her company he finds his earthly heaven. She is the light of his home, the comfort of his soul and (for this world) the soul of his comfort. Whatever fortune God may send him, he is rich so long as she lives. His rib is the best bone in his body.

> The man who weds a loving wife,
> Whate'er betideth him in life,
>   Shall bear up under all;
> But he that finds an evil mate,
> No good can come within his gate,
>   His cup is fill'd with gall.

A good husband makes a good wife. Some men can neither do without wives nor with them; they are wretched alone in what is called single blessedness, and they make their homes miserable when they get married. They are like Tompkin's dog, which could not bear to be loose and howled when it was tied up.

Happy bachelors are likely to be happy husbands, and a happy husband is the happiest of men.

Bird of Paradise

A well-matched couple carry a joyful life between them, as the two spies carried the cluster of Eshcol. They are a brace of birds of Paradise. They multiply their joys by sharing them and lessen their troubles by dividing them: this is fine arithmetic. The wagon of care rolls lightly along as they pull together, and when it drags a little heavily, or there's a hitch anywhere, they love each other all the more and so lighten the labor.

When a couple fall out, there are always faults on both sides, and generally there is a pound on one and sixteen ounces on the other. When a home is miserable, it is as often the husband's fault as the wife's. Darby is as much to blame as Joan and sometimes more. If the husband won't keep sugar in the cupboard, no wonder his wife gets sour.

Want of bread makes want of love; lean dogs fight. Poverty generally rides a home on the husband's back, for it is not often the woman's place to go out working for wages.

A man down our parts gave his wife a ring with this on it: "If thee don't work, thee sha'nt eat." He was a brute. It is no business of hers to bring in the grist. She is to see it is well used and not wasted; therefore, I say, short commons are not her fault. She is not the breadwinner but the bread maker. She earns more at home than any wages she can get abroad.

STICK TO IT AND DO IT

Set a stout heart to a stiff hill, and the wagon will get to the top of it. There's nothing so hard but a harder thing will get through it; a strong job can be managed by a strong resolution. Have at it and have it. Stick to it and succeed. Till a thing is done, men wonder that you think it can be done; and when you have done it, they wonder it was never done before.

In my picture the wagon is drawn by two horses; but I would have every man who wants to make his way in life pull as if all depended on himself. Very little is done right when it is left to others. The more hands to do work, the less there is done. One man will carry two pails of water for himself; two men will only carry one pail between them; and three will come home with never a drop at all. A child with several mothers will die before it runs alone. Know your business and give your mind to it, and you will find a buttered loaf where a sluggard loses his last crust.

In these times it's no use being a farmer if you don't mean work. The days are gone by for gentlemen to make a fortune off of a farm by going out shooting half their time. If foreign wheats keep on coming in, farmers will soon learn that—

> *He who by the plough would thrive,*
> *Himself must either hold or drive.*

Going to Australia is of no use to a man if he carries a set of lazy bones with him. There's a living to be got in old England at almost any trade if a fellow will give his mind to it. A man who works hard and has his health and strength is a great deal happier than my lord Tom Noddy, who does nothing and is always ailing.

Do you know the old song, "The Nobleman's Generous Kindness"? You should hear our Will sing it. I recollect some of the verses. The first one gives a picture of the hard-working laborer with a large family:

> *Thus careful and constant, each morning he went*
> *Unto his day labor with joy and content;*
> *So jocular and jolly he'd whistle and sing,*
> *As blithe and as brisk as the birds in the spring.*

The other lines are the ploughman's own story of how he spent his life, and I wish that all countrymen could say the same:

> *I reap and I mow, I harrow and I sow,*
> *Sometimes a-hedging and ditching I go;*
> *No work comes amiss, for I thrash and I plough,*
> *Thus my bread I do earn by the sweat of my brow.*
>
> *My wife she is willing to pull in a yoke,*
> *We live like two lambs, nor each other provoke;*
> *We both of us strive, like the laboring ant,*
> *And do our endeavors to keep us from want.*

And when I come home from my labor at night
To my wife and my children in whom I delight,
I see them come round me with prattling noise.
Now these are the riches a poor man enjoys.

Though I am as weary as weary may be,
The youngest I commonly dance on my knee.
I find in content a continual feast
And never repine at my lot in the least.

So, you see, the poor laborer may work hard and be happy all the same; surely those who are in higher stations may do the like if they like.

He is a sorry dog who wants game and will not hunt for it. Let us never lie down in idle despair, but follow on till we succeed.

"Little Sweat, Little Sweet"

Rome was not built in a day, nor much else, unless it be a dog kennel. Things which cost no pains are slender gains. Where there has been little sweat, there will be little sweet. Jonah's gourd came up in a night, but then it perished in a night.

Light come, light go; that which flies in at one window will be likely to fly out at another. It's a very lean hare that hounds catch without running for it, and a sheep that is no trouble to shear has very little wool. For this reason, a man who cannot push on against wind and weather stands a poor chance in this world.

Perseverance is the main thing in life. To hold on, and hold out to the end, is the chief matter. If the race could be won by a spurt, thousands would wear the blue ribbon; but they are short-winded and pull up after the first gallop. They begin with flying and end in crawling backward.

When it comes to collar work, many horses turn to jibbing. If the apples do not fall at the first shake of the tree, your hasty folks are too lazy to fetch a ladder and in too much of a hurry to wait till the fruit is ripe enough to fall of itself.

The hasty man is as hot as fire at the outset and as cold as ice at the end. He is like the Irishman's saucepan, which had many good points about it, but it had no bottom. He who cannot bear the burden and heat of the day is not worth his salt, much less his potatoes.

Before you begin a thing, make sure it is the right thing to do: ask Mr. Conscience about it. Do not try to do what is impossible: ask Common Sense. It is of no use to blow against a hurricane, or to fish for whales in a washing tub. Better give up a foolish plan than go on and burn your fingers with it. Better bend your neck than knock your forehead.

Brag and Perseverance

But when you have once made up your mind to go a certain road, don't let every molehill turn you out of the path. One stroke fells not an oak. Chop away, axe; you'll down with the tree at last!

A bit of iron does not soften the moment you put it into the fire. Blow, smith! Put on more coals! Get it red-hot and hit hard with the hammer, and you will make a ploughshare yet. Steady does it. Hold on, and you have it!

Brag is a fine fellow at crying "Tally-ho!" but Perseverance brings home the brush.

We ought not to be put out of heart by difficulties; they are sent on purpose to try the stuff we are made of—and depend upon it—they do us a world of good. There's a sound reason why there are bones in our meat and stones in our land. A world where everything was easy would be a nursery for babies, but not at all a fit place for men. Celery is not sweet till it has felt a frost, and men don't come to their perfection till disappointment has dropped a half-hundred weight or two on their toes.

Who would know good horses if there were no heavy loads? If the clay was not stiff, my old Dapper and Violet would be thought no more of than Tomkin's donkey. Besides, to work hard for success makes us fit to bear it. We enjoy the bacon all the more because we have got an appetite by earning it.

When prosperity pounces on a man like an eagle, it often throws him down. If we overtake the cart, it is a fine thing to get up and ride; but when it comes behind us at a tearing rate, it is very apt to knock us down and run over us. And when we are lifted into it, we find our leg is broken, or our arm out of joint, and we cannot enjoy the ride.

Patient Waiting

Work is always healthier for us than idleness; it is always better to wear out shoes than sheets. I sometimes think, when I put on my considering cap, that success in life is something like getting married: there's a very great deal of pleasure in the courting, and it is not a bad thing when it is a moderate time on the road. Therefore, young man, learn to wait—and work on.

Don't throw away your rod; the fish will bite some time or other. The cat watches long at the hole, but catches the mouse at last.

The spider mends her broken web, and the flies are taken before long. Stick to your calling, plod on and be content; for, make sure, if you can undergo you shall overcome.

> If bad be your prospects, don't sit still and cry,
> But jump up and say to yourself, "I will try."

Miracles will never cease! My neighbor, Simon Gripper, was taken generous about three months ago. The story is well worth telling. He saw a poor blind man, led by a little girl, playing on a fiddle. His heart was touched, for a wonder. He said to me, "Ploughman, lend me a penny; there's a good fellow."

I fumbled in my pocket, found two halfpence and handed them to him. More fool I, for he will never pay me again.

He gave the blind fiddler one of those halfpence and kept the other—and I have not seen either Gripper or my penny since. Nor shall I get the money back till the gatepost outside my garden grows Ribstone pippins. There's generosity for you!

Poor as a Church Mouse

The old saying which is put at the top of this bit of talk brought him into my mind, for he sticks to it most certainly. He lives as badly as a church mouse and works as hard as if he was paid by the piece and had twenty children to keep. But I would no more hold him up for an example than I would show a toad as a specimen of a pretty bird.

When I talk to you young people about getting on, I don't want you to think that hoarding up money is real success; nor do I wish you to rise an inch above an honest ploughman's lot if it cannot be done without being mean or wicked. The workhouse, prison as it is, is a world better than a mansion built by roguery and greed.

If you cannot get on honestly, be satisfied not to get on. The blessing of God is riches enough for a wise man, and all the world is not enough for a fool. Old Gripper's notion of how to prosper has, I dare say, a great deal of truth in it, and the more's the pity. The Lord deliver us from such a prospering, I say.

That old sinner has often hummed these lines into my ears when we have got into an argument, and very pretty lines they are **not**, certainly:

> To win the prize in the world's great race,
> A man should have a brazen face;
> An iron arm to give a stroke,
> And a heart as sturdy as an oak;
> Eyes like a cat, good in the dark,
> And teeth as piercing as a shark;
> Ears to hear the gentlest sound,
> Like moles that burrow in the ground;
> A mouth as close as patent locks,
> And stomach stronger than an ox.
> His tongue should be a razor blade,
> His conscience india-rubber made,
> His blood as cold as polar ice,
> His hand as grasping as a vice.
> His shoulders should be adequate
> To bear a couple thousand weight;
> His legs, like pillars, firm and strong,

To move the great machine along;
With supple knees to cringe and crawl,
And cloven feet placed under all.

It amounts to this: Be a devil in order to be happy. Sell yourself outright to the old dragon, and he will give you the world and the glory thereof. But remember the question of the old Book: "What shall it profit a man, if he gain the whole world, and lose his own soul?"

ALL IS LOST THAT IS POURED IN A CRACKED DISH

Cook is wasting her precious liquor, for it runs out almost as fast as it runs in. The sooner she stops that game, the better.

This makes me think of a good deal of preaching; it is labor in vain, because it does not stay in the minds of the hearers, but goes in at one ear and out at the other. When men go to market they are all alive to do a trade, but in a place of worship they are not more than half awake and do not seem to care whether they profit or not by what they hear.

I once heard a preacher say, "Half of you are asleep, half are inattentive, and the rest—" He never finished that sentence, for the people began to smile, and here and there one burst out laughing. Certainly, many only go to meeting to stare about.

Attend your church, the parson cries;
To church each fair one goes.
The old ones go to close their eyes,
The young to eye their clothes.

You might as well preach to the stone images in the old church as to people who are asleep. Some old fellows come into our meeting, pitch into their corner and settle themselves down for a quiet snooze as knowingly as if the pew was a sleeping car on the railway. Still, all the sleeping at service is not the fault of the poor people, for some parsons put a lot of sleeping stuff into their sermons. Will Shepherd says they *mesmerize* the people. (I think that is the right word, but I'm not sure.)

I saw a verse in a real live book by Mr. Cheales, the vicar of Brockham, a place which is handy to my home. I'll give it to you:

The ladies praise our curate's eyes:
I never see their light divine,
For when he prays he closes them,
And when he preaches, closes mine.

Well, if curates are heavy in style, the people will soon be heavy in sleep.

Even when hearers are awake, many are forgetful. It is like pouring a jug of ale between the bars of a gridiron, to try and teach them good doctrine. Water on a duck's back does have some effect, but sermons by the hundred are as much lost upon many men's hearts as if they had been spoken to a kennel of hounds.

Preaching to some fellows is like whipping the water or lashing the air. As well talk to a turnip, or whistle to a dead donkey, as preach to these dull ears. A year's sermons will not produce an hour's repentance till the grace of God comes in.

Argufying About Doctrine

We have a good many hangers-on who think that their duty

to God consists in hearing sermons, and that the best fruit of their hearing is to talk of what they have heard. How they do lay the law down when they get argufying about doctrines! Their religion all runs to ear and tongue; neither their heart nor their hand is a scrap the better. This is poor work, and will never pay the piper. The sermon which only gets as far as the ear is like a dinner eaten in a dream. It is ill to lie soaking in the Gospel like a bit of coal in a milkpan, never the whiter for it all.

What can be the good of being hearers only? It disappoints the poor preacher and brings no blessing to the man himself.

Looking at a plum won't sweeten your mouth; staring at a coat won't cover your back; lying on the bank won't catch the fish in the river. The cracked dish is never the better for all that is poured into it. It is like our forgetful heart—it wants to be taken away and a new one put instead of it.

A BLACK HEN LAYS A WHITE EGG

The egg is white enough, though the hen is black as a coal. This is a very simple thing, but it has pleased the simple mind of John Ploughman and made him cheer up when things have gone hard with him.

Out of evil comes good, through the great goodness of God. From threatening clouds we get refreshing showers; in dark mines men find bright jewels; and so from our worst troubles come our best blessings.

The bitter cold sweetens the ground, and the rough winds fasten the roots of the old oaks. God sends us letters of love in envelopes with black borders. Many a time have I plucked sweet fruit from bramble bushes and taken lovely roses from among prickly thorns. Trouble is to believing men and women like the sweet-brier in our hedges. And where it grows there is a delicious smell all around, if the dew do but fall upon it from above.

Cheer up, mates, all will come right in the end. The darkest night will turn to a fair morning in due time. Only let us trust in God and keep our heads above the waves of fear. When our hearts are right with God, everything is right. Let us look for the silver which lines every cloud; and when we do not see it, let us believe that it is there. We are all at school, and our great Teacher writes many a bright lesson on the blackboard of affliction.

Scant fare teaches us to live on heavenly bread; sickness bids us send off for the good Physician; loss of friends makes Jesus more precious; and even the sinking of our spirits brings us to live more entirely upon God. All things are working together for the good of those who love God, and even death itself will bring them their highest gain. Thus the black hen lays a white egg.

> *Since all that I meet shall work for my good,*
> *The bitter is sweet, the medicine is food.*
> *Though painful at present, 'twill cease before long,*
> *And then, oh, how pleasant the conqueror's song!*

HE HAS GOT THE FIDDLE, BUT NOT THE STICK

It often comes to pass that a man steps into another's shoes, yet cannot walk in them. A poor fool of a parson gets into a good man's pulpit, takes the same texts, but the sermons are chalk and not cheese. A half-baked young swell inherits his father's money but not his generosity; his barns but not his brains; his title but not his sense. He has the fiddle without the stick, and the more's the pity.

Some people imagine that they have only to get hold of the plough-handles and they would soon beat John Ploughman. If they had his fiddle, they are sure they could play on it. J. P. presents his compliments and wishes he may be there when it is done.

That I fain would see,
Quoth blind George of Hollowee.

However, between you and me and the bedpost, there is one
secret which John does not mind letting out. John's fiddle is poor
enough, but the stick is a right good one, too good to be called
a fiddlestick.

Do you want to see the stick with which John plays his fiddle?
Here it is. Looking to God for help, John always tries to do his
best, whatever he has to do, and he has found this to be the very
best way to play all kinds of tunes. What little music there is in
John's poor old fiddle comes out of it in that way. Listen to a
scrape or two:

If I were a cobbler, I'd make it my pride
The best of all cobblers to be;
If I were a tinker, no tinker beside
Should mend an old kettle like me.

And being a ploughman, I plough with the best,
No furrows run straighter than mine;
I waste not a moment, and stay not to rest,
Though idlers to tempt me combine.

Yet I wish not to boast, for trust I have none
In aught I can do or can be;
I rest in my Saviour and what He has done
To ransom poor sinners like me.

"GREAT CRY AND LITTLE WOOL," AS THE MAN SAID WHO CLIPPED THE SOW

Our friend Hodge does not seem to be making much of an out at shearing. It will take him all his time to get wool enough for a blanket. His neighbors are telling him so, but he does not heed them, for a man never listens to reason when he has made up his mind to act unreasonably. Hodge gets plenty of music of a sort. Hullah's system is nothing to it, and even Nebuchadnezzar's flutes, harps, sackbuts and dulcimers could not make more din. He gets "cry" enough to stock a Babylon of babies, but not wool enough to stop his ears with.

Now is not this very like the world with its notions of pleasure? There is noise enough—laughter and shouting and boasting—

but where is the comfort which can warm the heart and give peace to the spirit?

Generally there's plenty of smoke and very little fire in what is called pleasure. It promises a nag and gives an egg. Gayety is a sort of flash in the pan, a fifth-of-November squib—all fizz and bang and done for.

The Devil's meat is all bran, and the world's wine turns to vinegar. It is always making a great noise over nutshells. Thousands have had to weep over their blunder in looking for their heaven on earth; but they follow each other like sheep through a gap, not a bit the wiser for the experience of generations.

It seems that every man must have a clip at his own particular pig. He cannot be made to believe that, like all the rest, it will yield him nothing but bristles. Men are not all of one mind as to what is best for them. They no more agree than the clocks in our village, but they all hang together in following after vanity, for to the core of their hearts they are vain.

One shears the publican's hog, which is so fond of the swill tub; he reckons upon bringing home a wonderful lot of wool. But everybody knows that he who goes to the "Woolpack" for wool will come home shorn. The "Blue Boar" is an uncommonly ugly animal to shear, and so is the "Red Lion." Better sheer off as fast as you can; it will be sheer folly to stop.

You may loaf about the tap of the "Half Moon" till you get the full moon in your noodle and need a keeper; it is the place for men whose wits go wool-gathering, but wool there is none.

Another is covetous, who hopes to escape misery by being a miser. His greedy mind can no more be filled than a lawyer's purse. He never has enough, so he never has a feast. He makes money with his teeth by keeping them idle.

That is a very lean hog to clip at, for poverty wants some things, luxury many things, but covetousness wants all things. If we could hoard up all the money in the world, what would it be to us at last? Today at good cheer, tomorrow on the bier. In the midst of life we are in death.

Some, like old Mrs. Too-good, go in for self-righteousness. Their own mouths dub them saints. They are the pink of perfection, the cream of creation, the gems of their generation, yet a sensible man would not live in the same house with them for all the money you could count.

A Saint Abroad and a Devil at Home

They are saints abroad, but ask their maids what they are at home. Great cry and little wool is common enough in religion. You will find that those who crack themselves up are generally cracked, and those who despise their neighbors come to be despised themselves.

Many who try wickedness run into bad company and rake the kennels of vice. I warrant you they may shear the whole sty-ful of filthy creatures and never find a morsel of wool on the whole lot of them.

Loose characters, silly amusements, gambling, wantonness, and such like, are swine that none but a fool will try his shears upon. I don't deny that there's plenty of swinish music—who ever expected that there would be silence in a piggery? But then noise cannot fill the heart, nor laughter lighten the soul.

John Ploughman has tried for himself and knows by experience that all the world is nothing but a hog not worth the shearing: "Vanity of vanities, all is vanity." But yet there is wool to be had. There are real joys to be got for the asking if we ask aright. Below, all things deceive us, but above, there is a true Friend. "Wherefore do ye spend your money for that which is not bread, and your labour for that which satisfieth not?"

This is John Ploughman's verdict, which he wishes all his readers to take note of:

> Faith in Jesus Christ will give
> Sweetest pleasures while we live.
> Faith in Jesus must supply
> Solid comfort when we die.

YOU CAN'T CATCH THE WIND IN A NET

Some people get windmills in their heads and go in for all sorts of silly things. They talk of ruling the nation as if men were to be driven like sheep. They prate of reforms and systems as if they could cut out a world in brown paper with a pair of scissors.

Such a body thinks himself very deep, but he is as shallow as a milkpan. You can soon know him as well as if you had gone through him with a lighted candle, yet you will not know a great deal after all. He has a great head, but very little in it. He can talk by the dozen or the gross and say nothing. When he is fussing and boasting of his fine doings, you soon discover that he makes a long harvest of very little corn. His tongue is like a pig's tail—going all day long and nothing done.

Falling Into the Ditch

This is the man who can pay off the national debt and yet in his little shop he sells two apples in three days. He has the secret of high farming and loses more at it than any man in the county. The more he studies, the more he misses the mark.

He reminds me of a blind man on a blind horse who rode out in the middle of a dark night. The more he tried to keep out of ditches, the more he fell in.

When they catch live red herrings on Newmarket Heath, he will bring out a good thing and line his pockets with gold. Up till now, he says, he has been unlucky. He believes if he were to make a man a coffin he would be sure not to die. He is going to be rich next year, and you will then see what you shall see. Just now he would be glad of half a crown on account, for which he will give you a share in his invention for growing wheat without ploughing or sowing.

It is odd to see this wise man at times when his wits are all up in the moon. He is just like Chang the Chinaman who said, "Here's my umbrella, and here's my bundle; but *where am I?*" He cannot find his spectacles, though he is looking through them. And when he is out riding on his own ass, he pulls up and says, "Wherever is that donkey?"

I have heard of one learned man who boiled his watch and stood looking at the egg, and another who forgot that he was to be married that day, and would have lost his lady if his friend had not fetched him out of his study.

Think of that, my boy, and don't fret yourself because you are not so overdone with learning as to have forgotten your common sense.

Always Laying and Never Hatching

The regular wind catcher is soft as silk and as green as grass, yet he thinks himself very long-headed. Indeed he would be if his ears were taken into the measurement. He is going to do— well—there's no telling what. He is full of wishes but short of will, so his buds never come to flowers or fruit. He is like a hen that lays eggs and never sets on them long enough to hatch a single chick.

Moonshine is the article our friend deals in, and it is wonderful what he can see by it. He cries up his schemes, and it is said that he draws on his imagination for his facts. When he is in full swing with one of his notions, he does not stick at a trifle.

Will Shepherd heard one of these gentry the other day telling how his new company would lead all the shareholders on to Tom Tiddler's ground to pick up gold and silver.

When all the talk was over, Will said to me, "That's a lie with the lid on, and a brass handle to take hold of it."

Rather sharp this of Will, for I do believe the man was caught on his own hook and believed in his own dreams. Yet I did not like him, for he wanted us poor fellows to put our little savings into his hands, as if he could afford to fly kites with laborers' wages.

Wonderful Schemes

What a many good people there are who have religious crazes! They do nothing, but they have wonderful plans for doing everything in a jiffy. So many thousands of people are to give half a crown each, and so many more a crown, and so many more a sovereign, and the meeting house is to be built just so and nohow else.

The mischief is that the thousands of people do not rush forward with their money. The minister and a few hardworking friends have to get it together little by little in the old-fashioned style, while your wonderful schemer slinks out of the way and gives nothing.

I have long ago found out that pretty things on paper had better be kept there. Our master's eldest son had a plan for growing plum trees in our hedges as they do in Kent. But never looking to see whether the soil would suit, he lost the trees which he put in, and that was the end of his damsons.

> *Circumstances alter cases;*
> *Different ways suit different places.*

New brooms sweep clean, but they mostly sweep up dirt. Plough with what you please; I stick to the old horses which have served me so well. Fine schemes come to nothing; it is hard work that does it, whether it be in the world or in the church.

In the laborious husbandman you see
What all true Christians are or ought to be.

NEVER STOP THE PLOUGH TO CATCH A MOUSE

There's not much profit in this game. Think of a man, a boy and four horses all standing still for the sake of a mouse! What would old friend Tusser say to that? I think he would rhyme in this fashion:

> *A ploughman deserveth a cut of the whip,*
> *If for idle pretence he let the hours slip.*

Heaps of people act like the man in our picture. They have a great work in hand which wants all their wits, and they leave it to squabble over some pretty nothing not worth a fig. Old Master Tom would say to them:

> *No more tittle-tattle, go on with your cattle.*

He could not bear for a farmer to let his horses out for carting even, because it took their work away from the farm. So I am sure he would be in a great stew if he saw farmers wasting their time at matches and hunts and the like. He says:

Who slacketh his tillage a carter to be,
For groat got abroad, at home shall lose three;
For sure by so doing he brings out of heart
Both land for the corn and horse for the cart.

The main chance must be minded, and the little things must be borne with. Nobody would burn his house down to kill the black beetles. And it would never answer to kill the bullocks to feed the cats.

If our baker left off making bread for a week while he cracked the cockroaches, what should we all do for breakfast? If the butcher sold no more meat till he had killed all the blowflies, we should be many a day without mutton. If the water companies never gave the Londoners a drink till they had fished every gudgeon out of the Thames, how would the old ladies make their tea?

There's no use in stopping your fishing because of the seaweed, nor your riding because of the dust.

A Grand Mouse Hunt

Now, our minister said to me the other day, "John, if you were on the committees of some of our societies you would see this mouse-hunting done to perfection. Not only committees, but whole bodies of Christian people go mouse-hunting."

"Well," said I, "minister, just write me a bit, and I will stick it in my book; it will be beef to my horseradish."

Here is his writing:

A society of good Christian people will split into pieces over a petty quarrel, or mere matter of opinion, while all around them the masses are perishing for want of the Gospel. A miserable little mouse, which no cat would ever hunt, takes them off from their Lord's work. Again, intelligent men will spend months of time and heaps of money in inventing and publishing mere speculations, while the great field of the world lies unploughed.

They seem to care nothing how many may perish so long as they can ride their hobbies. In other matters a little common sense is allowed to rule, but in the weightiest matters, foolishness is sadly conspicuous.

As for you and me, John, let us kill a mouse when it nibbles our bread, but let us not spend our lives over it. What can be done by a mousetrap or a cat should not occupy all our thoughts.

The paltry trifles of this world are much of the same sort. Let us give our chief attention to the chief things—the glory of God, the winning of souls for Jesus and our own salvation. There are fools enough in the world, and there can be no need that Christian men should swell the number. Go on with your ploughing, John, and I will go on with my preaching and "in due season we shall reap if we faint not."

DON'T CUT OFF YOUR NOSE
TO SPITE YOUR FACE

Anger is a short madness. The less we do when we go mad, the better for everybody; and the less we go mad, the better for ourselves. He is far gone who hurts himself to wreak his vengeance on others. The old saying is, "Don't cut off your head because it aches"; another says, "Set not your house on fire to spite the moon."

If things go awry, it is a poor way of mending to make them worse, as the man did who took to drinking because he could not marry the girl he liked.

He must be a fool who cuts off his nose to spite his face. Yet this is what Dick did when he had vexed his old master, and because he was chid, must needs give up his place, throw himself out of work and starve his wife and family.

Jane had been idle, and she knew it; but sooner than let her mistress speak to her, she gave warning, and lost as good a service as a maid could wish for.

Old Griggs was wrong and could not deny it; yet because the parson's sermon fitted him rather close, he took the sulks and vowed never to hear the good man again. It was his own loss. He wouldn't listen to reason, but was as willful as a pig.

Do nothing when you are out of temper, then you will have less to undo. Let a hasty man's passion be a warning to you: if he scalds you, take heed that you do not let your own pot boil over. Many a man has given himself a box on the ear in his blind rage; ay, and ended his own life out of spite! He who cannot curb his temper carries gunpowder in his bosom, and he is neither safe for himself nor his neighbors.

When passion comes in at the door, what little sense there is indoors flies out at the window. By and by a hasty man cools and comes to himself, like McGibbon's gruel when he put it out of the window; but if his nose is off, in the meantime, who is to put it on again? He will only be sorry once, and that will be all the rest of his life.

Anger does a man more hurt than that which made him angry. It opens his mouth, shuts his eyes, fires his heart, drowns his sense and makes his wisdom folly.

Don't Hunt for a Lost Temper

Old Tompkins told me that he was sorry that he lost his temper. I could not help thinking that the pity was that he ever found it again, for it was like an old shoe with the sole gone and the upper leathers worn out—only fit for a dunghill. A hot-tempered man would be all the better for a new heart and a right spirit.

Anger is a fire which cooks no victuals and comforts no household. It cuts, curses and kills. No one knows what it may lead to; therefore, good reader, don't let it lodge in your bosom. But if it ever comes there, pass the vagrant on to the next parish.

Gently, gently, little pot;
Why so hasty to be hot?
Over you will surely boil,
And I know not what you'll spoil.

The old gent in our picture has a fine nose of his own, and though he will be a fool to cut it off, he would be wise to cut off the supplies which have made it such a size. That glass and jug on the table are the paint pots that he colors his nose with. Everybody knows—whether he knows it or knows it not—that his nose is the outward and visible sign of a good deal of inward and spirituous drink, and the sooner he drops his drops, the better.

So here we will cut off not our nose, but the present subject.

BEWARE OF THE DOG!

J ohn Ploughman has not wearied his friends by preaching; but he makes bold to try his hand at a sermon and hopes he will be excused if it should prove to be only a ploughman's preachment.

If this were a regular sermon—preached from a pulpit, of course—I should make it long and dismal, like a winter's night, for fear people should call me eccentric. As it is only meant to be read at home, I will make it short, though it will not be sweet, for I have not a sweet subject.

The text is one which has a great deal of meaning in it, and is to be read on many a wall: **"Beware of the Dog!"**

You know what dogs are, and you know how you beware of

them when a bulldog flies at you to the full length of his chain; so the words don't need any clearing up.

It is very odd that the Bible never says a good word for dogs. I suppose the breed must have been bad in those eastern parts, or else, as our minister tells me, they were nearly wild, had no master in particular, and were left to prowl about half-starved.

No doubt a dog is very like a man, and becomes a sad dog when he has himself for a master. We are all the better for having somebody to look up to. Those who say they care for nobody and nobody cares for them, are dogs of the worst breed and, for a certain reason, are never likely to be drowned.

1. Beware of Dirty Dogs

Dear friends, I shall have heads and tails like other parsons, and I am sure I have a right to them, for they are found in the subjects before us. Or, as the grand old Book calls them, "evil workers"—those who love filth and roll in it.

Dirty dogs will spoil your clothes, and make you as foul as themselves. A man is known by his company. If you go with loose fellows, your character will be tarred with the same brush as theirs.

People can't be very nice in their distinctions. If they see a bird always flying with the crow and feeding and nesting with them, they call it a crow, and ninety-nine times out of a hundred they are right. If you are fond of the kennel and like to run with the hounds, you will never make the world believe that you are a pet lamb. Besides, bad company does a man real harm, for, as the old proverb has it, if you lie down with dogs, you will get up with fleas.

You cannot keep too far off from a man with the fever and a man of wicked life. If a lady in a fine dress sees a big dog come out of a horse-pond and run about shaking himself dry, she is very particular to keep out of his way. From this we may learn a lesson: when we see a man half gone in liquor, sprinkling his dirty talk all around him, our best place is half a mile off at the least.

2. Beware of All Snarling Dogs

There are plenty of these about. They are generally very small creatures, but they more than make up for their size by their noise. They yap and snap without end. Dr. Watts said—

Let dogs delight to bark and bite,
For God has made them so.

But I cannot make such an excuse for the two-legged dogs I am writing about, for their own vile tempers and the Devil together have made them what they are. They find fault with anything and everything. When they dare they howl, and when they cannot do that they lie down and growl inwardly. Beware of these creatures!

Make no friends with an angry man. As well make a bed of stinging-nettles or wear a viper for a necklace. Perhaps the fellow is just now very fond of you, but beware of him, for he who barks at others today without a cause will one day howl at you for nothing. Don't offer him a kennel in your yard unless he will let you chain him up.

When you see that a man has a bitter spirit and gives nobody a good word, quietly walk away and keep out of his track if you can. Loaded guns and quick-tempered people are dangerous pieces of furniture. They don't mean any hurt, but they are apt to go off and do mischief before you dream of it.

Better go a mile out of your way than get into a fight. Better sit down on a dozen tin tacks with their points up than dispute with an angry neighbor.

3. Beware of Tail-Wagging, Crouching Dogs

They jump up upon you and leave the marks of their dirty paws. How they will lick your hand and fondle you as long as there are bones to be got: like the lover who said to the cook, "Leave you, dear girl? Never, while you have a shilling!"

Too much sugar in the talk should lead us to suspect that there is very little in the heart. The moment a man praises you to your face, mark him, for he is the very gentleman to rail at you behind your back.

If a fellow takes the trouble to flatter, he expects to be paid for it. He calculates he will get his wages out of the soft brains of those he tickles. When people stoop down, it generally is to pick something up. Men don't stoop to flatter you unless they reckon upon getting something out of you.

When you see too much politeness, you may generally smell a rat if you give a good sniff. Young people need to be on the watch against crafty flatterers. Young women with pretty faces and a little money should especially *beware of puppies*.

4. Beware of Greedy Dogs

or a man who never has enough. Grumbling is catching. One discontented man sets others complaining—a bad state of mind to fall into. Folks who are greedy are not always honest, and if they see a chance they will put their spoon into their neighbor's porridge; why not into yours? See how cleverly they skin a flint; before long you will find them skinning you, and as you are not quite so used to it as the eels are, you had better give Mr. Skinner a wide berth. When a man boasts that he never gives anything away, you may read it as a caution, "Beware of the dog!"

A liberal, kindhearted friend helps you keep down your selfishness, but a greedy grasper tempts you to put an extra button on your pocket. Hungry dogs will wolf down any quantity of meat, then look out for more; so will greedy men swallow farms and houses, then smell around for something else.

I am sick of the animals—I mean both dogs and men. Talking of nothing but gold, how to make money and how to save it— why, one had better live with the hounds at once, and howl over your share of dead horse. The mischief a miserly wretch may do to a man's heart no tongue can tell; one might as well be bitten by a mad dog, for greediness is as bad a madness as mortal can be tormented with.

Keep out of the company of screwdrivers, tight-fists, hold-fasts and bloodsuckers: "Beware of dogs."

5. Beware of a Yelping Dog

Those who talk much tell a great many lies, and if you love truth, you had better not love them. Those who talk much are likely enough to speak ill of their neighbors and of yourself among the rest; therefore, if you do not want to be town talk, you will be wise to find other friends.

Mr. Prate-apace will weary you out one day, so you will be wise to break off his acquaintance before it is made. Do not lodge in Clack Street, nor next door to the Gossip's Head. A lion's jaw is nothing compared to a talebearer's. If you have a dog which is always barking and should chance to lose him, don't spend a penny in advertising for him. Few are the blessings which are poured upon dogs which howl all night and wake up honest householders, but even these can be better put up with than those incessant chatterers who never let a man's character rest either day or night.

6. Beware of a Dog That Worries the Sheep

Such get into our churches and cause a world of misery. Some have new doctrines as rotten as they are new; others have new plans, whims and crotchets, and nothing will go right till these are tried. There is a third sort which are out of love with everybody and everything and only come into the churches to see if they can make a row. Mark these and keep clear of them. There are plenty of humble Christians who only want leave to be quiet and mind their own business, and these troublers are their plague.

To hear the Gospel and to be helped to do good is all most of our members want, but these worries come in with their "ologies," puzzlements and hard speeches causing sorrow upon sorrow. A good shepherd will soon fetch these dogs a crack of the head, but they will be at their work again if they see half a chance. What pleasure can they find in it? Surely they must have a touch of the wolf in their nature. At any rate, beware of the dog.

7. Beware of Dogs That Have Returned to Their Vomit

An apostate is like a leper. As a rule, none are more bitter enemies of the cross than those who once professed to be followers of Jesus. He who can turn away from Christ is not a fit companion for any honest man.

There are many abroad nowadays who have thrown off religion as easily as a ploughman puts off his jacket. It will be a terrible day for them when the heavens are on fire above them, and the world is ablaze under their feet.

If a man calls himself my friend, and leaves the ways of God, then his way and mine are different. He who is no friend to the good cause is no friend of mine.

Lastly, finally and to finish up,

8. Beware of a Dog That Has No Master

If a fellow makes free with the Bible, the laws of his country and common decency, it is time to make free to tell him we had rather have his room than his company. A certain set of wonderfully wise men are talking very big things and putting their smutty fingers upon everything which their fathers thought to be good and holy. Poor fools! They are not half as clever as they think they are.

Like hogs in a flower garden, they are for rooting up everything. And some people are so frightened that they stand as if they were struck, and hold up their hands in horror at the creatures.

When the hogs have been in my master's garden and I have had the big whip handy, I warrant you I have made a clearance. I only wish I was a scholar, for I would lay about me among these freethinking gentry and make them squeal to a long metre tune. As John Ploughman has other fish to fry and other tails to butter, he must leave these mischievous creatures and finish his rough ramshackle sermon.

"Beware of the dog!" Beware of all who will do you harm. Good company is to be had; why seek bad? It is said of Heaven, ". . . without are dogs." Let us make friends of those who can go inside of Heaven, for there we hope to go ourselves. We shall go to our own company when we die; let it be such that we shall be glad to go to it.

HOME

That word *"home"* always sounds like poetry to me. It rings like a peal of bells at a wedding, only more soft and sweet and chimes deeper into the ears of my heart. It does not matter whether it means thatched cottage or manor house, home is home, be it ever so homely, and there's no place on earth like it. Green grows the flowered plant on the roof forever, and let the moss flourish the thatch. Sweetly the sparrows chirrup and the swallows twitter around the chosen spot which is my joy and rest.

Every bird loves its own nest. The owl thinks the old ruins the fairest spot under the moon. The fox is of the opinion that his hole in the hill is remarkably cozy.

When my master's nag knows that his head is towards home, he wants no whip, but thinks it best to put on all steam. I am always of the same mind, for the way home to me is the best bit of road in the country. I like to see the smoke out of my own chimney better than the fire on another man's hearth; there's something so beautiful in the way it curls up among the trees.

Your Own Is Always the Best

Cold potatoes on my own table taste better than roast meat at my neighbor's. The honeysuckle at my own door is the sweetest I ever smell. When you are out, friends do their best, but still it is not home. "Make yourself at home," they say, because everybody knows that to feel at home is to feel at ease.

> *East and west,*
> *Home is best.*

Why, at home you are at home, and what more do you want? Nobody grudges you, whatever your appetite may be. And you don't get put into a damp bed. Safe in his own castle, like a king in his palace, a man feels himself somebody, and is not afraid of being thought proud for thinking so.

Every cock may crow on his own dunghill; and a dog is a lion when he is at home. A sweep is master inside his own door. No need to guard every word because some enemy is on the watch, no keeping the heart under lock and key; but as soon as the door is shut it is liberty hall, and none to peep and pry.

I cannot make out why so many workingmen spend their evenings at the public house, when their own fireside would be so much better and cheaper, too. There they sit, hour after hour, boozing and talking nonsense and forgetting the dear good souls at home who are half-starved and weary with waiting for them. Their money goes into the publican's till, when it ought to make their wives and children comfortable. As for the beer they get, it is just so much fool's milk to drown their wits in. Such fellows ought to be horsewhipped. And those who encourage them and live on their spendings deserve to feel the butt end of the whip.

England's Curse

Those beer shops are the curse of this country. No good ever can come of them, and the evil they do, no tongue can tell. The publics were bad enough, but the beer shops are a pest. I wish the man who made the law to open them had to keep all the families that they have brought to ruin. Beer shops are the enemies of home; therefore, the sooner their licenses are taken away, the better. Poor men don't need such places, nor rich men either; they are all worse and no better, like Tom Norton's wife. Anything that hurts the home is a curse and ought to be hunted down, as gamekeepers do the vermin in the copses.

Husbands should try to make home happy and holy. It is an ill bird that fouls its own nest, a bad man who makes his home wretched. Our house ought to be a little church, with holiness to the Lord over the door; but it ought never to be a prison, where there is plenty of rule and order but little love and no pleasure.

Married life is not all sugar, but grace in the heart will keep away most of the sours. Godliness and love can make a man, like a bird in a hedge, sing among thorns and briers, and set others a-singing, too. It should be the husband's pleasure to please his wife, and the wife's care to care for her husband. He is kind to himself who is kind to his wife.

When Husband-Wife Are Well Yoked

I am afraid some men live by the rule of self. When that is the case, home happiness is a mere sham. When husbands and wives are well yoked, how light their load becomes! It is not every couple that is a pair, and the more's the pity. In a true home, all the strife is which can do the most to make the family happy.

A home should be a Bethel, not Babel. The husband should be the house-band, binding all together like a cornerstone, but not crushing everything like a millstone. Unkind and domineering husbands ought not pretend to be Christians, for they act clean contrary to Christ's demands.

Yet a home must be well ordered, or it will become a Bedlam and be a scandal to the parish. If the father drops the reins, the family coach will soon be in the ditch. A wise mixture of love and firmness will do it, but neither harshness nor softness alone will keep home in happy order.

Home is no home where the children are not in obedience: it is rather a pain than a pleasure to be in it. Happy is he who is happy in his children, and happy are the children who are happy in their father.

All fathers are not wise. Some are like Eli and spoil their children. Not to cross our children is the way to make a cross of them. Those who never give their children the rod must not wonder if their children become a rod to them. Solomon says, "Correct thy son, and he shall give thee rest; yea, he shall give delight to thy soul." I am not clear that anybody wiser than Solomon lives in our time, though some think they are.

Home May Be a Hell

Young colts must be broken in, or they will make wild horses. Some fathers are all fire and fury, filled with passion at the smallest fault. This is worse than the other and makes home a little hell instead of a heaven. No wind makes the miller idle, but too much upsets the mill altogether. Men who strike in their anger generally miss their mark. When God helps us to hold the reins firmly, but not to hurt the horses' mouths, all goes well. When home is ruled according to God's Word, angels might be asked to stay a night with us, and they would not find themselves out of their element.

Wives should feel that home is their place and their kingdom, the happiness of which depends mostly upon them. She is a wicked wife who drives her husband away by her long tongue.

A man said to his wife the other day, "Double up your whip." He meant, "Keep your tongue quiet." It is wretched living with such a whip always lashing you.

When God gave to men ten measures of speech, they say the women ran away with nine; and in some cases, I am afraid the saying is true. A dirty, slatternly, gossiping wife is enough to drive her husband mad; and if he goes to the public house of an evening for liquor, she is the cause of it.

It is doleful living where the wife, instead of reverencing her husband, is always wrangling and railing at him. It must be a good thing when such women are hoarse, and it is a pity that they have not as many blisters on their tongues as they have teeth in their jaws.

God save us all from wives who are angels in the streets, saints in the church and devils at home! I have never tasted of such bitter herbs, but I pity from my very heart those who have this diet every day of their lives.

Show me a loving husband, a worthy wife, good children; and no pair of horses that ever flew along the road could take me in a year where I could see a more pleasing sight.

Home is the grandest of all institutions. Talk about parliament! Give me a quiet little parlor. Boast about voting and the Reform Bill if you like, but I go in for weeding the little garden and teaching the children their hymns. Franchise may be a very fine thing, but I should a good deal sooner get the freehold of my cottage, if I could find the money to buy it. Magna Carta I don't know much about; but if it means a quiet home for everybody, three cheers for it.

LIKE CAT, LIKE KIT

Most men are what their mothers made them. The father is away from home all day, and has not half the influence over the children that the mother has. The cow has most to do with the calf. If a ragged colt grows into a good horse, we know who it is that combed him. A mother is therefore a very responsible woman, even though she may be the poorest in the land, for the bad or the good of her boys and girls very much depends upon her.

As is the gardener, such is the garden; as is the wife, such is the family.

Samuel's mother made him a little coat every year, but she had done a deal for him before that. Samuel would not have been Samuel if Hannah had not been Hannah. We shall never see a better set of men till the mothers are better. We must have Sarahs and Rebekahs before we shall see Isaacs and Jacobs. Grace does not run in the blood, but we generally find that the Timothys have mothers of a goodly sort.

Spoiled Children

Little children give their mother the headache; but if she lets them have their own way, when they grow up, they will give her the heartache.

Foolish fondness spoils many, and letting faults alone spoils more. Gardens that are never weeded will grow very little worth gathering. All watering and no hoeing will make a bad crop. A child may have too much of his mother's love, and in the long run, it may turn out that he had too little.

Softhearted mothers rear softhearted children. They hurt them for life because they are afraid of hurting them when they are young. Coddle your children, and they will turn out noodles. You may sugar a child till everybody is sick of it. Boys' jackets need a little dusting every now and then. And girls' dresses are all the better for occasional trimming.

Children without chastisement are fields without ploughing. The very best colts want breaking in. Not that we like severity; cruel mothers are not mothers, and those who are always flogging and faultfinding ought to be flogged themselves. There is reason in all things, as the madman said when he cut off his nose.

Good mothers are very dear to their children. There's no mother in the world like our own mother. My friend Sanders from Glasgow says, "The mither's breath is aye sweet." Every woman is a handsome woman to her own son. That man is not worth hanging who does not love his mother. When good women lead their little ones to the Saviour, the Lord Jesus blesses not only the children, but their mothers as well. Happy are they among women who see their sons and daughters walking in the truth.

He who thinks it easy to bring up a family never had one of his own. A mother who trains her children aright had need be wiser than Solomon, for his son turned out a fool.

Some children are perverse from their infancy: none are born perfect, but some have a double share of imperfections. Do what you will with some children, still they don't improve. Wash a dog, comb a dog, still a dog is but a dog. Trouble seems thrown away on some children. Such cases are meant to drive us to God, for He can turn a blackamoor white and cleanse out the leopard's spots.

It is clear that whatever faults our children have, we are their parents so cannot find fault with the stock they came of. Wild geese do not lay tame eggs. That which is born of a hen will be sure to scratch in the dust. The child of a cat will hunt after mice. Every creature follows its kind. If we are black, we cannot blame our offspring if they are dark, too. Let us do our best with them and pray the mighty Lord to put His hand to the work.

Children of prayer will grow up to be children of praise. Mothers who have wept before God for their sons will one day sing a new song over them. Some colts often break the halter, yet become quiet in harness. God can make those new whom we cannot mend; therefore, let mothers never despair of their children as long as they live.

Are they away from you across the sea? Remember—the Lord is there as well as here. Prodigals may wander, but they are never out of sight of the Great Father, even though they may be "a great way off."

Let mothers labor to make home the happiest place in the world. Those who are always nagging and grumbling will lose hold on their children. The boys will be tempted to spend their evenings away from home. Home is the best place for boys and men, and a good mother is the soul of home.

The smile of a mother's face has enticed many into the right path, and the fear of bringing a tear into her eye has called off many a man from evil ways. The boy may have a heart of iron, but his mother can hold him like a magnet. The Devil never reckons a man to be lost so long as he has a good mother alive.

O woman! Great is thy power! See to it that it be used for Him who thought of His mother even in the agonies of death.

VERY IGNORANT PEOPLE

I have heard tell of a man who did not know a great A from a bull's foot. I know a good many who certainly could not tell what great A or little *a* may mean. But some of these people are not the most ignorant in the world for all that.

For instance, they know a cow's head from its tail. One of the election gentlemen said lately that the candidate from London did not know that. They know that turnips don't grow on trees. And they can tell a mangel-wurzel from a beet root and a rabbit from a hare. There are fine folk who play on pianos who could hardly know as much as that. If they cannot read, they can plough and mow, reap and sow and bring up seven children on ten shillings a week, yet pay their way; and there's a sight of people who are much too ignorant to do that.

The Worst Ignorance

Ignorance of spelling books is very bad, but ignorance of hard work is worse. Wisdom does not always speak Latin. People laugh at smock frocks, and indeed they are about as ugly garments as could well be contrived; but some who wear them are not half such fools as people take them for. If no ignorant people ate bread but those who wear hobnail shoes, corn would be a great deal cheaper.

Wisdom in a poor man is like a diamond set in lead: only judges can see its value. Wisdom walks often in patched shoes and men admire her not; but I say, never mind the coat, give me the man: nutshells are nothing, the kernel is everything. You need not go to Pirbright to find ignoramuses; there are heaps of them near St. Paul's.

I would have everybody able to read and write and cipher; indeed, I don't think a man can know too much. But, mark you, the knowing of these things is not education. There are millions of your reading and writing people who are as ignorant as neighbor Norton's calf that did not know its own mother. This is plain as the nose on your face, if you only think a little.

Horses Not Intended to Fly

To know how to read and write is like having tools to work with; but if you don't use these tools, and your eyes and your ears too, you will be none the better off.

Everybody should know what most concerns him and makes him most useful. It is little use for a horse to know how to fly; it will do well enough if it can trot.

A man on a farm ought to learn all that belongs to farming; a blacksmith should study a horse's foot; a dairymaid should be well up in skimming the milk and making the butter; and a laborer's wife should be a good scholar in the sciences of boiling and baking, washing and mending. And John Ploughman ventures to say that those men and women who have not learned the duties of their callings are very ignorant people, even if they can tell the Greek name for a crocodile, or write an ode on a black beetle.

It is too often very true—

Jack has been to school
To learn to be a fool.

When a man falls into the water, to know how to swim will be of more use to him than all his mathematics, yet how very few boys learn swimming. Girls are taught dancing and French, when stitching and English would be a hundred percent more use to them.

When men have to earn their livings in these hard times, a good trade and industrious habits will serve their turn a world better than all the classics in Cambridge and Oxford; but who nowadays advocates practical training at our schools? Schoolmasters would go into fits if they were asked to teach poor people's boys to hoe potatoes and plant cauliflowers.

If you want a dog to be a pointer or a setter, you train him accordingly; why ever don't they do the same with men? It ought to be, "Every man for his business, and every man master of his business."

Let Jack and Tom learn geography by all means, but don't forget to teach them how to black their own boots and put a button onto their own trousers. And as for Jane and Sally, let them sing and play the music if they like, but not till they can darn a stocking and make a shirt.

When they bring on the new act for general education, I hope they will put in a clause to teach children practical common sense home duties as well as the three Rs and the folderols which I think they call "accomplishments."

There's poor Gent with six girls and about fifty pounds a year to keep his family on, yet not one of them can do a hand's turn, because their mother would go into fits lest Miss Sophis Elfrida should have chapped hands through washing the family linen or lest Alexandra Theodora should spoil her complexion in picking a few gooseberries for a pudding.

It's enough to make a cat laugh to hear the poor things talk about fashion and etiquette, when they are not half so well off as the higgler's daughters down the lane, who earn their own living and are laying money by against the time when some young farmer will pick them up.

Trust me: he who marries these highty-tighty young ladies will have as bad a bargain as if he married a wax doll. How the fat would be in the fire if Mrs. Gent heard me say it! But I do say it for all that. She and the girls are *ignorant, very ignorant,* because they do not know what would be of most service to them.

Every sprat nowadays calls itself a herring; every donkey thinks itself fit to be one of the queen's horses; every candle thinks itself the sun. But when a man with his best coat on, and a paper collar, a glass in his eye, a brass chain on his waistcoat, a cane in his hand, an emptiness in his head, fancies that people cannot see through his swaggers and brags, he must be *ignorant, very ignorant,* for he does not know himself.

Flats, dressed up to the top of the fashion, think themselves somebodies, but nobody else does. Dancing masters and tailors may rig up a fop, but they cannot make a nothing into a man.

You may color a millstone as much as you like, but you cannot improve it into a cheese.

When tradesmen put their earnings into companies and expect to see it again; when they take shares in railways and look for dividends; when they lend money at high interest and think to make their fortunes, they must be *ignorant, very ignorant*. As well hang a wooden kettle over the fire and get ready for tea, or sow beans in a river and look for a fine crop.

When men believe in lawyers and moneylenders (whether Jews or Gentiles), and borrow money and speculate, and think themselves lucky fellows, they are shamefully *ignorant*. The very gander on the common would not make such a stupid of himself, for he knows when anyone tries to pluck him, and won't lose his feathers and pride himself in the operation.

The man who spends his money with the publican and thinks that the landlord's bows and "How do ye do, my good fellow?" mean true respect, is a perfect natural; for with them it is—

> *If you have money, take a seat;*
> *If you have none, take to your feet.*

The fox admires the cheese, not the raven. The bait is not put into the trap to feed the mouse but to catch him. We don't light a fire for the herring's comfort, but to roast him.

He who believes in promises made at elections has long ears and may try to eat thistles. Mr. Plausible has been round asking all the workingmen for their votes, and he will do all sorts of good things for them. Will he? Yes, the day after tomorrow, a little later than never.

Poor men who expect the "friends of the workingman" to do anything for them must be *ignorant, very ignorant*. When they get their seats, of course they cannot stand up for their principles, except when it is to their interest to do so.

Stupid as a Donkey

To lend umbrellas and look to have them sent home; to do a

man a good turn and expect another from him when you want it; to hope to stop some women's tongues; to try to please everybody; to hope to hear gossips speak well of you; or to get the truth of a story from common report—is all evidence of great ignorance. Those who know the world best trust it least; those who trust it at all are not wise. As well trust a horse's heel or a dog's tooth.

Trusting to others ruins many. The mouse knows when the cat is out of the house. Servants know when the master is away. No sooner is the eye of the master gone than the hand of the workman slackens. "I'll go myself" and "I'll see to it" are two good servants on a farm. Those who lie in bed and reckon that their trade will carry on itself are *ignorant, very ignorant.*

When I see a young lady with a flower garden on her head and a draper's shop on her body, tossing her head about as if she thought everybody was charmed with her, I am sure she must be *ignorant, very ignorant.* Sensible men don't marry a wardrobe or a bonnet box; they want a woman of sense, and such dress sensibly.

To my mind, those who sneer at religion and set themselves up to be too knowing to believe in the Bible are shallow fellows. They generally use big words and bluster a great deal; but if they fancy they can overturn the faith of thinking people who have tried and proved the power of the grace of God, they must be *ignorant, very ignorant.* He who looks at the sunrise and the sunset and does not see the footprints of God, must be inwardly blinder than a mole and only fit to live underground. God seems to talk to me in every primrose and daisy, to smile upon me from every star, to whisper to me in every breath of morning air, and call aloud to me in every storm.

They say that man is the god of the dog; that man must be worse than a dog who will not listen to the voice of God, for a dog follows at his master's whistle. They call themselves philosophers, don't they? Their proper name is fools, for the fool hath said in his heart, "There is no God."

The sheep know when rain is coming, the swallows foresee the winter, and even the pigs, they say, can see the wind. Then how much worse than a brute must he be who lives where God is everywhere present, yet sees Him not!

So you see, a man may be a great hand at learning, yet be *ignorant, very ignorant.*

HE LOOKS ONE WAY AND PULLS THE OTHER

He faces the shore, but he is pulling for the ship. This is the way of those who row in boats, and also of a great many who never trust themselves on the water. The boatman is all right, but the hypocrite is all wrong, whatever rites he may practice. I cannot endure Mr. Facing-both-ways, yet he has swarms of cousins.

It is ill to be a saint without and a devil within—to be a servant of Christ before the world in order to serve the ends of self and the Devil, while inwardly the heart hates all good things.

There are good and bad of all classes. Hypocrites can be found among ploughmen as well as among parsons. It used to be so in the olden times, for I remember an old verse which draws out just such a character. The man says:

> I'll have a religion all of my own,
> Whether Papist or Protestant shall not be known;
> And if it proves troublesome I will have none.

In our Lord's day many followed Him, but it was only for the loaves and fishes. They do say that some in our parish don't go quite so straight as the Jews did, for they go to the church for the loaves, then go over to the Baptist chapel for the fishes. I don't want to judge, but I certainly do know some who, if they do not care much for faith, are always following after charity.

Better die than sell your soul to the highest bidder. Better be shut up in the workhouse than fatten upon hypocrisy. Whatever else we barter, let us never try to turn a penny by religion, for hypocrisy is the meanest vice a man can come to.

It is a base thing to call yourself Christ's horse and yet carry the Devil's saddle. The worst kind of wolf is that which wears a sheep's skin. Jezebel was never so ugly as when she had finished painting her face.

Above all things, then, brother laborers, let us be straight as an arrow and true as a die. Never let us be timeservers or turncoats. Never let us carry two faces under one hat, nor blow hot and cold with the same breath.

RUNNING IN DEBT

When I was a very small boy in pinafores and went to a woman's school, it so happened that I wanted a stick of slate pencil, yet I had no money to buy it with. For fear of being scolded for losing my pencils so often—I was a really careless little fellow—I did not dare to ask at home. What then was John to do?

There was a little shop in the place where nuts and tops and cakes and balls were sold by old Mrs. Dearson. Sometimes I had seen boys and girls get trusted by the old lady. I argued with myself that Christmas was coming and that somebody or other would be sure to give me a penny then, and perhaps even a whole silver sixpence. I would therefore go into debt for a stick of slate pencil and be sure to pay at Christmas.

I did not feel easy about it, but still I screwed my courage up and went into the shop. One farthing was the amount. As I had never owed anything before and my credit was good, the pencil was handed over by the kind dame, and *I was in debt*. It did not please me much, and I felt as if I had done wrong, but I little knew how soon I should smart for it.

How my father came to hear of this little stroke of business I never knew, but some little bird or other whistled it to him, and he was very soon down upon me in right earnest. God bless him for it!

Powerful Lecture on the Side of the Head

He was a sensible man and no children spoiler. He did not intend to bring up his children to speculate and play at what big rogues called financing; therefore, he knocked my getting into debt on the head at once, and no mistake. He gave me a very powerful lecture upon getting into debt, how like it was to stealing, and upon the way in which people were ruined by it, and how a boy who would owe a farthing might one day owe a hundred pounds and get into prison and bring his family into disgrace. It was a lecture indeed. I think I can hear it now, and I can feel my ears tingling at the recollection of it.

Then I was marched off to the shop like a deserter marched into barracks, crying bitterly all down the street and feeling dreadfully ashamed, because I thought everybody knew I was in debt.

The farthing was paid amid many solemn warnings, and the poor debtor was set free, like a bird let out of a cage. How sweet it felt to be out of debt! How did my little heart vow and declare that nothing should ever tempt me into debt again! It was a fine lesson, and I have never forgotten it. If all boys were inoculated with the same doctrine when they were young, it would be as good as a fortune to them and save them wagonloads of trouble in life.

God bless my father, say I, and send a breed of such fathers into old England to save her from being eaten up with villainy. What with companies and schemes and paper money, the nation is getting to be as rotten as touch wood.

Debt, Dirt and the Devil

Ever since that early sickening I have hated debt as Luther hated the Pope, so if I say some fierce things about it, you must not wonder. To keep debt, dirt and the Devil out of my cottage has been my greatest wish ever since I set up housekeeping. Although the last of the three has sometimes got in by the door or the window, for the old serpent will wriggle through the smallest crack, yet thanks to a good wife, hard work, honesty and scrubbing brushes, the two others have not crossed the threshold.

Debt is so degrading that if I owed a man a penny I would walk twenty miles in the depth of winter to pay him, sooner than feel that I was under an obligation.

I should be as comfortable with peas in my shoes, or a hedgehog in my bed, or a snake up my back, as with bills hanging over my head at the grocer's and the baker's and the tailor's. Poverty is hard, but debt is horrible; a man as well have a smoky house and a scolding wife, which are said to be the two worst evils of our life.

We may be poor, yet respectable, which John Ploughman and

wife hope they are and will be. But a man in debt cannot even respect himself. And he is sure to be talked about by the neighbors, and that talk will not be much to his credit.

Some persons appear to like to be owing money; but I would as soon be a cat up a chimney with the fire alight, or a fox with the hounds at my heels, or a hedgehog on a pitchfork, or a mouse under an owl's claw. An honest man thinks a purse full of other people's money to be worse than an empty one. He cannot bear to eat other people's cheese, wear other people's shirts and walk about in other people's shoes.

Neither will he be easy while his wife is decked out in the milliner's bonnets and wears the draper's flannels. The jackdaw in the peacock's feathers was soon plucked, and borrowers will surely come to poverty—a poverty of the bitterest sort, because there is shame in it.

Living beyond their incomes is the ruin of many of my neighbors. They can hardly afford to keep a rabbit, and must needs drive a pony and chaise. I am afraid extravagance is the common disease of the times, and many professing Christians have caught it, to their shame and sorrow. Good cotton or stuff gowns are not good enough nowadays; girls must have silks and satins, then there's a bill at the dressmaker's as long as a winter's night and quite as dismal.

Show and style and smartness run away with a man's means, keep the family poor and the father's nose down on the grindstone. Frogs who try to look as big as bulls, burst themselves. A pound a week apes five hundred a year, and comes to the county court. Men burn the candle at both ends, then say they are very unfortunate. Why don't they put the saddle on the right horse and say they are extravagant?

Economy is half the battle in life. It is not so hard to earn money as to spend it well. Hundreds would never have known *want* if they had not first known *waste*. If all poor men's wives knew how to cook, how far a little might go!

Our minister says the French and the Germans beat us hollow

in nice cheap cookery. I wish they would send missionaries over to convert our gossiping women into good managers. This is a French fashion which would be a deal more useful than those fine pictures in Mrs. Frippery's window, with ladies rigged out in a new style every month.

Dear me! Some people, too fine nowadays to eat what their fathers were thankful to see on the table, please their palates with costly feeding, so come to the workhouse and expect everybody to pity them. They turned up their noses at bread and butter and came to eat raw turnips stolen out of the fields. They who live like fighting cocks at other men's costs will get their combs cut, or perhaps get roasted for it one of these days.

If you have a great store of peas, you may put the more in the soup; but everybody should fare according to his earnings. He is both a fool and a knave who has a shilling coming in and on the strength of it, spends a pound which does not belong to him.

Cut your coat according to your cloth, is sound advice. But cutting other people's cloth by running into debt is as like thieving as fourpence is like a groat.

If I meant to be a rogue, I would deal in marine stores, or be a pettifogging lawyer, or a priest, or open a loan office, or go out picking pockets. But I would scorn the dirty art of getting into debt without a prospect of being able to pay.

Debtors can hardly help being liars, for they promise to pay when they know they cannot. When they have made up a lot of false excuses, they promise again; so they lie as fast as a horse can trot.

> *You have debts, and make debts still,*
> *If you've not lied, lie you will.*

Now if owing leads to lying, who shall say that it is not a most evil thing? Of course there are exceptions. I do not want to bear hard upon an honest man who is brought down by sickness or heavy losses. But taking the rule as a rule, you will find debt to be a great dismal swamp, a huge mudhole, a dirty ditch. Happy is the man who gets out of it after once tumbling in, but happiest of all is he who has been by God's goodness kept out of the mire altogether.

If you once ask the Devil to dinner, it will be hard to get him out of the house again: better to have nothing to do with him. Where a hen has laid one egg, she is very likely to lay another. When a man is once in debt, he is likely to get into it again. Better keep clear of it from the first. He who gets in for a penny will soon be in for a pound. And when a man is over shoes, he is very liable to be over boots. Never owe a farthing and you will never owe a guinea.

Out of Debt, Out of Danger

If you want to sleep soundly, buy a bed of a man who is in debt. Surely it must be a very soft one, or he never could have rested so easy on it. I suppose people get hardened to it, as Smith's donkey did when its master broke so many sticks across its back.

It seems to me that a real honest man would sooner get as lean as a greyhound than feast on borrowed money, and would choke up his throat with March dust before he would let the landlord make chalks against him behind the door for a beer score.

What pins and needles tradesmen's bills must stick in a fellow's soul!

A pig on credit always grunts. Without debt, without care. Out of debt, out of danger. But owing and borrowing are bramble-bushes full of thorns.

If ever I borrow a spade of my next-door neighbor I never feel safe with it for fear I should break it. I never can dig in peace as I do with my own. But if I had a spade at the shop and knew I could not pay for it, I think I should set to dig my own grave out of shame. Scripture says, "Owe no man any thing," which does not mean pay your debts, but means never have any to pay. And my opinion is that those who wilfully break this law ought to be turned out of the Christian church, neck and crop as we say.

Our laws are shamefully full of encouragement to credit. Nobody need be a thief now. He has only to open a shop and make a fail of it, and it will pay him much better. As the proverb is, "He who never fails will never grow rich." Why, I know tradesmen who have failed five or six times, yet think they are on the road to Heaven. The scoundrels! What would they do if they got there? They are a deal more likely to go where they shall never come out till they have paid the uttermost farthing. But people say, "How liberal they are!" Yes, with other people's money.

I hate to see a man steal a goose, then give religion the giblets. Piety by all means, but pay your way as part of it. Honesty first, then generosity.

But how often religion is a cloak for deceiving! There's Mrs. Scamp as fine as a peacock. All the girls are out at boarding school learning French and the piano. The boys are swelling about in kid gloves. And G. B. Scamp, Esq., is driving a fast-trotting mare and taking the chair at public meetings. All this while his poor creditors cannot get more than enough to live from hand to mouth.

It is shameful and beyond endurance to see how genteel swindling is winked at by many in this country. I'd off with their white waistcoats and kid gloves and patent leather boots if I had my way and give them the county crop and the prison livery for six months. Gentlemen or not, I'd let them see that big rogues could dance on the treadmill to the same tune as little ones. I'd make the land too hot to hold such scamping gentry if I were a member of Parliament or a prime minister. As I've no such power, I can at least write against the fellows and let off the steam of my wrath in that way.

My motto is: Pay as you go, and keep from small scores. Short reckonings are soon cleared. Pay what you owe, and what you're worth you'll know. Let the clock tick, but no *"tick"* for me. Better go to bed without your supper than get up in debt. Sins and debt are always more than we think them to be. Little by little a man gets over his head and ears. It is the petty expenses that empty the purse. Money is round and rolls away easily.

Buying What You Don't Want

Tom Thriftless buys what he does not want because it is a great bargain, so is soon brought to sell what he does want and finds it a very little bargain. He cannot say "no" to his friend who wants him to be security. He gives grand dinners, makes many holidays, keeps a fat table, lets his wife dress fine, never looks after his servants. By and by he is quite surprised to find the quarter days come round so very fast and that his creditors bark so loud. He has sowed his money in the field of thoughtlessness, now he wonders that he has to reap the harvest of poverty.

Still hoping for something to turn up to help him out of difficulty, he muddles himself into more trouble, forgetting that hope and expectations are fools' income. Being hard up, he goes to market with empty pockets and buys at whatever prices trades-men like to charge him. So he pays them double and gets deeper and deeper into the mire.

This leads him to scheming and trying little tricks and mean dodges, for it is hard for an empty sack to stand upright. This is sure not to answer, for schemes are like spiders' webs, which never catch anything better than flies, and are soon swept away.

As well attempt to mend your shoes with brown paper, or stop a broken window with a sheet of ice, as try to patch up falling business with maneuvering and scheming. When the schemer is found out, he is like a dog in church whom everybody kicks at, and like a barrel of powder which nobody wants for a neighbor.

Paying by Borrowing

They say poverty is a sixth sense. It had need be, for many debt-ors seem to have lost the other five, or were born without common sense. They appear to fancy that you not only make debts, but pay them by borrowing. A man pays Peter with what he has borrowed of Paul and thinks he is getting out of his difficulties, when he is putting one foot in the mud to pull his other foot out.

It is hard to shave an egg, or pull hairs out of a bald pate; but they are both easier than paying debts out of an empty pocket.

Samson was a strong man, but he could not pay debts without money. And he is a fool who thinks he can do it by scheming.

As to borrowing money of loan societies, it's like a drowning man catching at razors. Both Jews and Gentiles, when they lend money, generally pluck the geese as long as they have any feathers. A man must cut down his outgoings and save his incomings if he wants to clear himself. You can't spend your penny and pay debts with it, too. Stint the kitchen if your purse is bare. Don't believe in any way of wiping out debts except by paying hard cash.

Promises make debts, and debts make promises, but promises never pay debts. Promising is one thing and performing is quite another. A good man's word should be as binding as an oath. He should never promise to pay unless he has clear prospect of doing so in due time. Those who stave off payment by false promises deserve no mercy. It is all very well to say, "I'm very sorry," but

A hundred years of regret
Pay not a farthing of debt.

Now I'm afraid all this sound advice might as well have been given to my master's cocks and hens as to those who have got in the way of spending what is not their own, for advice to such people goes in at one ear and out at the other.

Well, those who won't listen will have to feel, and those who refuse cheap advice will have to buy dear repentance. But to young people beginning life, a word may be worth a world, and this shall be John Ploughman's short sermon, with three heads to it—always live a little below your means, never get into debt, and remember

He who goes a borrowing
Goes a sorrowing.

A MAN IN A PASSION RIDES A HORSE
THAT RUNS AWAY WITH HIM

When passion has run away with a man, who knows where it will carry him? Once let a rider lose power over his horse, and he may go over hedge and ditch and end with a tumble into the stone quarry and a broken neck.

No one can tell in cold blood what he may do when he gets angry; therefore, it is best to run no risks. Those who feel their temper rising will be wise if they rise themselves and walk off to the pump. Let them fill their mouths with cold water, hold it there ten minutes at the least, then go indoors and keep there till they feel cool as a cucumber.

If you carry loose gunpowder in your pocket, you had better

not go where sparks are flying. And if you are bothered with an irritable nature, you should move off when folks begin teasing you. Better keep out of a quarrel than fight your way through it.

Nothing is improved by anger, unless it be the arch of a cat's back. A man with his back up is spoiling his figure. People look none the handsomer for being red in the face. It takes a great deal out of a man to get into a towering rage; it is almost as unhealthy as having a fit. Time has been when men have actually choked themselves with passion, and died on the spot. Whatever wrong I suffer, it cannot do me half so much hurt as being angry about it; for passion shortens life and poisons peace.

When once we give way to temper, temper will claim a right of way and come in easier every time. He that will be in a peeve for any little thing will soon be out at elbows about nothing at all. A thunderstorm curdles the milk, and so does a passion sour the heart and spoil the character.

He who is in a tantrum shuts his eyes and opens his mouth and very soon says what he will be sorry for. Better bite your lips now than smart for life. It is easier to keep a bull out of a china shop than it is to get him out again. Besides, there's no end of a bill to pay for damages.

A man burning with anger carries a murderer inside his waistcoat; so the sooner he can cool down, the better for himself and all around him. He will have to give an account for his feelings as well as for his words and actions, and that account will cost him many tears.

It is a cruel thing to tease quick-tempered people, for though it may be sport to you, it is death to them—at least death to their peace and may be something worse. We know who said, "Woe to that man by whom the offence cometh."

Shun a furious man as you would a mad dog, but do it kindly, or you may make him worse than he would be. Don't put a man out when you know he is out with himself. When his monkey is up, be very careful, for he means mischief.

A man in a rage
Needs a great iron cage;

He'll tear and he'll dash
Till he comes to a smash;
So let's out of his way
As quick as we may.

As we quietly move off, let us pray for the angry person, for a man in a thorough passion is as sad a sight as to see a neighbor's house on fire and no water handy to put out the flames.

Let us wish the fellow on the runaway horse a soft ditch to tumble in and sense enough never to get on the creature's back again.

EVERY BIRD LIKES ITS OWN NEST

It pleases me to see how fond the birds are of their little homes. No doubt each one thinks his own nest is the very best: and so it is for him, just as my home is the best palace for me, even for me, King John, the king of the Cottage of Content. I will ask no more if Providence only continues to give me

> *A little field well tilled,*
> *A little house well filled,*
> *And a little wife well willed.*

An Englishman's house is his castle, and the true Briton is always fond of the old roof tree. Green grows the houseleek on the thatch, sweet is the honeysuckle at the porch, and dear are the gillyflowers in the front garden. But best of all is the good wife within who keeps all as neat as a new pin. Frenchmen may live in their coffeehouses, but an Englishman's best life is seen at home:

> My own house, though small
> Is the best house of all.

When boys get tired of eating tarts, and maids have done with winning hearts, and lawyers cease to take their fees, and leaves leave off to grow on trees, then will John Ploughman cease to love his own dear home. John likes to hear some sweet voice sing—

> 'Mid pleasures and palaces though we may roam,
> Be it ever so humble, there's no place like home;
> A charm from the sky seems to hallow us there,
> Which, wherever we rove, is not met with elsewhere.
> Home! Home! sweet, sweet home!
> There's no place like home!

People who take no pleasure in their own homes are queer folks and no better than they should be. Every dog is a lion at his own door. And a man should make most of those who make most of him. Women should be housekeepers and keep in the house.

That man is to be pitied who has married one of the Miss Gadabouts. Mrs. Cackle and her friend Mrs. Dressemout are enough to drive their husbands into the county jail for shelter. There can be no peace where such a piece of goods as either of them is to be found. Old Tusser said:

> Ill huswifery pricketh
>   Herself up with pride;
> Good huswifery tricketh
>   Her house as a bride.

> Ill huswifery moveth
>   With gossip to spend;
> Good huswifery loveth
>   Her household to tend.

The woman whose husband wastes his evenings with low

fellows at the beer shop is as badly off as a slave, and when the act of Parliament shuts up most of these ruin houses, it will be an act of emancipation for her.

Good husbands cannot have too much of their homes; and if their wives make their homes comfortable, they will soon grow proud of them. When good fathers get among their children, they are as merry as mice in malt.

Our Joe Scroggs says he is tired of his house, and the house certainly looks tired of him. It is all out of windows and would get out of doors if it knew how. He will never be weary in well-doing, for he never began. What a different fellow he would be if he could believe that the best side of the world is a man's own fireside! I know it is so, and so do many more.

> Seek home for rest,
> For home is best.

What can it be that so deludes lots of people who ought to know better? They have sweet wives, nice families and comfortable houses. They are several cuts above us poor country bumpkins, yet they must be out of an evening. What is it for? Surely it can't be the company; for the society of the woman you love, who is the mother of your children, is worth all the companies that ever met together. I fear they are away soaking their clay and washing all their wits away. If so, it is a great shame, and those guilty of it ought to be trounced. Oh! that drink, that drink!

The Best Homebrewed

Dear, dear! What stuff people will pour into their insides! Even if I had to be poisoned, I should like to know what I was swallowing. A cup of tea at home does people a sight more good than all the mixtures you get abroad. There's nothing like the best homebrewed, and there's no better mash-tub for making it in than the old-fashioned earthenware teapot.

Our little children sing, "Please, Father, come home," and John Ploughman joins with thousands of little children in that simple prayer, which every man who is a man should be glad to answer. I like to see husband and wife longing to see each other.

> *An ear that waits to catch*
> *A hand upon the latch;*
> *A step that hastens its sweet rest to win.*
> *A world of care without,*
> *A world of strife shut out,*
> *A world of love shut in.*

Fellow-workmen, try to let it be so with you and your wives. Come home and bring your wages with you. Make yourselves happy by making everyone happy around you.

A Thankful Heart

My printer jogs my elbow, and says, "That will do; I can't get any more in." Then, Mr. Passmore, I must pass over many things, but I cannot leave off without praising God for His goodness to me and mine, and all my brother ploughmen; for it is of His great mercy that He lets us live in this dear old country and loads us with so many benefits.

This bit of poetry shall be my finish. I mean every word of it. Let us sing it together:

> *What pleasant groves, what goodly fields!*
> *What fruitful hills and vales have we!*
> *How sweet an air our climate yields!*
> *How blest with flocks and herds we be!*
> *How milk and honey doth o'erflow!*
> *How clear and wholesome are our springs!*
> *How safe from ravenous beasts we go!*
> *And, oh, how free from poisonous things!*
>
> *For these and for our grass, our corn,*
> *For all that springs from blade or bough,*
> *For all those blessings that adorn*
> *Both wood and field, this kingdom through—*
> *For all of these Thy praise we sing;*
> *And humbly, Lord, entreat Thee, too,*
> *That fruit to Thee we forth may bring,*
> *As unto us Thy creatures do.*

TRY

O f all the pretty little songs I have ever heard my youngsters sing, that is one of the best which winds up,

> *If at first you don't succeed,*
> *Try, try, try again.*

I recommend it to grown-up people who are down-in-the-mouth, and fancy that the best thing they can do is to give up. Nobody knows what he can do till he tries. "We shall get through it now," said Jack to Harry as they finished up the pudding. Everything new is hard work, but a little of the "try" ointment rubbed on the hand and worked into the heart makes all things easy.

Can't do it sticks in the mud, but Try soon drags the wagon out of the rut.

The fox said Try, and he got away from the hounds when they almost snapped at him.

The bees said Try and turned flowers into honey.

The squirrel said Try, and up he went to the top of the beech tree.

The snowdrop said Try and bloomed in the cold snows of winter.

The sun said Try, and the spring soon threw Jack Frost out of the saddle.

The young lark said Try, and he found his new wings took him over hedges and ditches, and up where his father was singing.

The ox said Try and ploughed the field from end to end.

No hill too steep for Try to climb, no clay too stiff for Try to plough, no field too wet for Try to drain, no hole too big for Try to mend.

> *By little strokes*
> *Men fell great oaks.*

By a spadeful at a time the navvies digged the cutting, cut a big hole through the hill, and heaped up the embankment.

> *The stone is hard, and the drop is small,*
> *But a hole is made by the constant fall.*

For a complete list of books available from the Sword of the Lord, write to Sword of the Lord Publishers, P. O. Box 1099, Murfreesboro, Tennessee 37133.

(800) 251-4100
(615) 893-6700
FAX (615) 848-6943
www.swordofthelord.com